Hits, Flops, and Other Illusions

Hits, Flops, and Other Illusions

MY FORTYSOMETHING YEARS IN HOLLYWOOD

ED ZWICK

G

GALLERY BOOKS

New York   London   Toronto   Sydney   New Delhi

G

Gallery Books

An Imprint of Simon & Schuster, LLC

1230 Avenue of the Americas

New York, NY 10020

First Gallery Books hardcover edition February 2024

GALLERY BOOKS and colophon are registered trademarks
of Simon & Schuster, LLC

Simon & Schuster: Celebrating 100 Years of Publishing in 2024

For information about special discounts for bulk purchases,
please contact Simon & Schuster Special Sales at
1-866-506-1949 or business@simonandschuster.com.

The Simon & Schuster Speakers Bureau can bring authors
to your live event. For more information or to book an event,
contact the Simon & Schuster Speakers Bureau at
1-866-248-3049 or visit our website at www.simonspeakers.com.

Interior design by Kathryn A. Kenney-Peterson

Manufactured in the United States of America

10 9 8 7 6 5 4 3 2

Library of Congress Cataloging-in-Publication Data has been applied for.

ISBN 978-1-6680-4699-9
ISBN 978-1-6680-4701-9 (ebook)

Contents

FILMOGRAPHY

Television

1978–1980	*Family*
1983	*Special Bulletin*
1987–1991	*thirtysomething*
1994–1995	*My So-Called Life*
1996–1997	*Relativity*
1999–2002	*Once and Again*
2020	*Away*

Film

1983	*Special Bulletin*	2001	*I Am Sam*
1986	*About Last Night*	2002	*Abandon*
1989	*Glory*	2003	*The Last Samurai*
1992	*Leaving Normal*	2006	*Blood Diamond*
1994	*Legends of the Fall*	2008	*Defiance*
1996	*Courage Under Fire*	2010	*Love & Other Drugs*
1998	*The Siege*	2014	*Pawn Sacrifice*
1998	*Dangerous Beauty*	2016	*Jack Reacher: Never Go Back*
1998	*Shakespeare in Love*	2017	*Woman Walks Ahead*
2000	*Traffic*	2018	*Trial by Fire*

I did not tell half of what I saw.

—Marco Polo, on his deathbed

INTRODUCTION

Taking Note

I tell stories for a living.

I've told them to friends over too much wine at dinner. I've told them while waiting for long lighting setups on distant locations. Sometimes lying awake in the middle of the night, I've even told them to myself. Hollywood stories are necessarily suspect. What's worse, time has sanded the rough edges of certain memories. And though I've resisted, as best I could, the impulse to straighten the narratives, shape the second acts, sharpen the dialogue, I'm afraid nearly fifty years of telling stories for a living has left its mark. Let's just say they're as true as they can be given a reflexive impulse to please and the hope not to be excommunicated from certain Hollywood parties that I don't care to attend anyway. And while I'd like to think I've been at least as hard on myself as I am on others, I'll admit that some names have been omitted while others have been kept. In certain cases, this is so as not to be hurtful, in others it's payback, pure and simple.

Speaking of names, I'll be dropping a few. I've come to accept there's no way to tell these stories without being falsely modest or pretentiously unpretentious. Call it the Director's Paradox—a mere mortal hiding behind the camera watching the drama of gods and goddesses in the golden glow of the stage lights, then wading into a shitstorm where he presumes to tell everybody what they're doing wrong. To be a director is to be a changeling. I have played both good cop and bad, psychoanalyst, flirt, camp counselor, drug counselor, scourge, tutor, BFF, coach, con artist, confidant, and co-conspirator. Also, a heartless son of a bitch. On set I can be downright jolly, joking with the cast and crew. It's all a big party until they learn I want what I want when I want it, and I morph into a muttering Napoleon determined to bend the world to my will.

A shooting company is like the crew of a nineteenth-century sailing ship. Each member is a master: the key grip is the ship's carpenter, the gaffer a sailmaker, the first assistant director (AD) is chief mate. And lurking in the prow is the ship's captain, long beard blown back by the salt spray, howling, *I know the way! Follow me!* The truth is he's only guessing. But someone has to say it.

Over the years I have worked with self-proclaimed masters of the universe, unheralded geniuses, hacks, sociopaths, savants, and saints. Mostly, I've found myself surrounded by brilliant, talented, funny-as-fuck artists, many of whom I've admired for years, and who to my surprise seemed interested in my ideas. As for tolerating the appalling behavior of the random beautiful narcissist, well, that's what my grandfather called "the cost of doing business." It also must be said they make for the best stories.

Rereading these chapters, I realize that while setting out to write about what I've learned making movies, I've in fact ended up highlighting what moviemaking has taught me about life. Though told in the guise of Hollywood anecdotes, each one turns out to be a surprising lesson: about mentors, monsters, and the meaning of friendship, about the perils of meeting your idols, the complexity of success and the nobility of failure. Taken together, these stories can also be read as a kind of pilgrim's progress: a sentimental journey from innocence to experience. More parable than practical instruction, some are moral tales, others aspire to high comedy. There are also turgid melodramas, crushing tragedies, political thrillers, and at least one horror story featuring the appearance of true evil. There are tales of love and loss, loyalty, betrayal, unexpected heartbreak, and even less anticipated triumph. Inevitably, each one becomes a meditation on working—that thing we do every day to which we give so much of ourselves, often at the expense of our families, our health, and a piece of our soul. The work we choose defines us. It creates meaning and purpose all its own; it peoples your life with an entirely different cast of characters from those waiting at home, offers a separate identity, sometimes even a contingent existence. I've been work-addicted since childhood, and I know I'm not alone in that on the set.

My notebooks on working fill an entire shelf in my office. On the inside cover of my first one—a black Moleskine, unlined—I wrote "creation is memory." I think it was Kurosawa who said it, I certainly didn't make it up, yet in retrospect it begins to explain what I was up to. I couldn't possibly use what I was witnessing, yet I was desperate to preserve it all, believing that by storing it away it might someday give me a leg up as a filmmaker. I couldn't have known that the value of these notes would only become clear years later, after a decade of scrambling, scheming, striving, and the repeated humiliation and abject mortification of knowing I was doing mediocre work. But I'm getting ahead of myself. Humiliation and mortification are subjects that will get more than their share of attention in the stories to come.

When one notebook would fill up or the spine would crack and the pages begin to fall out, I'd buy another. To this day I continue to scour my old notebooks for inspiration. I covered page after page with Hollywood lore. I loved the autobiographies of Billy Wilder, Sidney Lumet, Nunnally Johnson, Akira Kurosawa, and so many others. To discover that these Olympian talents were forced to deal with the same indignities I would eventually endure was perversely comforting. As I continue to be buffeted by the chutes and ladders of the biz, William Goldman's *Adventures in the Screen Trade* serves as both bible and Baedeker. There was no point transcribing his brilliant and laugh-out-loud observations into my notebooks; there were simply too many. Better to buy several copies and wear them out, one after another.

Having admired so many great memoirs, I will admit to being more than a little sheepish at having written one. I am reconciled that my career will never rival those of my heroes, and it seems more than a little presumptuous to assume anybody will be interested in my own misadventures. I've always taken comfort *behind* the camera. The words spoken on-screen may be mine but I'm more than happy having the lights shine on the actors. My most personal thoughts can be safely disguised in the mouth of a character while the notion of writing in the first person holds a unique terror. I was trying to explain this to Liberty, my wife of more than forty years, feeling a little vulnerable about revealing myself to the world. She set down the manuscript on the bedside table, smiled gently, and said, "Let's just say it reveals *some* of you, sweetheart."

Four years ago, I had never considered writing a memoir. But everything changed at 4 a.m. on a March morning in Tribeca as I was getting ready to direct the first day of shooting on our reboot of *thirtysomething* called, unsurprisingly, *thirtysomethingelse*, a project my partner and I had contemplated but managed to procrastinate writing for thirty years. The stillness of a big city at dawn has always been one of the pleasures of directing; standing alone on a deserted avenue before the endless barrage of questions begin—what an assistant director likes to describe as "trying to herd cats." I remember cursing when my phone rang. It could only mean something was wrong.

"The city is locking down," said our unit production manager. "The studios are scuttling every show in the country." We had all known the pandemic was spreading, but few of us could have anticipated how rapidly, and only the most alarmist had imagined what the next two years would portend. I flew back to LA on the last plane out of JFK. Back home, I watched, benumbed, as the death toll climbed. As for the postponement of our production, I had long ago grown accustomed to such sudden reversals of fortune. *Legends of the Fall* had been delayed twice, once for over a year. *Shakespeare in Love* was canceled only weeks before shooting with huge sets built and costumes fitted and ready. It took six years to bring it back to life. Alas, to this day, *thirtysomethingelse* remains stillborn.

Like everyone else, I sat home wondering how quickly things might get back to normal. As weeks turned to months and months blurred into years, I knew I should start writing something new. But my head wasn't in it. I now know that I was grieving. Something about losing the opportunity to revisit halcyon days, the chance to reconnect, after thirty years, with a group of actors and writers who had meant so much to me—it knocked the wind out of me. I have always been aggressively forward-looking, mostly immune to regret, and never interested in looking at past work. But for the first time in my life, having been stripped of the work addiction that's defined me since second grade, I decided to sit down and take a hard look at what I'd made over the years.

Once I got past all the moments that made me cringe—creaky exposition, clunky dialogue, awkward staging, a funky camera move, a joke falling flat (nobody can write worse reviews than a movie's director), something strange and unexpected began to happen. Instead of watching the movies themselves, I began to reflect on what it had taken to make them: the twenty rewrites, the fights with the studio, the endless casting process, the mind-numbing budget meetings, the hours in the scouting van. Had it all really happened? Had *I* made these? Under pain of death, I couldn't reconstruct the plots of the twenty movies and two hundred hours of television I'd made, yet as I watched one after another I marveled at the scale of the enterprise, the amount of effort, not just mine, but the combined efforts of hundreds, no, thousands of people. I could see their faces clearly, passing in and out of view like shuffling a deck of cards.

Where were they now? Why were we no longer in touch? So many treasured relationships—with the directors of photography (DPs), ADs, production designers, producers, and most obviously, as their faces filled the screen, the actors. They'd been important relationships, too, passionate and abiding. Or hadn't they? There'd been feuds, affairs, breakups, high hilarity, and tears. We'd spent hours in dingy rehearsal rooms, worked six-day weeks of sixteen-hour days in foreign cities where we knew only one another. There'd been endless personal conversations on airplanes, screaming fights in hotel rooms, tearful reconciliations, hysterical laughter, secret revelations, public triumphs and private betrayals, succès d'estime and colossal disasters. And that was all on one movie.

When I started filling my notebooks, I couldn't have known how all-consuming making movies would be, what a manic-depressive roller-coaster life it augured. The juxtapositions were just so wrenching: weeks in dismal hotel rooms and a night on the red carpet, anxiety attacks and acceptance speeches. How many months, years even, had I spent waiting to see if a movie was going to happen only to genially accept the crushing disappointment when it didn't? Even as a life in the movies has given me so much joy, such personal fulfillment and so many material perks, it has also taken a toll on my marriage, my children, my friendships, not to mention my physical and mental health. Could I write about what it's really like to make movies? Could I reveal certain ugly truths, not just about the creativity and the craft, but also the cost—the personal cost?

Could I tell stories about telling stories?

A hopeful image comes to me as I write this. It is of a young filmmaker, bent over a copy of my book, scribbling something I'd written into a notebook of her own.

CHAPTER ONE

An Origins Story

Claire, Nina, Marshall, and the AFI, 1975

I bought my first notebook the day I set foot on a film set. I had always been a theater kid, writing and directing plays since I was twelve. I was just as obsessed with movies but couldn't figure out even the most basic understanding of how they were made. Then the movie gods smiled on me.

I was living in Paris after college on a fellowship to observe experimental theater companies—Peter Brook at the Bouffes du Nord, Ariane Mnouchkine at the Cartoucherie de Vincennes—when I scored a dream job as an assistant to Woody Allen (yes, the name-dropping begins). He was there shooting *Love and Death*. I'd hover as close to the camera as the scowling French crew would allow, pestering him with the kind of clueless, impertinent questions only an entitled twenty-one-year-old would dare ask. That he always responded patiently and with generosity is a kindness for which I will always be grateful. But what most impressed me about Woody (first names now) was his willingness to admit what he didn't know. He was, foremost, a writer who knew what he wanted, and he surrounded himself with experienced, talented people who could help realize his vision. Watching him gave me license to believe I could do the same someday.

He even let me peek at a new script he was writing—a bittersweet romantic comedy called "Anhedonia," later to become *Annie Hall*. I'd gotten to know Diane Keaton a little on the set of *Love and Death* and knew of Woody's past relationship with her, but I was astonished by her comic manifestation in the script. Her sweetness, her wonderful, daffy locutions, it was all there. He was using personal experience, not for its details but for its essence as inspiration in his writing. It was the kind of teachable moment that would have major implications for me when, in years to come, I somehow managed to put an idealized version of my own marriage (and my writing partner's) on national television.

Woody also had the most amazing work ethic; at lunch, he'd hide out in his trailer and practice the clarinet, then after a day of shooting from 6 a.m. to 6 p.m., instead of going out to dinner (in Paris!) he'd return to his hotel and go back to work writing his next movie.

Courtesy of the author

Whenever I could, I would sneak off and scribble what I'd observed from his set on the back of call sheets and the cast's lunch orders, sometimes adding snippets of dialogue from the scenes I'd watched (and one I'd actually been in). Riding back on the Métro, I'd pull the crumpled scraps from my pocket and transcribe them into my notebooks. Once ensconced in my fourth-floor walk-up, I'd underline passages of a secondhand copy of Sergei Eisenstein's *Film Form* or a French edition of Robert Bresson's *Notes on the Cinematographer* (which I couldn't understand in English either). Weekends were spent at the Cinémathèque where, for the equivalent of a dollar, I would sit on the cement floor and watch classic films, one at 8 p.m., one at 10 p.m., and with help from some strong hashish, a midnight feature. I began to keep pen and paper on my bedside table to record the grand visions of films I would someday make. Some nights I wouldn't sleep at all because I was too busy shooting them in my head.

With my production assistant (PA) job over, I returned to the States and fumbled around trying to come up with what to do next. While in college I'd written for *Rolling Stone*, and then for *The New Republic*, yet it never felt like journalism was my calling, and my editors tended to agree. I'd had small professional jobs directing plays in summer stock and had received a tentative offer to work at the Public Theater, but I had to admit that I'd been bitten by the movie bug. And so, on a wing and a prayer, never having made a short film or held a camera, I applied to the director's program of the American Film Institute. Inexplicably, I was accepted. All I can surmise is that admission was much less competitive back then.

The day I arrived in Los Angeles it was a hundred and two. As I drove around looking for a place to stay, falling ash from a brush fire in a canyon whose Spanish name I couldn't pronounce covered the used Volkswagen Rabbit I'd bought from an out-of-work sound editor. Half its dashboard had been gnawed away by a German shepherd left in the car with the windows rolled up, the air-conditioning didn't work, and sweat pooled on the polyester seats. Not long ago I'd been drinking pastis in Saint-Germain-des-Prés, now I was lost in a featureless city, not knowing a soul. I checked into a shabby motel on Pico with an over-chlorinated, leaf-strewn pool and spent the week before classes began in my darkened room watching reruns of sixties TV shows with a wet towel on my chest or seeking the cool refuge of a matinee in the Village Theatre. At night I haunted the Westwood bookstore or trolled the UCLA campus unsuccessfully hitting on coeds.

Every first day of school bears the same terrors. Within minutes of arriving at the AFI—formerly a grand Beverly Hills mansion—I could tell my classmates were all better prepared than me, having graduated from NYU film school, worked for production companies, or made their own films. They talked easily of agents, executives, and development deals. Their conversations were peppered with a strange patois of "grosses," "release patterns," and something called "the trades." Even more daunting was their technical proficiency. Standing beside the lunch truck, I eavesdropped on passionate arguments over the merits of the Panavision camera versus Arriflex, and whether a 1:85 aspect ratio was more conducive than an anamorphic lens for shooting action.

The structure of the AFI conservatory in those early days was based on the nineteenth-century European model. Twenty-six of us were invited as first-year fellows with the understanding that only six would be invited back for the second year and given financing to shoot a half-hour movie on film. Though only in the fifth year of its existence, the program had already produced a remarkable crop of graduates: among them, Terrence Malick, Caleb Deschanel, Amy Heckerling, Marty Brest, and Bob Richardson. We'd also heard about a strange young man in the basement finishing what was rumored to be a masterpiece. His name was David Lynch. It was a high bar, and the atmosphere was charged with the desperate ambition and intensity common in young filmmakers everywhere.

I had made a terrible mistake—I didn't belong there—a conviction borne out by the reception to the screening of my first student project in the program's weekly narrative workshop. In a tradition perhaps inspired by the struggle sessions of China's Cultural Revolution, the unfortunate director was forced to sit in a hard chair and forbidden to speak while twenty-five director-classmates gleefully analyzed (read, brutalized) their work. Ever the diligent student, I was unaccustomed to such overt failure. The humiliation would have been bad enough, but it was amplified by the derision of the artistic director, an Italian martinet named Antonio Vellani, formerly George Steven's assistant of many years. His summation of my first effort, a turgid, lugubrious Bertolucci homage about a boy returning home to see his dying mother: "Mood," he intoned, "is doom spelled backwards."

That afternoon I returned to the hateful motel room, flung myself face down on my bare mattress, and cried myself to sleep. While in Paris I'd fallen in love with the idea of being a filmmaker, but I clearly had no idea how to actually make a movie. Waking up sometime after dark, sweaty and disoriented, I resolved to quit film school and return to Europe. In this spirit I wrote a plaintive letter to Woody.

"L.A. is horrible. Nobody understands the kind of sophisticated, intellectual films they make in Europe." I knew he would understand, his revulsion for L.A. was part of his comedy: "Q: What's the difference between L.A. and Dannon Yogurt? A: Dannon Yogurt has active culture." So, I was surprised when he not only encouraged me to stick it out, but also gave me the name of a young woman he had met on his last trip to L.A. He said he'd been impressed by her and thought we might like each other.

Her name was Claire. An L.A. native, she had spent her first year out of Princeton working for Ralph Nader's NGO on the abuse of seniors in nursing homes. Having done her part for the good of mankind, she had made her way back to the embrace of family—and the family mansion—in Bel Air, where she was presently passing the time, poolside, writing poetry. Claire and I met and slept together in the same afternoon; it was 1975, that kind of thing happened. I was enchanted with her wit, her self-assurance, and the vanity plate on her late-model BMW that read BEL JAR. A week later, she withdrew money from her trust fund and rented the top floor of a falling-down shack in Laurel Canyon. I moved in soon after, humping two duffel bags and a guitar up the rickety steps. There, we read poetry to each other by candlelight. Overwhelmed by the decision to be artists, we clung to each other like two forest animals lost in the city.

Meanwhile, my experience at AFI continued to be torturous. My early efforts at screenwriting were universally derided, as was my next project for the narrative workshop. I might well have quit had it not been for the presence of two sublime artists who rounded out the faculty. Nina Foch, an Academy Award–nominated actress and legendary teacher, rode herd on us as we directed scenes, while the great European filmmaker Ján Kadár mercilessly analyzed our work frame by frame. The pain of their harsh critiques was outdone by the acuity of their insight. Every artist has a teacher who changed their life. I had two.

To have encountered Nina Foch at twenty-two was akin to the horrors of my first acid trip mixed with the rapture of my first love affair. I thought I knew

something about directing actors before meeting her, but the depth of her observations opened my mind to an unseen world. She was a protégée of Stella Adler, a
disciple of a tradition begun at the Group Theatre and carried on by such legendary teachers as Sanford Meisner and Uta Hagen.

Ján's approach was utterly different. A product of a European conservatory
himself, he was as exacting about lenses, editing, and mise-en-scène as he was
about politics and purpose. His life had also been harrowing. A Jew imprisoned
by the Nazis in World War II, later jailed as a socialist when the Russians took over
Czechoslovakia, his grim view of humanity was leavened by irrepressible humor.
He taught us that no movie, no matter how serious, could ever be funny enough.

In what was intended as a gift to the student body, a celebrity guest speaker
would come to campus every week. We, the Fellows (in the conservatory spirit,
that's what we were called), sat in a circle and listened spellbound to the words of
a parade of past masters—David Lean, Paul Newman, King Vidor—praying their
greatness would somehow rub off on us by proximity. In fact, their dazzling anecdotes about making classic films with the world's biggest stars had the opposite
effect, only making me feel worse about my own miserable efforts.

Then one day in Nina's class, something marvelous happened. I met someone
who would change my life. Marshall Herskovitz had graduated from Brandeis the
year before and decided to use his bar mitzvah money to make a short film. Undaunted by knowing nothing about filmmaking—a fact borne out on his first day
of shooting when he attempted to film the entire script one line at a time—he had
come to California believing his masterpiece would get him work in the business.
Alas, his self-financed short turned out to be—in his words—the most expensive
application to film school in history. (I should add that by the second day of shooting his opus, Marshall had deduced it made more sense to shoot an entire scene
and then cut and assemble it afterward, thus singlehandedly discovering modern
filmmaking, albeit not for the first time.)

I felt myself drawn to this tall, underweight, curly-haired, bespectacled young
man who bore, in my mind at least, a slight resemblance to the young Groucho
Marx. We were doing an exercise about "hot objects," intended to teach us how

an actor's connection to his props can generate deep emotion. Marshall brought in an antique carpenter's ruler that had belonged to his late grandfather, a cabinet-maker. As instructed, he first described the tool with great precision, then, at Nina's command, began to reminisce about his connection to Max Herskovitz. I watched, fascinated, as a remarkable transformation took place. No longer was he a geeky twenty-two-year-old standing awkwardly before a group of skeptical student filmmakers. Instead, here was a master storyteller spinning a tale that had us all leaning forward in our seats. Looking around, I saw that some of us were deeply moved. When it was my turn to stand before the class and I took out a broken pocket watch belonging to *my* grandfather and told the story of his immigrant journey to America, I could see the look of recognition and delight on Marshall's face.

Each day at lunch the Fellows would hang out by the roach coach wolfing down terrible burritos. I can't recall who first spoke to whom, but within minutes Marshall and I were deep in a conversation that has now lasted almost fifty years. It's not just that he was smart and eccentric—his senior thesis had been a screenplay of *Beowulf*, he could speak passable Middle English, and for some morbid reason I chose not to think about, possessed an encyclopedic knowledge of firearms and edged weapons. He was also funny, psychologically astute—he'd been in therapy since age ten—and animated by a brimming passion for making movies. As soon as we began to shoot our short films it was clear he was light-years ahead of me. Technically proficient, with a great ear for dialogue, he was quickly recognized as the star of the class. There's a line from August Strindberg's *The Stronger* that epitomizes our early relationship.

"I couldn't risk becoming your enemy," says Madame X, "so I became your friend."

Competitive as the program was, we were also expected to work together on each other's films as DPs, sound mixers, even actors. Given that setting, it's impossible to downplay the meaning of the unspoken alliance Marshall and I formed. It's remarkable just how much a single friendship can be a tonic to the alienation and self-doubt of a gestating career—especially in such a strange hothouse environment. Marshall recognized strengths of mine he considered weaknesses in his own work. Often bedeviled by structure, his storytelling was sometimes squishy and rambling, whereas the only virtue I seemed to possess was the ability to be dropped anywhere in a story and be able to say what scene came before and what beat should come after. As we worked together, it became clear that, between the two of us, we might be at least one complete filmmaker.

Meanwhile, I was spending more time with Claire and her family in Bel Air. Whenever possible, I would flee the intensity of school, winding my way up Bellagio Road for lavish dinners and weekends by the pool. I'd been around money before, but it was old money—the subdued, underplayed, Ivy League version. Bel Air had an allure all its own. One morning at a Sunday brunch buffet catered by Nate'n Al's, I found myself in the kitchen with Claire's sister, Jill, an actress I'd seen starring on Broadway in *Inadmissable Evidence*. Sitting beside her was her husband, the renowned Shakespearean thespian Nicol Williamson. Also present was Claire's other sister, Joey, and her girlfriend, Maria Schneider, who had recently starred with Marlon Brando in *Last Tango in Paris*. I will never forget how casually Maria unbuttoned Joey's shirt to hold her breast with one hand while eating a bagel with the other. Other Sundays, a celebrity pal or two could be counted on to stop by to say hi. Ever the rube from the Midwest, I was more than a little starstruck.

Claire's father, Robert, had been a legendary ad exec on Madison Avenue who later became CEO of Avis, and then wrote a huge bestseller called *Up the Organization*. I still recall his slightly aggrieved smile at my hovering presence around his youngest daughter. He was somehow connected to 20th Century Fox, and one day I was invited to join Claire at a screening there. To her mortification, I was far too excited being on a studio lot, craning my neck as if on a tour bus at a celebrity sighting of, say, Burt Reynolds. To Claire, this was all old hat, but I will never forget watching a 70mm print of Kurosawa's *Dersu Uzala* on a screen thirty feet high and seventy feet across.

Marshall was wary of Claire. He and his longtime girlfriend, Susan Shilliday, had met in college and moved west together. Susan was working as a script reader and supporting him while he was in school. Their relationship was flagging; as a couple they were almost hermetic and didn't socialize much. When I managed to persuade them to go out with us on a double date, Claire's confidence, her name-dropping, and her obvious entitlement were too much for Marshall to bear. Despite my labored explanation that it was born of the same insecurity we all felt, he was unconvinced and remained suspicious of her. Our first real fight took place when I accused him of being intimidated by Claire. "She didn't even know I was there," he said. "I'm not even sure she knew that you were."

Soon after moving into Claire's aerie, I chose to use it as a location for my next narrative project. On the second day of shooting, a C-stand fell, shattering a valuable stained glass window, and I spent the next three months doing landscape work around the house to repay the owners. This disaster was followed soon after by another when she stepped off our bed and put her foot through the body of a 1947 Martin D-28 guitar, my most prized possession. (I'd bought it after selling a long freelance piece to *Rolling Stone*.) Still, I was unconcerned by these portents, convinced that ours was a love straight out of a Crosby, Stills & Nash ballad: Claire wrote poems while I chopped wood for the potbelly stove, the little shack's only heat. Yet as the days grew shorter and an L.A. winter crept up the dark canyon, I had to acknowledge a chill in the relationship. At first, I thought I was imagining it. But was it natural for a young couple's torrid sex life to wane after only a few months? Was it a sign that Claire began spending several late evenings each week with her Princeton friends and chose never to invite me? What did it mean that her wardrobe, haircut, makeup, and demeanor had changed radically after accepting a job from one of her father's producer-friends? A D-girl, as they were called in those days, was a junior executive role to which smart women were often assigned, working closely with writers on the development of their scripts. I chose to ignore the strangeness of watching her wholeheartedly embrace a role in a business she had only months before claimed to revile.

Okay, so I was a fool in love.

I was twenty-two, remember, and afraid my ardent desire to make movies was fading along with my chances of matriculating to the second year. Unlike

Marshall, I didn't have bar mitzvah money to shoot my own short film. I'd used it all when my father had declared bankruptcy (for the third time) and couldn't pay the tuition for my last year of college. In fact, Allen Zwick and I hadn't spoken since I'd had the hubris—his word was *insanity*—to turn down an acceptance to Harvard Law School. To him this was tantamount to passing on what he called a "golden ticket."

"C'mon, Eddie . . ." he said, during an ugly argument, "get your head out of your ass!"

Now, two years later, not only was I doubting my ability as a filmmaker, but it was dawning on me I might lack any talent whatsoever. As a kid with overweening ambition and no money, can I be forgiven for seeing in Claire an entrée into a world I desperately wanted to be a part of? I realize how biddable that sounds, but I couldn't bring myself to confront her about our dissolving relationship. Especially after we both received an invitation to Woody Allen's New Year's Eve black-tie gala in New York City. That we never entertained the thought of not attending says it all. I'm sure the invitation was sent as a courtesy. I couldn't afford the flight, couldn't pay for a hotel room, and didn't own a tuxedo, yet I didn't hesitate to RSVP. I said nothing to Claire about my misgivings and we made plans to be in NYC over the holidays.

Claire decided to leave early and visit friends back east while I finished the semester. On the morning of her departure, having booked an early flight, she slipped out of bed while I was still asleep. Her morning ritual was to sequester herself in the bathroom with a cup of coffee, a cigarette, and her journal—after which she would hurriedly dress, give me a quick kiss, and head for the studio. That morning as I lay in bed, I could smell the cigarette smoke wafting in from the bathroom. A while later I heard her grab her bags and head out to meet the waiting cab.

There was no kiss. I feigned sleep.

Eventually I got out of bed, stoked the potbelly stove, and walked into the bathroom. There on the counter, lying open, was Claire's journal. Some people like to snoop. They take great pleasure in learning other people's secrets. I don't happen to be one of them. In my early years in L.A. I often housesat for friends and scrupulously avoided doing that kind of thing. What's more, a writer's journal is private. Sacred, even.

Of course, I read it.

Page after page described recent affairs, each with a successful older man from her new Hollywood incarnation. It was, I have to say, a prodigious number of conquests for such a short period of employment, but I will refrain from naming names. One was a big producer, another a top executive, the third a movie star. Somehow worse were the entries about me.

"I love Edward . . ." (To this day, she remains the only person ever to call me by my full name.) "He is sweet and adoring, but so callow. And so hungry. I need someone older, more comfortable in his skin, more established in a world I want to inhabit."

My day of horrors wouldn't end. In class, after presenting what I thought was a clever "romantic comedy" scene I'd written, Nina eviscerated me in front of all the Fellows, proclaiming in her stentorian voice, "You know your problem, Mr. Zwick? You have a case of the cutes. You have no idea who you are, or who women are . . . Maybe someday you'll find out and then you can write about it."

I barely managed to hold back tears. Of course, Nina was right. But did that stop me from flying off to New York in pursuit of Claire and my ill-fated dreams?

It was a blustery New Year's Eve when we met as planned in my tiny hotel room. I stood there in my rented tux with the cuffs rolled and pinned (I hadn't had time to have them hemmed) watching Claire get dressed and wondering who'd be attending the party. I needed to tell her how devastated I was by what I'd read in her journal. Though awash with bile and ego-crushing resentment, I choked it down and merely said, "I read your journal."

"Oh, dear."

"It's cool," I said mildly. "It's over. I get it."

"I'm so sorry."

"Wish you could've said something."

"I didn't know how . . ."

"Forget it."

And that was that. So cool. So grown-up. So uncallow.

A storm was moving in as we walked past the limos disgorging the great, the greater, and the greatest into the Harkness Ballet Foundation on East Seventy-Fifth Street. According to the *New York Times*, "Anybody who was anybody" was attending: a miscellany ranging from Lillian Hellman to Walt "Clyde" Frazier to Mick and Bianca Jagger. I couldn't help keeping a mental list as we sauntered past Candice Bergen and Mike Nichols laughing together; Meryl Streep and Joe Papp sipping champagne; and Kurt Vonnegut, Edgar Doctorow, and Liza Minnelli in a serious tête-à-tête with New York senator Jacob Javits. To enter that ballroom, with its huge chandeliers sparkling above and the din of animated conversation echoing off the mirrored walls, was both disorienting and oddly pleasing. Discomfiting because I knew no one; liberating because I was completely invisible.

Within minutes Claire was whisked away by Polly Bergen (a family friend?). Every now and then I spotted her through the scrum, chatting away. I know I must have said hello to Woody at some point but just as quickly slunk away as he was besieged by three hundred of his closest friends. At one point I jostled Lauren Bacall, nearly causing her to spill her drink. I did get up the nerve to introduce myself to Peter Bogdanovich. He seemed genuinely happy to be singled out and indulged me for three minutes before glimpsing someone more famous over my shoulder and drifting off.

What was I doing here? Did I think I was going to impress Neil Simon with such dazzling repartee that he'd invite me to adapt his next hit play? Maybe Richard Zanuck would screen my pathetic narrative projects and offer me a three-picture deal! I had become the modern incarnation of Sammy Glick (writer Budd Schulberg's legendary literary avatar of sweaty, grasping Hollywood). Finding myself near the bar I ordered vodka. I was never much of a drinker; my father's history of binge drinking had bequeathed to me a mortal fear of alcoholism. But I was feeling bloody-minded and ordered another. At one point I saw Claire laughing flirtatiously with Woody. My mood darkened. Was it possible she'd slept with him, too? And why exactly had I passed up law school? Already, friends of mine were being offered clerkships for Supreme Court justices. Soon they'd join powerful law firms, marry svelte girls from Wellesley, have babies, and move to penthouses on Central Park West while I would grow old and bitter in my dingy L.A. apartment reading scripts for other directors. I was cratering. I'd lost count of how much I'd drunk. The world was tilting, and I'd begun mumbling to myself.

Midnight was approaching. As if in a scene staged by that great director in the sky, I found myself standing near Claire. Should we kiss at the stroke of twelve? Could I strangle her in public and get away with it? I had no idea what I was going to say when I grabbed her arm; I was way beyond thought.

"You bitch," I hissed. "How could you do that to me?"

I have no specific memory of the torrent of profanity that followed. All I know is that my banked rage, my bruised ego, and my epic self-loathing gushed out in an inarticulate spew. Claire tried to pull away, but I tightened my grip, and she must have cried out, because I suddenly felt two pairs of arms grabbing me and leading me away in a bum's rush.

"Just settle down, pal."

It was a familiar voice. I turned and recognized Tom Brokaw holding one arm. Tom Brokaw! I'm not certain, but it's possible Bill Bradley was holding the other.

Moments later I found myself deposited on Seventy-Fifth Street where a winter monsoon had just turned the streets of the Upper East Side into rivers two feet deep. A cloud of exhaust from the waiting limos billowed in what had become a freezing rain and the thought of finding a cab at midnight on such a New Year's Eve was ludicrous. I began to run. By the time I'd covered the forty blocks back to my hotel I was almost hypothermic. I tried to warm up in the rusty bathtub, but the water wouldn't get hot. A few hours later I made my way to La Guardia and flew back "student standby" to L.A., collected my clothes and my damaged guitar from Claire's shack, and moved back into my pathetic apartment.

Marshall called that night. He and Susan had broken up and he needed a place to stay. I said yes—masking my gratitude at not having to be alone with real sympathy for his predicament. Within hours he was on my couch, sobbing.

If it's true that misery loves company, then my lifelong bond with Marshall can be said to have begun in earnest that night. He told his tale of woe, I spilled mine, and we talked with a ferocious authenticity, shedding the inhibitions and guardedness young men harbor. We dissected everything: our childhoods, our parents, and the secret grandeur of our ambitions. With a wisdom beyond his years—alluding to my time with Claire but never lording it over me—he said there was no such thing as a free pass to a career. He goaded us to work harder, intimating that together we could conquer Hollywood. The next day he dragged me to a run-down movie house in West Hollywood—later to become a porn theater—where we watched a terrible print of a movie he said I needed to see. After I had sobbed through the end credits, we took a long walk and decided if we ever had a company, we'd name it after the town George Bailey couldn't leave, Bedford Falls.

By the end of that school year, Marshall had written and directed a wildly ambitious love story set amid the student protest movement. (Happily, my performance in the lead role has been lost in the mists of time.) Meanwhile, I adapted a John Guare one-act on which Marshall was the DP. *Something I'll Tell You Tuesday* is the story of an old couple on the eve of a life-and-death surgery. What could have been a morbid bummer, Guare had written so deftly, weaving humor with pathos, that when I screened it in the dreaded narrative workshop, it was greeted with boisterous laughter and even a few tears. After the screening, Tony Vellani patted me on the back, and I realized I might be asked back for a second year. In fact, Marshall and I were both invited to make films.

Over the next decades I would come to meet, and even work with, many of the people in that ballroom on New Year's Eve, but I would only see Claire once more, many years later. We ran into each other at a friend's birthday party in the midnineties and shared carefully gilded memories of our brief time together. A year later she was dead. Breast cancer. I still have her poems in my notebooks.

TEN THINGS THEY TRIED TO TEACH ME IN FILM SCHOOL

Which took me years of humiliating mistakes to learn.

1. **REMEMBER TO BREATHE**

   You've worked for two years to get to this moment, and there's no guarantee you'll ever get to do it again. You might as well enjoy it.

2. **THE CAMERA IS A BUDDHA**

   It sees the world as it is. It doesn't photograph your expectations or your fantasies. Try to see as the camera sees.

3. **NO PLAN SURVIVES CONTACT WITH THE ENEMY**

   Overprepare and then be ready to throw it all away when the actor feels their character wouldn't do it that way. Or you're behind. Or both.

4. **A GOOD IDEA CAN COME FROM ANYWHERE**

   You might as well listen to what others have to say because you're going to get the credit (and the blame) anyway. Remember, the key grip has probably made six times as many movies as you have.

5. **NO MOVIE CAN BE FUNNY ENOUGH**

   Laughter lets the audience know they're in good hands. They let their guard down and become vulnerable to the serious stuff.

6. **ON EVERY PRODUCTION**

   The director loses faith in the movie, the actors lose faith in the director, the crew hates the actors. Somehow it all works out.

7. **THE AUDIENCE'S ATTENTION SPAN IS EVEN SHORTER THAN YOURS**

   Fill every moment. Be generous. Give them gifts: jokes, secrets, surprises, truths. The minute they're bored, they'll check their email.

8. **THE ACTORS MOVE THE CAMERA, THE CAMERA DOESN'T MOVE THE ACTORS**

   Unless you have a style, don't pretend you do.

9. **MAKE THE MOVIE FOR ONE PERSON AT A TIME**

   Imagine your fourth-grade teacher sitting alone in the dark.

10. **WHERE THERE IS NO SOLUTION, THERE IS NO PROBLEM**

   As Hannibal said while deciding to cross the Alps, "I will find a way or I will make one."

P.S. NONE OF THESE RULES make any difference if you don't have a good script.

CHAPTER TWO

The Learn-As-You-Earn
School of Filmmaking

Family, 1978–1980

While struggling to finish my student film, I found work as a reader for United Artists. Twenty-five bucks for a script, forty for a novel. I must have read at least ten bad scripts a week as well as a novel or two. It was brutal work but instructive. Writing a synopsis, even of a weak script, helped me internalize the rhythms of narrative structure, while offering my half-assed comments forced me to consider why something did or didn't work, and how I might fix it. It also paid the rent and kept my battered Volkswagen running often enough that I didn't have to take the bus.

Around this time, I fell in with a group of young filmmakers, several years older than me—brash, driven, opinionated, and, to their own amazement, wildly successful. They had no reason to pay attention to me, let alone take me in, except maybe to have someone hanging around to remind them of their extraordinary good fortune. Michael Phillips, who at thirty-one, along with his wife, Julia, had already produced *Taxi Driver* and (joined by Tony Bill) *The Sting*, welcomed me into his warm, convivial circle. He invited me to visit the set of *Close Encounters of the Third Kind*, fed me often, and included me at his anarchic, wine-soaked Passover seders. Writer Jeff Fiskin (*Cutter's Way*) allowed me to sit in with a group of talented musicians at "music nights" at his Moorish castle in the Hollywood Hills. At a weekly coed softball game, comprised mostly of wannabe screenwriters, I first met Paul Schrader—already revered among us—and was happily reunited with writer Clay Frohman (*Under Fire*)—a childhood pal I hadn't seen since Hebrew school. Nick Meyer, in addition to letting me house-sit his rustic home in Laurel Canyon while he was in London working on the adaption of his bestselling novel *The Seven Percent Solution*, loaned me a thousand dollars to pry the release print of my student film out of hock to the lab at Technicolor (an extraordinary gesture I'm not sure I ever repaid). Oliver Stone, Ivan Passer, Jon Brauer, Liz Gill, David Ward, and Jeremy Kagan rounded out the merry band. Without ever demanding any kind of fealty or adulation—although both were abundant on my part—they were the midwives to my new Hollywood life. Justifiably pretentious, but never superior, they demystified its rituals, its protocols and nomenclature. For their generosity and lavish friendship, I am forever grateful.

Everyone has a tale of how they landed their first real job. Mine had nothing to do with my new circle of friends. It began conventionally enough but soon became as improbable and serendipitous as a Busby Berkeley movie. My agent had sent a script of mine to Richard Kramer, the freshly hired story editor of a new TV show called *James at 15*. Richard had been hired by Dan Wakefield, the creator of the show, who was fired in a network purge the day Richard arrived in town. Having moved from New York with only a six-week guarantee, Richard found himself under the thumb of the new executive story editor, a mean hack who took an instant dislike to him. It's easy to see how Richard, then only twenty-five and having recently published a short story in the *New Yorker*, might have been threatening to the much older TV writer. In any case, Richard knew he would soon be out of a job, and my screenplay was possibly the first (and only) submission he ever had time to read. Undaunted, he invited me to come up with a few story ideas. I duly read the show's first ten episodes, did my best to contrive a plot or two, and having no idea how to do a pitch, drove onto the Fox lot for my first grown-up, professional meeting. It was a disaster. The executive was rude to Richard and dismissive of me. We were in and out of his office in fifteen minutes. The next day, in their wisdom, the network deemed that James would never make it to sixteen; the show was canceled, and Richard was paid off.

Embarrassed and unnecessarily apologetic, he offered to send my script to the story editor of *Family*—for which he had once written a script. It was a remarkable, openhearted gesture in a town not known for its generosity of spirit. I had watched the pilot of *Family* when it came on the air. It seemed to me the first show that at least made an honest effort to portray flawed people who nonetheless loved each other enough to work things out. Its lovely pilot had been written by Jay Presson Allen, the brilliant playwright and screenwriter of *The Prime of Miss Jean Brodie* and *Prince of the City*. It was directed by Mark Rydell (*The Rose*) and featured a formidable ensemble led by Sada Thompson, a Tony-winning actress, and James Broderick (father of Matthew), who had recently starred in Sydney Lumet's *Dog Day Afternoon*. Notably, its producer was Mike Nichols (everything else good since 1968). Fancy people doing network TV. A first.

Carol and Nigel McKeand were the showrunners, although at the time such worker bees were called producers. Carol had once been a writers' assistant for Chuck Barris (later the subject of Charlie Kaufmann's *Confessions of a Dangerous Mind*) and written a funny, scabrous novel about it, *Glad and Sorry Seasons*, which caught the attention of a few TV producers. Until then, one-hour drama was mostly a boy's club, but Carol's prodigious talent was so undeniable they had no choice but to make way. I was never quite clear on Nigel's background. I knew he'd been an actor and that he was English and very smart about story structure, and that he and Carol were married. Leonard Goldberg was the executive producer. Together with Aaron Spelling, he had been responsible for an endless string of commercial hits including *Charlie's Angels*, *Fantasy Island*, and other triumphs of dubious artistic merit.

I was thrilled such bigshots might read my work. Okay, I was thrilled *anybody* would read it. No more than a week later, I got a call from my agent. They had all liked my writing and wanted to give me an assignment. Six weeks after that, only days after turning in my first draft, the story editor, David Jacobs, told me he had sold a pilot of his own (a melodrama about a scheming, rich family in Dallas . . . yes, that one) and would be leaving the show. Was I interested in becoming the story editor of *Family*?

Six months before, I had been reading scripts and writing coverage, mooching off my loving girlfriend, Lucy Bingham, able to contribute to the rent only when UA gave me enough scripts to cover. Suddenly, I found myself making more money per week than I had made in the previous two years. I was so afraid it would all come crashing down, I spent only enough to help with the rent and fix my car, and kept the rest of the checks inside a copy of Thomas Mann's *Confessions of Felix Krull, Confidence Man*. When, after a year, somebody suggested I needed to pay taxes, the guy at H&R Block thought I was kidding when I handed over forty weeks' worth of uncashed checks.

It's possible the most exciting moment of my young life was pulling into a studio parking space with my name on it. I was going to be working with Mike Nichols! The same Mike Nichols who'd directed *The Graduate* and *Who's Afraid of Virginia Woolf*. Of course, I couldn't have known that Mike had little to do with the show once the pilot was done and the series was picked up (although I'm sure he endorsed the checks that arrived weekly). In fact, Mike never said a word to me for several months, until one day we found ourselves alone in an elevator. After a moment he turned to me and said, "And you are?"

Jay Presson Allen, on the other hand, would stop by when she was in town. She took me to the Polo Lounge at the Beverly Hills hotel and told ribald stories about her early years in Hollywood working with "Hitch." (I eventually figured out she was talking about Alfred Hitchcock.) She'd stop by the stage for an hour or two, say hi to the cast and roam the sets, praising the décor before casually dropping an ashtray she fancied into her purse—not stealing, really, more like *droit du seigneur*, as if it was all hers by virtue of having created the show.

My Cinderella story began to lose its luster when I discovered what it meant to work in episodic television. We made twenty-two episodes of *Family* a year. There was no writing staff: no one had ever heard of a writers' room for one-hour drama.

I worked around the clock, taking pitches, writing outlines. Carol wrote or rewrote everything, including my horrible first drafts. I think she needed someone to talk to, so I wasn't fired. The following year, Carol decided she was tired—I can't imagine why—and that she and Nigel were leaving to create a show of their own. (It lasted six episodes.) Len Goldberg realized there was no one left to run our show. He had no choice but to hire me. I was twenty-seven. You'd think I'd be anxious taking on such responsibility, but I was much too full of myself to know how little I knew. Rather than hire anyone who understood what they were doing, I hired Liz Coe, a friend from my college theater days, as well as Marshall, who turned out to be even less prepared than I was to stay up all night doing rewrites scheduled to shoot the next morning. The episodes of *Family* we made were . . . underwhelming.

It was my first encounter with real stress, and I didn't do well. My back was in constant spasm. I lost fifteen pounds and began a decade-long relationship with Valium. Yet it turned out to be the kind of learn-as-you-earn experience I desperately needed. My film school idealism, my arrogance about directing, it all came crashing down. In those days, the measure of a good TV director was their speed. If they could shoot the day's work without going into overtime, they were pretty much guaranteed to be rehired. That meant pre-lit sets, very little discussion with the actors, and the kind of rudimentary staging that inevitably ended up with two actors standing opposite each other trading dialogue like broadside salvos from two ships at sea. But even amid such by-the-numbers technique I learned how long it took the grips to pull a wall, spent hours working with an AD breaking down a script, and figured out how to fashion a shooting schedule. Mostly, I made one humiliating mistake after another. I did get to spend hours in the cutting room with the fabled editor Marge Fowler. I was so anxious and self-absorbed I never bothered to talk to her about her career and she never got around to mentioning it; she was too busy excoriating me for my inept directing. (To my eternal shame, I learned years later that she had cut *Elmer Gantry*.) But shooting episode after episode eventually had an effect. After two years of this, I was no longer a mediocre writer; I was now a mediocre writer-director.

It was then that I experienced the first of many humiliating episodes on the bumpy path to becoming a movie director. My agent (the affable and kind Jeff Sanford) contrived to arrange a screening of my student film for David Puttnam, whose *Chariots of Fire* had won the Best Picture Oscar. Thrilled beyond description—after all, Steven Spielberg's short *Amblin'* had captured the imagination of the head of Universal and jump-started his career—I scammed a screening room on the Fox lot claiming it was for our TV show, and at the appointed time loitered outside until I saw Puttnam walk in. A few minutes later, when I heard the opening music cue, I snuck into the darkened theater, ostensibly to see how the film looked on a big screen but in truth to check on his reaction. Five minutes later, Puttnam stood up. I ducked down in my seat and watched in horror as he left the room. He had watched less than six minutes.

So much for being the next Spielberg.

I then failed at one writing assignment after another. During the summer hiatus of *Family*, I pitched an original story to Fox about an American G.I. during the Korean War suffering from battle fatigue (no such thing yet as PTSD) who is pulled out of combat and dropped into Tibet to aid the young Dalai Lama in his escape from the Chinese. Long before I handed it in, the studio executive who had commissioned the script was fired, and to my knowledge it was never read. Except by Michael Douglas, that is, who believed in it enough to team me with a wonderfully talented writer named Diane Thomas for a crash-and-burn six-week rewrite of a movie he was to produce and star in called *Starman*. Diane had met Michael while working as a waitress at Coogie's in Malibu. She had pestered him for months to read her original script, and at last he agreed. It was called *Romancing the Stone*. Even while writing under intense pressure, not to mention certain criminalized substances (such was eighties Hollywood), Diane and I got along famously and so we were crushed when, for reasons high above our pay grade, Michael was taken off the movie and our script was thrown away. I was struggling with a mortgage I couldn't afford and was paid in the normal fashion, but in an extravagant gesture Michael bought Diane a Porsche 911, in which she was killed shortly after, hitting a power pole on the Pacific Coast Highway.

There was one particularly gratifying moment in this tumultuous period. Len

Goldberg was friends with Joanne Woodward. When she told him she was interested in trying her hand at directing, he handed her over to me. I can only shake my head at the thought of myself at twenty-seven presuming to teach Joanne Woodward about directing. We sat in my office where I did my best to explain screen direction and lenses, aspects of which I still didn't entirely understand. The rest of the time I sat there saying to myself, *I'm sitting with Joanne Woodward!* Joanne (first names again) was so singularly sweet and avid, while I was so intent on being the serious pro rather than the starstruck fan I really was, that I never asked a single question about her astonishing body of work. It only got worse when she invited me to her home in Beverly Hills to work on the script for the episode of *Family* she would direct and there sat Paul Newman on the sofa in his undershirt, beer in hand, watching NASCAR. I imagined him chuckling to himself as he listened to me coaching his Academy Award–winning wife on the nuances of staging. As it turned out, Paul and I did end up having a conversation. It was during a commercial that he turned his eyes from the TV and said, "Hey, kid, want a beer?" I considered my reply and said yes.

Later, when Joanne casually mentioned asking "Hank" Fonda to be the guest star in her episode, I thought she was putting me on.

When he arrived on the stage, Henry Fonda insisted on calling me Mr. Zwick and refused to leave his chair all day whether he was in the scene or not.

"That was how Mr. Ford did it," he said. "At dawn, all our chairs would be lined up outdoors, and we would sit there as he looked up at the clouds and decided what we'd be shooting that day."

I tried to imagine the scene. John Wayne sitting beside Linda Darnell and Ward Bond under the towering skies of Monument Valley. *Someday*, I said to myself . . .

Len was a kind and generous man who went out of his way to support me. Sometimes he'd invite me to lunch in his office, where he'd give me advice about the business. Our relationship wasn't without its eccentricities. Long married, he'd apparently done his share of carousing in his younger years and sometimes the conversation would turn to what he called "Young Hollywood." It wasn't as creepy as it sounds; he was genuinely curious about my generation, and I was as close as he was likely to get to a young person in "the sexual revolution." He was convinced I was something of a player—a conviction based entirely on a misunderstanding of his own devising. The year before, as producer of *Charlie's Angels*, he had created a media event out of the search to replace Kate Jackson, one of the original Angels. By sheer coincidence, the young woman cast in the part was an old friend of mine named Shelley Hack. Finding herself besieged by the media, Shelley had asked if she could escape her pursuers by camping out at my house for a few days. I agreed, only to discover paparazzi hiding in the bushes the next day and my bewildered face on the front page of the tabloids as the newest Angel's "Mystery Man."

From then on, Len was convinced I was a lothario. I'd like to think it was for more than this that he continued to show an interest in me, but I suspect it didn't hurt. He began inviting me to play tennis at his Beverly Hills home with the likes of Sidney Poitier and Charlton Heston (who once raised a large welt on my ass when, as my doubles partner, he hit me in the rear with a first serve). More significantly, he hired me to direct my first TV movie, a story about teenage fashion models called *Paper Dolls*. I knew nothing about its world, nor did anybody think it necessary that I research it. The script, despite my efforts, was risible, as inauthentic and sugarcoated as network TV could be. But it was a big made-for-TV movie shooting on the streets of Manhattan—yet another course in my learn-as-you-earn school of filmmaking. The only good thing I can think to say about the experience is that I had the good sense to cast Eric Stoltz in his first major role, and we remain friends to this day.

To my surprise, *Paper Dolls* was picked up as a "backdoor" pilot. Len took avuncular pride watching my ascendance from story editor to producer to director. As a newbie, I had loved nothing more than goofing on the set with the actors and palling around with the crew, but once I was in charge, the fun stopped. I was now an authority figure, and nobody was interested in my jokes. It was all very confusing. I didn't feel entirely comfortable in my new role, yet for the first time in my life I was making real money. Ever since my father's financial bankruptcies I had been struggling. Being able to pay rent and pick up a check had real meaning. Len had been raised in modest circumstances and then enjoyed early success as head of programming at ABC in his thirties. He loved to play the wizened sage and once said something to me that still resonates: "You pay to get paid."

You never forget your first job, its unique confusion of giddiness, arrogance, and mortification. *Family* was the second-best thing that ever happened to me. The best was when it was canceled, and I went looking for my own voice.

NINE LESSONS FROM NINA

The oracle speaks.

1. **A HELPING HAND**

   If an actor is nervous, tell him his power emanates from the ground, rising from the earth into the sky like lightning. If he's scared, insist "This is going to be fun." Appeal to the child in the actor, who then appeals to the child in himself.

2. **BE HERE NOW**

   Everything is happening for the first time. There's never time in real life to think. Throw in a curve ball before a take now and then. Create an unforeseen obstacle. Watch life happen. If something is easy, it's usually wrong.

3. **THE DIALECTIC**

   Every scene has two truths that collide and change each other. Pretty much every scene should go from dark to light, or light to dark. Try to identify the moment in a scene that a dark bird flies in and flies out. Everything else is just sleight of hand.

4. **THE GLASS IS HALF-FULL**

   When we say a performance is "generous" it means the actor is constantly giving the audience little gifts. Unexpected humor, sudden rage, mysterious secrets, unflagging intensity. That's the actor you want to cast.

5. **THE LUCKY ONES**

   The best actors can be reading items from a dinner menu and leave you breathless as you wait to hear the entrées. Some people simply appear to have more vivid inner lives than others even when they don't. The life in their eyes never seems to dim and the camera wants to know why. We call this Being Kissed by the Angel.

6. **VINTAGE NINA, Part I**

   As they grow older, actors tend to become less than men and actresses become more than women. She hastened to add, "They used to tell me I didn't have enough cleavage. Now I do but it's on my face."

7. **VINTAGE NINA, Part II**

Cut scenes whenever you can. There are only two things that are too short: life and penises. Everything else is too long.

8. **VINTAGE NINA, Part III**

One evening, after a cocktail or two, Nina whispered to me: "If you've ever listened to actors talk in private, you won't let them improvise."

9. **DEFAULT MODE**

If the script and the staging and the set and the costumes are right, it should feel like cheating. The key to acting is to stop acting.

CHAPTER THREE

The Year of Loving Dangerously

Special Bulletin and *thirtysomething*, 1982–1991

The year I turned thirty everything happened at once. Love, illness, success, tragedy. Throw in marriage, friendship, pregnancy, and therapy and you begin to get the picture. The problem about opening yourself to the improvisation of life is having to admit you aren't in control. Especially when life is coming at you head-on like a speeding truck in the wrong lane and there's no way to avoid the collision.

I almost forgot the fatal car accident. That happened too.

It was 1982. My career was going nowhere. After the ridiculous good luck of getting the chance to produce a network TV series at twenty-seven, I had spent the next four years writing scripts no one wanted to make and directing TV that wasn't worth seeing. It was as if there was this chasm between what I intended and what ended up on the page and screen. No matter how determined I was to be daring and original, the work came out ordinary and inauthentic. In the years since film school, Marshall and I had become inseparable. As we struggled to assimilate what they had tried to teach us in class, we became each other's scourge as well as best friend. If you find one person in your life who can always be counted on to tell you the truth, you're lucky. If you can find him in Hollywood, you've won the lottery. We were then and remain each other's first reader. After finishing a new script of mine, he would get this compassionate yet anguished look in his eye, and I knew he agreed that it sucked. To this day, fifty years on, his casually withering criticism occasionally makes me want to murder him. He'll look up from a page and say, "This part makes me tired."

Flushed with early success on *Family*, I had bought a little house I could no longer afford and desperately took whatever work I could to pay the mortgage, such as a low-budget indie about the Kentucky Derby where I never got to attend the race, nor go to Kentucky for that matter. Meanwhile, Marshall wasn't doing much better writing for such unchallenging fare as *CHiPs* (California Highway Patrol) and *Seven Brides for Seven Brothers*. He finally had to borrow money from his father to write an original script, promising to pay him back with interest, should it sell. It didn't. Every afternoon, when we could no longer tolerate another fruitless day of writing, one of us would call the other and we would meet at a video arcade and pour quarters into a road-racing game. Afterward we would lie on the living room floor of the house I was about to lose, whining and moaning. During one such sob session, I told him about a terrifying dream I'd had the night before about seeing TV news of imminent nuclear annihilation, and how I woke up, sweating and unable to breathe, still believing it to be real.

"We should do it!" he said.

"Do what?"

"Pitch it as a movie!"

"I'm talking about an anxiety attack, not a development deal!"

"I'm serious," he said. "What if we were to tell a story on TV but we did it only through what you would be able to see on the news."

"You mean, like Orson Welles's *War of the Worlds*?"

"Except not about aliens. We'll choose something more plausible and terrifying."

"Like nuclear annihilation, you mean."

"And we'll create all the news footage ourselves."

"Like *The Battle of Algiers?*"

"Never heard of it."

And so it began.

I won't try to describe the labyrinth we had to navigate before getting NBC to agree to pay us for a script. Had they not been languishing at the bottom of the Nielsen ratings, I'm convinced they would never have given us a chance. The moment we began writing, though, it was as if fortune's wheel had turned, and our names spun to the top. We couldn't believe our luck. I imagine the movie gods gazing down on our giddy optimism, chuckling, *So they want to disrupt the universe? Let's see how much disruption these two geniuses can handle . . .*

Here are some of the things that happen that year, 1982:

The day after we begin writing, I meet a girl in the parking garage of the old Santa Monica mall. My battered car is in the shop. I've borrowed a friend's car and can't remember where I'm parked. She is driving a beater from Dave Schwartz's Rent-A-Wreck and can't remember what it looks like. We chat as we wander from one level to another. I manage to get her number before she finds her car (which has a copy of Pascal's *Pensées* on the front seat).

I tell Marshall about the girl in the parking lot, rhapsodizing about her beauty, wit, and intelligence and that I think I could fall in love with her. He says, "What else is new? You say that every other week. Let's get back to work." The next day I call her, only to learn she is living with someone else. I have no choice but to get back to work. Days later, Marshall learns his now-wife Susan (yes, they had gotten back together, for now, at least) is pregnant with their first child. He's too distracted to work. The following week, the girl from the parking lot, whose name is Liberty, calls to tell me she has left the man she'd been living with. Now Marshall and I are both too excited to work. We all spend an idyllic summer watching Susan's belly grow. I ask Liberty to marry me. She says yes. Marshall and I finish a first draft.

In September we hear the network likes it. The next day Marshall gets a call that his father has been diagnosed with a brain tumor. The prognosis isn't good.

He flies to Philadelphia to see him. Afterward, he joins us on Liberty's farm in rural Pennsylvania to be my best man. The day of the wedding we hear the network wants us to come to NYC to observe NBC News. After the ceremony, Susan returns to L.A. while Liberty, Marshall, and I head to Manhattan for our honeymoon. The next morning, we begin observing at NBC News.

By mid-November, the rewrite is done. Two weeks later, the network gives us the go-ahead, and everything speeds up. We begin prep in L.A., casting unknown actors since the premise only works if the audience doesn't recognize them. (This is how we first get to know David Clennon, later to become the infamous Miles Drentell on *thirtysomething*.) During rehearsals, I operate the video camera myself as if I am the news cameraman in the scene. When I review the footage, for the first time in my life the work is exactly as I imagined it. That night I am too excited to sleep, believing I might have a future as a director. The next day at the production office, my sister calls to tell me my mother has been killed in a car accident. I collapse in Marshall's arms.

That night I fly home to Chicago to help my sisters prepare for the funeral. Their lives had already been buffeted by my parents' messy divorce, but now they are shattered. I'd like to be able to give them the support they need, but the truth is, I am a wreck myself. On the morning after my mother is buried, I fly to Charleston, South Carolina, to meet Marshall and scout locations, burying my grief in work, not the last time that charming habit will serve me. We begin production in January. It's a grueling shoot with challenging material made even more emotional by the tumultuous events in our lives. On the first day of shooting, something is wrong with the lead actress. Whether it's nerves or a medical condition, she has a vocal problem that makes her sound nothing like a professional news anchor. Marshall and I huddle in a corner. We realize we're going to have to fire her. I've never fired anyone in my life. So, while I continue shooting, knowing everything we do will have to be redone, Marshall is on the phone with the casting director frantically looking for a replacement. We decide on Kathryn Walker and send her a script at 7 p.m. She reads it by 9 p.m. Arrives on set the next morning at 4:30 a.m. Goes on camera at 6 a.m., letter perfect and brilliant. Kathryn Walker is a goddess.

When we finish production, the network informs us they need our movie—
now called *Special Bulletin*—on the air in six weeks. There is no such thing as a
video editing system that allows for the kind of elasticity used in film editing, nor
are there any film editors trained on video editing systems. That means we must
cut the movie online, with little help from a news editor unfamiliar with narrative. Marshall and I hunker down in a facility in Burbank, essentially making final
decisions about each sequence, one cut at a time, in sequence. And then tearing
it apart when it doesn't work and beginning again. Midway through the process,
Susan goes into labor. Two days later, sleepless beyond recognition, the proud father of a baby girl, Marshall stumbles back into the editing room to do the offline
cut of the "news packages" to be dropped into the final cut I am finishing.

The show is due to air in two weeks, but before that can happen, Reuven
Frank, the head of NBC News, insists on seeing the movie and goes berserk. He
calls Brandon Tartikoff, the president of NBC, demanding that it not be aired,
fearing the depiction of a nuclear event, shot as if it were really happening, would
not only cause widespread panic but also bring the news division into disrepute.
When we get word that the network is seriously considering not putting it on, we
call Howard Rosenberg at the *L.A. Times* and John O'Connor at the *New York
Times* to tell them what the network is thinking of doing. They ask to see the film.
Following Werner Herzog's adage to ask forgiveness and not permission, we send
it to them without the network's consent. All hell breaks loose. The controversy
plays out on the front page of every entertainment outlet in the country. Everyone
wants to see the movie the network won't air. Tartikoff has no choice; he must air
it. But to pacify the news division, he agrees to run a disclaimer at the bottom of
the screen coming out of each commercial break. We aren't happy about it, but
nobody seems to notice them when they air because they were too busy raiding the
refrigerator during the commercials.

The velocity of events is relentless. Rave reviews are followed by six Emmy
nominations, including best movie, writing, and directing. Two days before the
ceremony, Marshall's father dies. He returns from the funeral in Philadelphia
barely in time to put on his new tuxedo and accept an armful of Emmys. Days

later, Liberty tells me she is pregnant. I am undone with happiness, but also stupe-fied. Dazed after yet another acceptance speech—it could have been the Writers Guild, the Directors Guild, the Peabody, we won them all—Marshall and I find ourselves sitting on the curb outside the Beverly Hilton, clutching our little stat-uettes. I don't know whether to laugh or cry. I turn to Marshall, or maybe it was Marshall turning to me, and affecting a comic Yiddish accent, *"So, nu . . . ?"*

It was more dark than funny, but soon we are laughing so hard that tears pour down our cheeks. Passersby stop to stare at the two bearded guys in ill-fitting new tuxedos doubled over in paroxysms of hilarity and grief. For an entire year, no sooner had we managed to internalize one overwhelming event than we were over-whelmed by another. Was this what adult life would be like from now on? It was Newton's third law of motion made flesh: For every success there is an equal and opposite trauma. We were learning that in life it is never one thing *or* another, it is always one thing *and* another. That phrase would soon become a kind of mantra for our creative lives.

Marshall had been very close to his father. Two years later, he would win an-other Emmy writing about his father's death. My mother had been only fifty when the drunk driver hit her head-on two blocks from our house on a road she had driven every day for thirty years. From the time I was very young, she had sensed in me a seriousness about a life in the arts and took it upon herself to cultivate it. Marshall's father had done the same. Neither of them had lived to see our first triumph, or even our firstborn children. In many ways their loss still informs a certain tragic sensibility in our work.

We couldn't have known it then, but it was in that moment of absurdity and heartbreak, of reckoning with confusion and celebration, that *thirtysomething* was born. It wasn't until some months later that we realized we couldn't rest on our laurels forever, and that this might be a good moment to cash in on our success with a paycheck or two, so we began to think in concrete terms about doing a tel-evision series. After more than a year playing around with hackneyed ideas about spies and epic heroes, detectives, and family shows, it occurred to us there might be something to write about in what had befallen us the year before.

In Hellenistic Egypt, alchemists claimed to be able to transform base metal into gold. They called it "transmutation." It was, of course, impossible. But isn't this what a writer presumes to do when he conjures up ordinary experience and tries to magically transform it into the splendor of art? Pasted into one of my notebooks is a George Booth cartoon I clipped from the *New Yorker* at the time. Sitting at a desk before an old typewriter is an unshaven, frustrated writer, obviously blocked. Surrounding him are a collection of mangy dogs. Large dogs, small dogs, the flea-ridden and the feckless. Behind him in the doorway stands his long-suffering wife. You can almost hear her shrill voice as she bitches him out.

"Write about dogs!" she says.

"Write about dogs!"

And so we did.

There is some dispute about who first suggested we write a show about ourselves and our friends. Liberty—formerly the girl in the parking lot, now known as the mother of our newborn son, Jesse—claims she was tired of listening to us lounging around our living room coming up with one lousy idea after another and suggested the trials and tribulations of our circle as fodder for a show. Marshall maintains he had always wanted to do this kind of show but was afraid to say it out loud for fear of me pointing out that John Sayles and Larry Kasdan had already explored our generation's angst in *The Return of the Secaucus 7* and *The Big Chill*, respectively. My claim of authorship dates to watching Woody Allen avail himself of his relationship with Diane Keaton as the inspiration for *Annie Hall*. But no matter how it came to pass, from the moment we pitched the idea to ABC—no sizzle reel, no pitch deck, just a couple of thirty-two-year-olds talking about our lives—we were convinced it didn't have a prayer of getting picked up. And until the eighty-fifth episode, four years later, Marshall, Susan, Liberty, and I were as close to Camelot as any of us were ever going to get and closer to getting divorced than any of us would have liked.

Too much has already been said—mostly by us—in self-serving magazine pieces and TV interviews about our theories of the dialectic in relationships, about the personal politics of truth-telling, and how hard it can be, even for articulate, privileged, whiny white boomers, to get through the day. I'm not at all sure how acute our insights really were, no matter how penetrating and provocative they seemed at the time. We certainly weren't the first generation to have children, struggle to reconcile work and family, deal with love and loss. I can't help but recall the indulgent smiles of our parents, who tended to see the show as more nostalgic than revolutionary. Then again, we only knew what we knew; how could we possibly have known more? I do think it's important to resist the temptation of seeing it all in prettified retrospect. It was so much more complex than that, so much more overwhelming than any of us could ever have anticipated. We were stupid and wised up, arrogant and innocent, brilliant and imitative, impossibly young and old beyond our years.

And it all went by so quickly, which is something that happens anyway in your thirties. Time blurs. To find ourselves on talk shows and the covers of magazines, to be recognized on the street, win awards, and be invited to fancy Hollywood parties was wonderful and disorienting. No one sets out to create a phenomenon; all we'd hoped was to be true to ourselves. It was head-turning to watch *thirtysomething* become common parlance and giddy to be hailed as generational spokesmen, but it was hard to reconcile all that with changing a blown-out diaper, eating dinner straight out of the refrigerator, removing our clothes from the backs of chairs where they'd been draped for months, barking our shin as we stumbled out of bed for the midnight feeding, and waking up four hours later to head into the studio for an early call.

The strain on our marriages would have been intense enough had the four of us not all been writing for the show. Consider the dynamics. Marshall and I were writing about Michael and Hope raising a newborn while Liberty and I were raising a newborn. Liberty, meanwhile, was writing about Michael being too obsessed with work and that he wasn't sharing the burden of raising a newborn. As showrunners, Marshall and I gave Liberty notes suggesting that she wasn't being fair to me, I mean Michael, who was overwhelmed by work. Liberty was also overwhelmed by work, simultaneously writing for a TV show *and* doing the lion's share of raising a newborn, and who the fuck did I think I was giving her notes about raising a newborn? Susan, meanwhile, was writing about Elliot and Nancy's troubled marriage and their decision to go into therapy while Marshall and Susan were *in* therapy. Marshall thought Susan's depiction of . . . er . . . Elliot was a bit harsh but was reluctant to say so, so he deputized me to give his wife notes. Susan knew full well that I was giving her Marshall's notes and confronted Marshall about it in therapy. A fictionalized version of their confrontation in therapy emerged as a wonderful scene written by Susan, directed by Marshall, and starring Marshall as the therapist.

Meanwhile, Ken Olin and Patty Wettig were married to each other in real life but married to Mel Harris and Tim Busfield, respectively, on the show. Having to watch each other play intimate bedroom scenes with someone else's partner wasn't easy, but possibly added a certain charge to a union that was already tempestuous enough, given the inevitable volatility of a marriage between two actors. Peter Horton and Polly Draper played Michael and Hope's single friends, which was no small irony since Peter's marriage was falling apart, and Polly's would soon follow. Tim Busfield was recently divorced and would remarry during season two. A firm believer in the triumph of hope over experience, Mel Harris ended her third marriage midway through the show's run and began her fourth. Melanie Mayron was the only genius with no intention of getting married, yet she eagerly offered marriage counseling to the rest of us, whether we wanted it or not.

What was most remarkable about this Bloomsbury in blue jeans was how little these complications interfered with the job at hand. Many of us had come from the theater and the fervor of our commitment was an attempt to recapitulate the best of those experiences. Every day we would crowd together in a tiny, windowless room, knee to knee, greasy Styrofoam lunch containers clutched in our laps, to watch dailies. It didn't matter whether your work appearing on the tiny screen in the corner was as an actor, writer, or director, you wanted to see what everyone else was up to. For Marshall and me as directors, this was an opportunity to test-drive one of Nina Foch's favorite admonitions: "Life doesn't stop when we're talking on the phone."

People multitask. We all graze in the refrigerator, doodle, do dishes, check our email, look in the mirror. We stretch, sit on countertops, hang upside down from sofas. Rarely do we ever stand opposite each other and just talk. Our goal in staging was to constantly keep all the balls up in the air, filling every moment with a joke, a pratfall, a sly bit of revealing behavior. And then, when you least expect it, whether in the middle of a plumbing emergency, or telling a funny story, or making love, a dark bird flies into the room and back out (metaphorically speaking) and a new truth is revealed. By overstuffing eight pounds into a six-pound bag and keeping it all moving at a blistering pace, we could hide the seams of clunky exposition or awkward character development. The same went for blocking. Instead of having actors nailed to the floor while declaiming into each other's face, we were fanatics for behavior, any kind of behavior, the funnier the better.

"Idiosyncratic, contrapuntal juxtaposition" is what Nina had called it.

Pace and rhythm were everything. Preston Sturges and Howard Hawks were our gods. There was no greater sin than an actor taking "a beat" before saying his line. Because in real life, we only listen to the end of someone else's sentence out of politeness. Midway through, we think we know what they're going to say. The truth is, there's only talking and waiting to talk.

Our emphasis was always on how the breakdown of a scene was the legacy of its content rather than an exercise in form. A dolly move may be stylish, but did it tell the story? How did the choice of a lens and the placement of the camera affect the emotional temperature? We preached that every scene had two truths colliding, with a winner and a loser. In life, people don't easily say hurtful things, or reveal hidden feelings. A price must be paid. And that deep emotion, when it happened—and boy, it happened often on *thirtysomething*—had to be earned. It's like sex. You don't want to get to the good part too fast.

For Marshall and me, those dailies-watching sessions were our reinvention of the tough love we'd endured in film school. Harshly critical one minute, supportive the next, we were pushing the cast and pushing each other, scene by scene, take by take, to experiment, to push the envelope of what episodic television had looked and felt like in the past. In other words, to do better.

It's no surprise that the cult of the director infected everyone. Peter Horton had already directed an *ABC Afterschool Special* the year before. His stipulation before joining the cast was that he would get to direct. He was first on the firing line. His maiden voyage was a little rocky, and I have since been told how terrifying, even cruel, a taskmaster I could be. One of the other cast members who directed for the first time that year dubbed Marshall and me "the rabbi and the terrorist." (I'm loath to admit who was who.) But by the end of the season, Peter had become a mainstay behind the camera, his work possessing a signature elegance we all came to envy. Ken Olin's searching intellect was never quite satisfied with acting. The minute he began to direct it was obvious this was his calling. The burdensome anxiety he carried with him as an actor would disappear when he stepped behind the camera, and his rapport with the other actors was beautiful to watch. Having two of our leads sharing the directing chores with me and Marshall gave the show the kind of continuity we'd always hoped for.

Tim Busfield came next. The ultimate team player, Tim and his brother had run their own children's theater for years. He brought a level of enthusiasm and a "let's put on a show" playfulness to each moment. Even as he sometimes drove the crew mad with his irrepressible energy, the actors adored working for him. As a director, Melanie Mayron's offbeat sensibility and comic chops meant that she always found the funny in unexpected ways. Mel Harris directed only once, quite well, and Polly Draper waited until the show ended to demonstrate her prodigious ability in movies she has since written and directed herself. From the moment Scott Winant, our supervising producer, got behind the camera for the first time, he revealed a wildly innovative technique we all sought to imitate. Claudia Weill, Dan Lerner, Rob Cohen, Gary Sinise, Rob Lieberman, and our costume designer, Patrick Norris, all pushed the envelope. Only Patty Wettig didn't get the bug. What we didn't know was that as she was raising two kids and winning three Emmys, she was secretly writing plays in her spare time.

Looking at the richness of their résumés since *thirtysomething* ended, it's hard not to admit a certain measure of parental pride as these talented professionals have gone forth to spread the good word. As producer-directors, executive producers, and showrunners, their work has had an undeniable influence on the best television has had to offer. *Alias, My So-Called Life, Friday Night Lights, Brothers & Sisters, Grey's Anatomy, Parenthood, New Amsterdam, Breaking Bad, Without a Trace, Nashville, Once and Again, Damages, Jane the Virgin, In Treatment*, and *This Is Us*, to name just a few. It's more than their felicity in staging or their skill with actors; there's an ineffable humanist signature common to each show they do that feels like a legacy of what we started.

But how to describe that legacy? The best way I can put it is that *thirtysomething* was always a show in search of itself, which is also a polite way of saying it was self-absorbed. The most radical thing about it wasn't that we were trying to elevate what we called "the octane of truth," or that we were willing to talk about ambivalence in marriage and friendships, or even that the searing episodes of loss that both Marshall and I had experienced led us to hold the audience's hands over a flame. What distinguished the show was the absence of anything but a close examination of the characters in it— radical at the time, old hat these days. Nobody was a cop or a doctor or a lawyer. With no franchise to fall back on for story ideas other than the web of relationships connecting seven characters, we had no choice but to dig deeper into each one, until the same network that had given us such freedom on the pilot began to grow uncomfortable the closer to the bone we got.

After reading our first few scripts they called:

"Don't you think these episodes are a little depressing?"

"I guess so."

"Do you think maybe you could lighten them up?"

"Nope."

And that was the last note we ever got. These were the halcyon days before the networks owned their own shows, a fleeting moment of prelapsarian Eden when creators still ruled. To sell a show today, you need to have the pilot worked out beat for beat, character arcs set for at least three seasons, and a cliffhanger for every episode. Not to mention a sizzle reel and a pitch deck. On spec. In our one and only meeting with the creative execs at ABC (bless you, Mireille Soría and Chad Hoffman), we started off by saying we didn't recognize anyone on television who looked or talked like us and went on to describe our lives in a way that was self-mocking and self-serious. Beyond that, we had no plan at all. The furthest we had gone in our thinking was that one marriage would survive while another might not. We knew someone should die but not who or how. We assumed the characters would have parents, work and sex lives, but mostly we wanted to raise the internal stakes as a kind of bulwark against TV's usual melodramatic clichés. To concentrate on what was epic in ordinary life, we based our characters on people we knew and experiences we'd had. It helped that the execs were in their thirties and facing the same upheaval in their lives that we were. The notion that their boss, Brandon Stoddard, then president of ABC, felt that was enough to put a show on the air was corporate lunacy. If we were to go into a meeting at Netflix tomorrow with only that, we'd be escorted out by security before we had time to sip our spring water.

The first episodes we shot were wildly uneven but that turned out to be a blessing. It forced us to reinvent the show every week to see what worked and what didn't. A *Scenes from a Marriage* rip-off, yes; a Mel Brooks satire, not so much. To have overdetermined the trajectory of our characters would have proscribed the creativity of a brilliant writing staff. With their first scripts, each writer was lobbying, consciously or not, for what they wanted the show to be. Having written the first three episodes, Marshall and I had already made an aggressive case for the currency of the show. Allowing other strong writers to influence its direction expanded the show's voice as well as its worldview. Different writers naturally felt drawn to writing for different actors, allowing each to shine in turn.

Everyone had their pet concerns, political, cultural, moral, and literary. For an early episode, Richard Kramer (the first writer I invited to join us) wrote an *Umbrellas of Cherbourg* homage describing Michael and Hope's first date since having a baby, with Michael Feinstein as the musical narrator. Paul Haggis wrote a Hitchcock spoof. Liberty wrote an entire show about weaning. Susan channeled Ingmar Bergman. Anne Hamilton wrote an episode told backward. Marshall and I wrote a version of *Rashomon*. We didn't have a writers' room. Marshall and I would work with each writer, one at a time, working out each story beat for beat. The writer would then go off and write, eventually turning in a draft (usually late) on which we would give notes—infuriating notes, I'm sure—draft after draft, but never rewriting them. We were already writing plenty as it was, not to mention directing, editing, and overseeing the scoring. Since the writers were all gifted creators in their own right, we were determined to treat them as such.

We were all in search of the same elusive grail, a show that would celebrate the examined life, honor our contradictory desires, forbidden dreams, and secret inhibitions, and somehow manage to be funny and entertaining at the same time. Each episode aspired to be a meditation on a serious theme—ambition, envy, shame—but leavened by witty dialogue, absurd fantasies, and discomfiting farce. When we ran out of ideas from our own lives we stole from the actors'. Once things they told us in private began to appear in the next week's episode, they became more circumspect.

Every week we would gather in the same tiny conference room for a table read. Each one felt like an event, with writers and crew crowded in among the principals and guest cast. One week, Joe Dougherty would delight us with a script about the latest depredations of Miles Drentell; next week's episode would have an entirely different tone with Susan's latest installment in the sad saga of Elliot and Nancy's marriage. A week later, Jill Gordon (Scott Winant's wife!) might deliver a slapstick comedy about Melanie and Polly falling in love with the same gynecologist, or Winnie Holzman would concoct a lovely, squirmy take on *La Ronde* on the difference between men and women. When Richard Kramer decided it was time we showed two men in bed, every advertiser dropped out and the network refused to rerun it. The details of Marshall's life and mine were laid bare as well. Marshall wrote a touching episode about the death of his father in the guise of Michael's dad, and when Liberty was in a car accident while pregnant and rushed to the hospital in danger of delivering prematurely, it appeared very much as it happened as the climax to a takeoff episode on sixties sitcoms we wrote called "The Mike Van Dyke Show."

Every week there was some new challenge: a tricky visual effect, a stunt, a down-and-dirty way to do something the studio said wasn't possible on our budget. I never could have gone on to make the movies I've made had I not learned all there was to be mined in making eighty-five hours of television. I also know that, after four years, neither Marshall nor I could have imagined making even one minute more. By the time we resolved the outcome of Nancy's illness and balanced the karmic ledger with Gary's death, we felt we had done everything we had set out to do, particularly as it pertained to the hard lessons we had confronted the year we turned thirty. Besides, any good vaudevillian knows to get the hell off the stage and leave the audience wanting more. Unfortunately, the network didn't agree and threatened to sue us when we told them we wanted to call it quits. We worked that out by promising to do another show, which eventually became *My So-Called Life*. In fact, we ended up doing a few more shows over the years but that's another story.

Keeping a promise to an audience to deliver your best work each week for four seasons takes its toll. Burnout is real. Especially when you add sick children and sleepless nights, marital issues, and garden-variety anxieties like death and taxes. Everybody gets tired and cranky and tempted to phone it in. But this cast never did. When Mel was nine months pregnant and two days past her due date, I didn't think twice about asking her to reshoot an emotional final scene between her and Ken in an episode I was directing. Without any hesitation she came back to work the next morning, and with an ambulance waiting outside the stage door with its motor running, she waddled in, nailed the scene, and gave birth eight hours later.

A long-running show inevitably becomes a kind of ad hoc family. Over four intense years at close quarters there were fights, romances, rivalries, and the occasional blowout followed by a tearful reconciliation. What was truly inspiring was how supportive and loving the cast was to each other throughout the run, which lasted until 1991. I don't recall a single incident of the kind of toxicity or sabotage I've heard about on other shows. They were troupers, indefatigable and determined to bring their A game to every scene.

There was just so much to celebrate: out of forty-two Emmy nominations we won a baker's dozen, including best drama in our first season. We also made at least that many clunkers I wish could be buried at the bottom of the sea. But we never stopped pushing ourselves and each other. When one of us would despair, someone else would pick up the slack, and the work in season four was every bit as strong as in the previous three seasons. The only thing we had ever done for that long was attend college. Over those four years we spent as much time with each other as with our partners and children. Which is perhaps why thirtysomething years later we were ready to do it again.

In 2020, we were hours from the first day of shooting the reboot, called *thirtysomethingelse*, when Covid brought it all crashing down. The subject of the show was, predictably enough, how it felt to be the parents of children who were now the same age as we were when we made the show. We all gathered for a week of rehearsal in New Jersey (filling in for Philadelphia), and it made for a lovely blending of old and new, a passing of the baton from the veterans to the rookies. Although our new cast wasn't nearly as uniformly white as the previous incarnation, the ensemble dynamic was eerily familiar: a heady cocktail of collegiality and competitiveness, anticipation and anxiety, self-absorption and self-revealment, vanity, vulgarity, jests, jibes, and lunch orders. And all on ABC's dime. I can report, based on those too-few delightful days as well as various dinners, emails, and Zoom calls since, that we're all still fond of each other. Even more reassuring is that none of us have yet to appear in one of those horrible Twitter threads under the heading "Whatever Became of . . ."

Everyone still looks remarkably hale and well-preserved, even in HD. Ken, Peter, and Tim are big-deal showrunners. Melanie is booked as a director every week and still manages to have a skincare line. Polly writes and directs her own movies, and did I mention both her kids are movie stars? At last count Patty has written three plays and Mel has an IMDb list of credits longer than my arm. She is also married for the sixth time and this one has every chance of sticking. Meanwhile, Winnie has written one of the biggest musicals of all time, and Richard has written a touching novel. In addition to tolerating me all these years, Liberty still writes marvelously when we manage to drag her away from her political activism to work on our shows, while Susan has blown off Hollywood and can be found writing poetry in a used bookstore she bought in a seventeenth-century gristmill in Northampton, Massachusetts.

And my partnership with Marshall—already the longest on record in Hollywood—is still thriving. Mostly it feels like one long conversation interrupted regularly by the same argument about whose dialogue is better, followed by the same grilled chicken salad for lunch. Yet somehow the work keeps getting done. The key to our partnership, as best I can explain it, is having had the good sense to choose someone who's a better writer than I am. Also, a nicer person. While I tend to go overboard emphasizing structure and mise-en-scène (literally, "put in the scene," aka "staging"), his insistence on digging relentlessly for the hidden truth beneath every scene and the subtext beneath every line is both maddening and invaluable. Over time we've assimilated each other's strengths—except for him having been in therapy since age ten and believing that makes him licensed to practice. On me. No, see . . . that's just the way we talk to each other. It confuses some people when they think we really mean the horrible things we say. In meetings we finish each other's sentences, interrupt each other, and even bicker. You know how sometimes at the dog park, a good dog will see another good dog he knows well and then suddenly, for no apparent reason, they begin barking and snarling at each other? Soon it escalates into a brawl until they have to be pulled apart. And the next day it's as if it never happened. Imagine seeing that same dog every day for forty-five years and you begin to get the idea.

Courtesy of the author

The best thing about working with Marshall is that he remembers nothing we've written the day before. Nothing. Tabula rasa. It's as if he's had anterograde amnesia since age twenty-two. This can be more than a little vexing, but it also turns out to be unexpectedly helpful. Because everything is new to him. Each morning when we begin work he looks at the script as if he's never seen it before. I sometimes tell him I wrote all his lines, and he believes me. On the other hand, he's just as likely to object to one of his ideas from the day before and want to rewrite it until I manage to convince him it was *my* idea and refuse to change it. Sometimes mine actually *is* the better idea. Sometimes it's his. Just as often it's a third idea that's better than either of us could have written alone; usually, it's something one of us was afraid to suggest because it's secret or shameful or worse, unconventional, and the other person recognizes it as the best.

On most days we begin work at ten. I've inevitably been up several times the night before anguishing about a scene while he hasn't given it a thought. Instead, he's read several articles from various obscure medical journals about a condition no one has ever heard of and is convinced he has symptoms.

"I don't feel well," he says. "Do we have any chocolate?"

By three we've put in a good five hours, but once you subtract his trips to the bathroom, calls from our children and wives, snacks, email, his daily recommendations of mysterious new supplements, waiting on hold to speak to our representatives only to be told they'll get back to us, more trips to the bathroom, and of course the obligatory grilled chicken salad, we will have done maybe twenty minutes' work. We're also in the final round of the world championship Toss the Crumpled-Up Page into the Wastebasket singles competition. He's hit nine in a row. If he sinks this one, I've agreed to use his cut of the final scene. As he's about to shoot, I sneeze to distract him. He misses but agrees to my version because I care more.

The phone rings. Another interruption, thank God. An actor has passed on a project. Or the studio hates my first cut. I'm immediately convinced I'll never work again and begin spiraling into full panic mode. I look over and see he has two pens sticking out of his ears, two pens in his nostrils, and two more between his teeth.

"What?" he asks.

"You used to be a child prodigy," I say. "Now you're just a child."

He smiles beatifically. I shake my head and we get back to work.

Partnerships tend not to last in Hollywood. You'd think ours might have ended during one of the many times we'd gone off and made movies on our own.

But when we're working together and I'm down on the set, over schedule, dealing with some disaster, and the studio threatens to pull the plug, he's the one who makes them back off. I never had a brother. Now I do. He would take a bullet for me. Like, in the leg or something.

What's appalling is how others try to divide you: "You don't need him; you could do better on your own." In a town defined by ego, it is commonplace to pay people to tell you how great you are. Agents. Managers. Lawyers. Publicists. Trainers. Yet I've willingly shared half my earnings for the privilege of having someone who eagerly tells me I'm full of shit. Still, there have been times I've considered ending it. So has he. Fortunately, neither of us has wanted to at the same time. One word best describes the secret of our longevity: *forbearance*.

THE TEN-PART *THIRTYSOMETHING* DIRECTOR'S HANDBOOK

Nina lives.

1. BASICS

Rather than give line readings, talk to actors in terms of discovery. Wonder. Awe. Pleasure, loss of pleasure. Love, loss of love. Fear. Rage. Grief. Give them something to think about instead of the line. The camera loves to watch the birth of the idea, not its execution.

2. MOTIVATION

Don't intellectualize. Engage the actor from the neck down, not the neck up. The farther south you can bring the conversation, from Norway, say, to Italy—meaning the more you can locate the motivation between the legs, the stronger the performance.

3. CHOICES, Part I

Directors talk a lot about "choices." Predictable choices are boring, but arbitrary ones are also distracting. Keep in mind Noel Coward's advice to actors: "Just say the lines and don't trip over the furniture."

4. CHOICES, Part II

Small is usually better than big. Skilled actors open a little window behind their eyes allowing the audience to glimpse their inner life and then shut it just as quickly. Such blessed creatures are why God invented the close-up.

5. THE REAL WORK

Vocal training. Fight training. Accents. Movement. Such things take practice, but emotional work requires courage and the willingness to pay a price. Critics like the technical stuff because it's showy and describable. Gifted actors know better.

6. THE DOCTOR IS IN

You're not really a psychiatrist but some basic understanding can unlock a performance. An actor playing "depressed" is unwatchable, but his work can come alive if you tell him depression is really anger turned inward. You don't have to have been in therapy. But it helps.

7. **ADJUSTMENTS, Part I**

   When an actor does something you don't like, never say, "I have a better idea." Say, "You've just given me a great idea!" If his next take is over the top, say, "You don't know your power." If you want another take, blame the camera operator.

8. **ADJUSTMENTS, Part II**

   When an actor does something you do like, try not to point it out or he'll never be able to repeat it for the next take. Instead, just tell him he looks incredible in that coat.

9. **ADJUSTMENTS, Part III**

   When a line reading is wrong, it's usually the beat before that's at fault. When trying to decide between two different interpretations, always make the colder choice. Always remember, a character never lies, he's just telling his own truth.

10. **CHEMISTRY**

    Chemistry can be real (Bogart and Bacall) or fake (Bruce Willis and Cybill Shepherd). Many actors dislike each other yet seem magical on-screen. Part of that is acting, most of it is good writing and directing. It doesn't matter, really, as long as it's in focus.

CHAPTER FOUR

The Anxiety of Influence

Drawing Fire and *About Last Night*, 1985–1986

Sydney Pollack was the closest thing to a mentor I ever had. I say *close* because it wasn't exactly the Mr. Chips version. Ours was at times a fond yet avuncular connection and just as often the contentious sparring of two hardheaded directors. There was also some unspoken fellow feeling based on both of us being, at heart, midwestern Jewish boys perpetually astonished to find ourselves in Hollywood. After seeing *Special Bulletin*, Sydney invited me to come work at a new studio called Tri-Star, for which he was consulting. It would be a good place to develop my first movie, he said. Sydney had done his time in TV before directing hit movies including *Tootsie* and *The Way We Were*. He was sympathetic to what it had taken to get such an opportunity. This was unquestionably the break that gave me a movie career.

In my first days there, he handed me a script he was producing called *Songwriter* and suggested I might be interested in directing it. I read it eagerly and hated it categorically. As best I could tell, it was trying to cash in on Hollywood's brief romance with ersatz cowboy culture (cf. *Urban Cowboy*). What could I say to him? If I told the truth, would I ruin everything? I *owed* him. For days I avoided his calls. When at last he tracked me down and asked what I thought of the script, I figured what the hell, and told him I thought it was middle-aged, Jewish shit-kicking. That was just before I happened to glance down and notice his cowboy boots, creased blue jeans, and silver rodeo buckle.

"Okay, smart-ass," he growled, "what *do* you want to do?"

"I have no idea," I said meekly, "but I'm hoping I'll know it when I see it."

Terry O'Neill / Iconic Images

He shook his head and sighed. One thing about Sydney, he'd seen it all. He wasn't about to be fazed by a pompous thirty-two-year-old who'd won a few Emmys and fancied himself the next Orson Welles. He offered to let me observe as he prepped *Out of Africa*, and promised he'd keep a lookout for interesting projects I might want to direct. He was soon up to his neck in preproduction but still made time for me to listen to him complain about the business as he made us lunch in his office. (Sydney claimed cooking calmed him.) I was fascinated to hear him talk openly about his complicated relationships with actors, especially with Robert Redford. They'd worked together many times and had a complicated symbiosis. Though they'd enjoyed extraordinary success together, they were also capable of driving each other crazy. They were as different as two men could be: Redford taciturn, laconic, and laid-back; Sydney voluble, excitable, and punctilious. Sydney was always early; Redford was infallibly late.

I couldn't know that Sydney was trying to warn me, but in the years since then I have come to understand his ambivalence toward Redford. My own relationships with movie stars have ranged from the deliriously happy to the unimaginably combative. No matter how much I've tried to treat movie stars as actors, and actors as movie stars, it hasn't always worked out that way. At times I have felt indistinguishable from the sycophants, handlers, and fluffers that feed off them like parasites on a whale. When asked what it was like to direct Barbra Streisand in the 1976 version of *A Star is Born*, Frank Pierson replied, "I wouldn't know."

By now, I've worked with certain actors many times over, yet a good experience on one movie is no guarantee the next won't be miserable. When passionate, reactive, oversensitive, occasionally irrational people (a category in which I include myself) work together in intense, intimate conditions, the results are unpredictable. In art as in life, all of us believe the way we want to make love is the only way anyone has ever wanted to be touched, whereas in truth the varieties and vagaries of the ways people get turned on are as diverse as the niche categories on a porn site. Which is another way of saying, some actors want to talk before, some don't want to talk at all, some yell and scream, while others are quiet and internal. One thing I've learned is always to be sure they've finished before you weigh in. And never ask, "Was it good for you?"

Before coming to Hollywood, my experience directing actors had been in the theater. It didn't take long to discover that working with them on a movie set is a world apart. To get a play on its feet, the director's job is to wean the actors. The goal is for them to be able to do it, night after night, by themselves long after he's gone. On a movie, there's often little and sometimes no rehearsal at all. But if the shot is in focus the actors need only get it right once. The umbilical cord between actor and director is never cut and they remain dependent. Does this mean movie actors are infantilized? Not necessarily, but I know I became a better director once I became a parent.

Having been an actor himself, Sydney had a special affinity for the craft. Calling someone an "'actors' director' is bullshit," he would say. "Anybody who isn't is just a shooter." He also reserved a special place in purgatory for those actors who'd tormented him over the years. His own performative self was never far away; he was an entertaining raconteur with tart anecdotes about those who'd humiliated him, and wonderful when he'd play a supporting role. Though he had a genial personality, he had a dark, self-loathing streak and could be equally harsh in his judgments of other artists. At times he was especially tough on me and I'm sure I deserved it. The first script we developed for Tri-Star—in 1984, before we started writing *thirtysomething*—was an original story Marshall and I came up with about a Secret Service agent and his relationship with a corrupt candidate, called *Drawing Fire*. (If the title sounds like a film with a similar subject that was made soon after, it does to me too.) After a great deal of research, which included spending time at the Secret Service training facility in Laurel, Maryland, and going on protective "movements," we showed Sydney the script. I have never had, nor hope ever to have again, a first draft so completely torn to pieces. When I made the rookie mistake of defending it, referring to its cool plot, he went for the jugular.

"Listen, kid," he said. "Plot is the rotting meat the burglar throws to the dogs so he can climb over the fence and get the jewels, which are the characters."

It took years for me to understand he was trying to tell me that if you make your characters interesting enough, you'll inevitably have a good plot. It's been a guiding principle ever since. To this day, it's the second-best piece of advice anybody ever gave me. The best piece of advice I've ever gotten also came from Sydney, but not until many years later.

Sydney's evisceration of the *Drawing Fire* script was only act one in what was to become my first high-end Hollywood story. Somehow, Dustin Hoffman had gotten hold of the script—presumably from someone at Tri-Star—and let it be known he wanted to play the lead. From the start, Sydney was opposed to Hoffman, whom he'd directed in *Tootsie*, doing it, but Dustin was a big catch and the studio agreed to his request that Marshall and I come to New York and work with him. It meant moving our families, as well as the word processor we had just learned to use. It was the size of a small car.

It was incredibly exciting to be working on our first feature script with a big star. For two months we'd leave our rented apartments uptown and walk down to Dustin's office on Fifty-Sixth Street. There, we would sit for hours listening to his extremely long-winded thoughts on our script as he pedaled a stationary bike as part of his preparation to star in a movie called *The Yellow Jersey* about the Tour de France—a movie that never got made, just as ours (as sophisticated readers will have already guessed) would eventually share the same fate. The hardest thing to get used to about working with Dustin was how what seemed like his endless and irrelevant digressions would eventually turn into brilliant observations. It just took him so damn long to get to the point.

Every day after our sessions, we would return to our behemoth writing machine and churn out new scenes. In those days it took hours to format a script and a minute a page to print it out. A tony benefit of our time in NYC was having several opportunities to see Dustin's performance as Willy in *Death of a Salesman*—still a high point in my theatergoing experience. At last, we finished our draft, waited three hours for it to print, and hurried to Midtown to hand it to him, excited and proud of what we'd come up with. Walking into Dustin's office we were surprised not to see him on the bike. Instead, we were met by a dapper man in a bespoke suit. This was Bert Fields, Dustin's attorney, who informed us Dustin couldn't accept our draft because Tri-Star refused to accept his deal.

Whiplashed and confused, we returned to L.A. and found ourselves in the middle of something between a pissing match and a power struggle neither of us could understand and no one would explain. As best as I was able to decipher the motives of the various players, Gary Hendler, a powerhouse lawyer who used to represent Sydney and was now the CEO of Tri-Star, didn't want to pay Dustin's exorbitant fee, while Mike Ovitz, head of Creative Artists Agency (CAA), who represented both Dustin and Sydney, was trying to mollify both while establishing Dustin's new price on our movie. After weeks of posturing by both sides, Hendler slipped our script to Nick Nolte, his former client, even as he was still negotiating with Dustin. Sydney encouraged me to meet with Nolte. When we did, Nolte didn't seem particularly interested in doing the movie.

Meanwhile, Dustin decided he was being dicked around (he was) and walked away. It was never clear to me whether Sydney was genuinely trying to serve in his role as advisor by protecting the studio from making a script he didn't believe in with a first-time director or was getting back at Dustin for reasons I didn't understand. The net result was that our movie didn't get made and Dustin for some reason decided I was a traitor and never wanted to speak to me again. (As fate would have it, we would later reconcile when I coached his son Max on a youth soccer team.) I don't believe Sydney consciously intended to sabotage us—he wasn't the Machiavellian type—but neither did he throw his weight behind our first effort to navigate the treacherous world of studio politics. This was only the beginning of what would turn out to be our long, fruitful, and ambivalent relationship. He continued to make himself available to me and, most significantly, encouraged the studio to send me scripts, one of which became my first movie, *About Last Night*. It's entirely possible that, even while I thought he was letting me down, he had saved my career from disaster.

One of the thrills of having a studio deal with Tri-Star was being invited to screenings. The studio's first release was *The Natural*. Not having been invited to many glitzy affairs, I was eager to go. Liberty, not so much. She had grown disenchanted with acting and its trappings, having spent the past five years doing guest-starring roles in bad episodic TV shows—the kind of parts she would struggle to get and then feel ashamed of having done. I have recently unearthed several incriminating photos online from this period. In one she is wearing a metallic bustier on an episode of *Buck Rogers* entitled "Planet of the Amazon Women"; in another she is snuggling in bed with J.R. on *Dallas*. For some reason, she adamantly refuses to let me include them in this book.

Though she had given up acting and sold an original screenplay of her own, she was nonetheless wary of my fascination with all things Hollywood, but agreed to go with me to a small after-party for Jessica Lange and the cast of *Sweet Dreams*. Once in the room, I tried not to gawk at the famous and more famous around us. I gravitated to a small group surrounding Bob Getchell, the film's gifted screenwriter, whom I'd always wanted to meet. Holding court in the center of the little group was a burly, bearded man I'd never met. He was wearing a kind of caftan cum moo-moo while liberally imposing his opinions on the others. When the conversation turned to recent movies, Liberty volunteered that she had seen and admired a new Argentine film, *The Official Story*, about *los disaparacidos* ("the disappeared"), the lost victims of Pinochet's brutal "Dirty War."

"Flop," said the bearded creature.

Liberty was taken aback. "I beg your pardon?" she said.

"Only two kinds of movies, babe. Hits and flops."

I think it was the use of "babe" that got to her. Ordinarily Liberty was quite well-behaved in social settings, at times even retiring. But I could tell by the glint in her eye that this would end badly.

"And what do you do?" she asked pleasantly.

Now it was he who was taken aback. He rolled his eyes. How was it possible she didn't know who he was?

"I'm a producer."

Liberty's lovely smile, the one for which she had always been hired to play the "pretty girl," suddenly looked more dangerous than beautiful.

"Only two kinds of producers, *babe*," she said, "artists and assholes."

If a single moment can explain why I've never much partaken of the industry's social scene, I need say no more. Not that my wife was antisocial, just that she'd had her fill of the industry bullshit. She had no stomach for fawning agents and hungry executives and took an especially dim view of watching how false and fawning I could be in their company. In fact, she soon developed a maddening habit of never recognizing studio executives or remembering their names, no matter how many times they'd been introduced. As for the tacky congratulatory gift baskets for a successful opening weekend, she dubbed them "Salami from Strangers." Likewise, the generic birthday and Christmas presents sent to our children and obviously bought by someone's assistant came to be known as "gifts of rage." Oddly, Liberty always seemed to welcome the occasional bottle of vintage champagne, but we all have our contradictions. Early in our marriage she decided there were better ways to spend her time than getting dressed up and standing around eating canapés with boors, and if I wanted our relationship to thrive, I had better get with the program, by which she meant having family dinners, driving carpool, coaching sports, and not being an asshole. I should add that, for years to come, I never made it onto any list of directors for the bearded producer's movies. Not that I would have wanted to, or that my wife's directness has adversely affected my career. But damn, *babe* . . .

One day at lunch in Sydney's office kitchen, I finally discovered the reason for his animus toward Dustin. He was about to leave for Africa and rhapsodizing about the genius of certain actors, in this case Meryl Streep. Somehow the conversation turned to Dustin, and he told me about his experience directing him in *Tootsie*. Apparently, Dustin had been driving him mad. No matter what direction he gave, Dustin would object, and it would devolve into an endless discussion as they fell further and further behind schedule. Sydney was beside himself. When I asked how he dealt with it, he said, "I went limp." When it was time to stage a new scene, rather than give direction he'd say nothing. As rehearsal began, if Dustin asked where he should sit Sydney's response was "Wherever you want." "How about over here?" Dustin would ask. "Whatever," Sydney would say. After a while Dustin knew his performance was suffering. Without someone to fight, he was lost. Finally, he apologized.

"Just let me be an asshole, Sydney, and I'll do whatever you want."

Sydney smiled and they got back to work. The rest is history.

The story would prove invaluable about a year later when I got the opportunity to direct *About Last Night*. One day while filming, I got into a pissing match with Jim Belushi. We were on the "L" in Chicago. I wanted him to begin speaking the moment the doors opened. For some reason he kept waiting until they closed. I got upset. After each blown take the train would make another loop around the city. We were losing the light. Finally, I couldn't take it any longer. In the middle of a take I yelled, "Cut!"

Belushi turned to me and bellowed, "What the fuck did you do that for?"

"Because you didn't take my direction," I said.

"Why the fuck should I?" he said, refusing to back down.

"Because I'm the fucking director!" I yelled back, without considering what a stupid thing I'd just done.

The train's doors opened, and Jim stormed out, muttering "Fuck you!" I followed. As we stood on the platform shouting, "Fuck you," "No, fuck you," the train sped off for another loop. With it went the crew. I remember the producers' horrified faces pressed against the window as they disappeared. Did I mention it was snowing? The deserted platform was suddenly quiet. After a few more "fuck you"s we were running out of dialogue. I stood there, snowflakes blurring my vision, feeling lost and disoriented. Is this how it all ends? I wondered. Was it possible my feature-film career was over before I'd finished the first week? Maybe I'd never work again . . .

Suddenly I heard myself say, "Jim . . . I'm scared. If we fall behind, I'll get fired. Maybe they'll fire us both."

He looked at me. "Aw, don't worry," he said, "I got ya." And pulled me into a hug.

From that moment on, Jim was my greatest ally, and his performance was brilliant. To this day, I don't know how I came to admit my fear as we stood yelling at each other in the snow. I do know, at that moment, I learned something that's served me ever since. I had believed a director had to be an authority figure. It turned out admitting I'm a human being worked even better. And the more real I was able to be, the more authentic the work became. As the years passed, I came to realize that since the actors are opening their hearts to me, I could stand to do a bit of the same. This isn't to suggest I pay the same deep emotional price as they do, but it's amazing how much I get in return for losing some of my own inhibitions and being more vulnerable. Even if it's only happening internally, I believe there's an unspoken, almost mystical exchange that transmits my intention to them. Such openness carries with it a certain amount of risk, but I'll get to that later.

About Last Night turned out to be the right choice as a first movie. Tim Kazurinsky and Denise DeClue, two Second City alumni, had written an adaptation of David Mamet's *Sexual Perversity in Chicago*. It was also the first film for Stuart Oken and Jason Brett, two Chicago theater producers who became lifelong friends. At one point, they had had Jonathan Demme attached to direct; it was my good fortune that he hadn't stuck with it. A profane comedy, it was also about something I had wrestled with myself not too many years before—trying to distinguish between love and sex. The story centered on two beginners, played by Rob Lowe and Demi Moore, trying to figure out the difference. Jim played Rob's friend and colleague.

The production wasn't especially challenging. Mostly two people in an apartment, on the street, or in bed. But there were still many lessons to learn. One day I arrived on the set twelve minutes late. My AD took me aside.

"Look around, how many people do you see?"

"Fifty?"

"Don't forget hair and makeup. And the guys outside in the trucks . . ."

"Seventy-five?"

"And they've all been waiting," he said. "Now multiply those twelve minutes by seventy-five. That makes you fifteen hours late."

I've never been late again.

Rob turned out to have a sharp sense of humor and was a great straight man to Jim. Demi was so emotionally available, and the camera loved her. Both actors were open and willing, especially given the nudity the scenes required. It wasn't until after casting them that I learned Rob and Demi had hooked up years before. To further complicate matters, Demi was the girlfriend of Rob's oldest friend, Emilio Estevez. Though they all knew such scenes to be more technical than sexual, they were still a little anxious. It all went surprisingly well, until an especially "passionate" (and athletic) moment when Rob began to groan quite loudly as they pretended to make love. Everyone looked away, embarrassed, trying to act like it wasn't happening until we realized that Rob had torn his ACL. Pro that he is, Rob kept "acting" until I said cut. The show, as they say, had to go on.

I was also lucky to complete the ensemble with an actress new to the movies. It's both a risk and a mitzvah to hire someone for their first job, but from the initial day of shooting, Elizabeth Perkins, playing Demi's friend, was as comfortable on a soundstage as she'd been in the Steppenwolf Theatre production of *Lydie Breeze*, where I'd noticed her. And the great work she has continued to do ever since has been no surprise.

Elizabeth's apartment was just down the street from where we were shooting. And I got to return to Chicago as a local boy made good. We shot in bars where I'd hung out, streets I'd walked my whole life, and in such favorite haunts as the baseball fields of Grant Park, 12th Street Beach, and Murphy's Bleachers high above Wrigley Field. Though the story wasn't explicitly autobiographical, it still felt deeply personal. As things turned out, it was my first step toward my next project, which would be much more self-revealing.

To top off a blissful experience, I cut the film on Market Street in Venice, California. Tony Bill's funky offices had become a kind of clubhouse for a generation of filmmakers. Every week I'd encounter someone new. Imagine my wide-eyed delight at meeting Barry Levinson, Hal Ashby, Randy Newman, and Frank Pierson, to name just a few.

When I finished my cut, the studio seemed surprised by how much they liked it, and our first preview scored much higher than anybody expected. The only problem arose when newspapers all over the country refused to run ads for the movie, which at the time still carried the name of Mamet's play, confusing *perversity* with *perversion*. I tried to convince the marketing department that this could prove to be a good thing, but they told me to stay in my lane. Not only did I have no leverage in the argument, but they had also left me alone to shoot the movie the way I'd wanted and imposed no notes on my cut. I shut up and let them do their jobs and so the milquetoast title *About Last Night* it was.

The movie did well in its first weekend—July 4, 1986—and just as well in its second. In what I came to understand was unusual, attendance remained at the same level from one weekend to the next. By the end of summer, we had far outperformed expectations. That fall we brought the movie to Europe and had our premiere as the midnight showing on opening night at the Venice Film Festival. Walking the red carpet on the Lido it began to sink in.

I was a movie director.

TEN TIPS FROM LONG LUNCHES
WITH SYDNEY

The anxiety of influence

1. **WORDS, WORDS, WORDS**

   Certain actors can't do speeches. Dialogue defeats them. They've made a career out of being the strong, silent type for a reason. Don't despair. Cut the scene in your head as you shoot: Takes one through three for the first half, Takes four through seven for the finish. It's why God invented the cutaway.

2. **IN THE PRESENCE OF GREATNESS**

   Certain actors are incapable of doing anything that isn't great. It may not be what you expected, but it's often better than you imagined. You watch, open-mouthed, and when the scene ends, the set is silent. You realize you've forgotten to say "Cut."

3. **"CAN I MOVE?"**

   Consider the scene in *Butch Cassidy* when Redford asks Strother Martin, "Can I shoot?" Certain actors are like great gunfighters: they can't be locked into rigid blocking. It kills their spontaneity and their spirit. Plan your blocking ahead of time but be prepared to let go of your expectations and experience life as it happens. Sundance hit the can every time.

4. **BRAVE NEW WORLD**

   You've loved the actor's work for years. He doesn't look great on Day One but maybe it's the lighting. Day Two is worse. "Don't worry," says the producer, "we'll fix it digitally. No more wrinkles, a few less pounds. It's a line item now." Dorian Gray lives.

5. **THE CUTTING ROOM FLOOR**

   There's gold to be found in the outtakes before you said "Action" or after you said "Cut." Before moving on, try shooting a take where the actors do it without any dialogue. You'll be surprised with what you find. There was great acting long before there were talkies.

6.   COLLABORATORS, Part I

Hire department heads with a strong point of view. Being challenged forces you to strengthen your own vision. But when you disagree, they must be willing to defer without feeling shut down. It's a delicate dance, especially when you haven't worked together. Choose wisely, they're your new family.

7.   COLLABORATORS, Part II

Department heads all want to make a great film, but sometimes their vision is myopic. The stunt coordinator thinks it's an action movie, the costumer thinks it's *Cleopatra*. They compete for your attention and a disproportionate share of the budget. Nicely suggest you're all making the same movie. Yours.

8.   THE DP & THE DESIGNER

Establish a common visual language. Watch films together, look at paintings, go out for wine-soaked dinners where you allow your imaginations to run wild. This is the time to overreach—before the crushing reality of time and money descends. Something beautiful will survive the onslaught.

9.   THE AD

You, the writer, the DP, the designer, and the stunt coordinator have dreamed up a marvelous movie. The AD is the reality police. He's made at least ten more movies than you have. When he says your plan is like trying to capture a bridge too far, ignore him at your peril.

10. IN THE VAN

Everyone hates location scouting. The scout doesn't understand the script, or you know you'll never get permission to shoot there. You get motion sickness looking at your notes. Ironically, those hours of frustration are when you and your team create a common vision. Like it or not, the movie is made in the van.

CHAPTER FIVE

In Search of Glory

Glory, 1989

In 1987, a first-draft screenplay entitled *Lay This Laurel* was being peddled around town by the fabled agent-turned-producer Freddie Fields. Freddie was sixty-four at the time. A loving scoundrel with mischief in his smile, a passion for the business, and a reputation for being fast and loose with the facts, Freddie had produced movies for Richard Brooks and John Huston, but was best known for having represented such superstars as Paul Newman, Robert Redford, and Barbra Streisand. He is often referred to as the first über agent, having created Creative Management Associates (later to become International Creative Management) and had once carried tourniquets in the trunk of his car for his client Judy Garland's many suicide attempts.

Freddie had come across a slim book by the same title as the screenplay, describing the role of the 54th Massachusetts Regiment in the failed assault on Fort Wagner on July 18, 1863, on Morris Island, South Carolina. The monograph was by Lincoln Kirstein, an important figure in American cultural history, a philanthropist, critic, and art connoisseur, who was perhaps best known for having collaborated with George Balanchine on the New York City Ballet. He was also a distant relative of Robert Gould Shaw, the twenty-five-year-old white commander of the Black regiment. As a young boy growing up, as did Shaw, in Beacon Hill, the wellspring of American abolitionism, Kirstein had thrilled to accounts of the regiment's courage. At that time the story was so beloved as to be taught in Boston's schools; there was even a junior high named after William C. Carney, the first Black recipient of the Medal of Honor, received for his valor during the attack. Though seriously wounded, Carney had crawled back to the Union lines carrying the regimental colors—a flag still displayed in the Boston statehouse.

Like Shaw and Kirstein, I loved reading history as a boy, especially about the Civil War. I'd haunt our little public library in Winnetka or hound my mother to bring home everything she could find. I devoured the Bruce Catton trilogy, Mac-Kinlay Kantor's *Gettysburg*, and Shelby Foote's narrative history. In fifth grade I convinced my mother to spend our spring break visiting the various Civil War battlefields. I can't help but smile thinking of her tromping up and down the hills at Gettysburg, acting like there was nowhere else she'd rather be, hanging on my every word as I went on and on about the various generals and their strategies— the doomed heroism of Pickett's Charge, Joshua Chamberlin's remarkable defense of Little Round Top. Even more than the vivid and gory descriptions of battle, my ten-year-old imagination was moved by the nobility of their conviction, by their willingness to sacrifice everything in the name of a cause they believed in.

As a student at Harvard College in the 1970s, I had often walked by a bas-relief monument on the Boston Commons with no more than the passing glance we give obscure memorials to patriotic gore. We tend to think statues belong to the world of the dead. (Until recently, that is, when racial politics have turned them into flash points.) Otherwise, they stand sentinel in anonymous disrepair, tucked away in the corner of parks, ignored by passersby, their meaning long forgotten, their majesty humbled by roosting pigeons and office picnickers. As a student, all I'd noticed of this particular statue was a man on a horse. Staged prominently in the foreground, his posture ramrod straight, he seemed no different from the equestrian statue on the village green in the Illinois town where I grew up. But it was only after looking into the shadows of the magnificent bas-relief sculpted by Augustus Saint-Gaudens that its politics were revealed.

Ian G Dagnall / Alamy Stock Photo

In fact, the man on the horse—Robert Gould Shaw—was originally intended to be the sole subject of the monument. But Shaw's parents, committed abolitionists, had insisted the brave Black enlisted men marching to battle on behalf of the Union—the men of the 54th Regiment—be featured as well. It was the first time in history that African Americans were portrayed publicly and heroically, in bronze. Thanks to Saint-Gaudens's masterful humanism, each face is a distinctive and soulful portrait: eyes cast forward, heads held high with solemn purpose, they seem to march beyond the confines of the relief and into history. With the kind of kismet Hollywood specializes in, I would be given a chance to bring it to life.

This extraordinary sequence of events began one September day, my first day of classes actually, in a freshman lecture on American history by the eminent scholar Oscar Handlin, where I found myself sitting beside a friendly redheaded kid from Wellesley named Jeff Sagansky. He claims we were both interested in the girl sitting between us. My recollection is that she paid no attention to us. Over the course of freshman year, Jeff and I would play tennis, chat after class, greet each other as we passed in the quad, and eventually became the kind of college friend you never really get to know well yet are always happy to see. After graduation we lost track of each other. I'd heard he'd gone to business school and so I was surprised to find him, ten years later, working in television in L.A. I shouldn't have been so shocked. A new breed of executive—many of them MBAs—were taking over Hollywood and Jeff was in the vanguard. I was glad to see him nonetheless. We started playing tennis again, and our casual friendship picked up where it had left off. Our careers were both accelerating. After rising rapidly in the executive ranks at NBC, Jeff had been named president of Tri-Star Pictures and was instrumental in me getting to make *About Last Night*.

Freddie Fields had hired Kevin Jarre, a young writer whose only previous credit had been "story by" for Sylvester Stallone's *Rambo*, to write the first draft of a script for *Lay This Laurel*. Freddie submitted it to Tri-Star with director Bruce Beresford attached. Beresford had made two of my favorite movies, *Breaker Morant* and *Tender Mercies*. Tri-Star agreed to buy the Civil War project, and Beresford was eager to get it into production, but Jeff didn't like the script and was dragging his feet about moving forward. Fed up with what he felt was the studio's waffling, Beresford accepted an offer to direct another movie called *Somebody Killed Her Husband* starring Tom Selleck and the supermodel Paulina Porizkova. Jeff rightly guessed I'd be interested in the Civil War subject matter and thought of me as a potential replacement to direct. But he didn't want Freddie to send me the script. Rather, Jeff wanted me to read the original monograph on which it was based.

I was sitting in my garden with my two-year-old son, Jesse, playing at my feet when I read the little forty-eight-page volume. Beautifully published, written in spare, unsentimental prose by Kirstein, it brought tears to my eyes. The story conformed remarkably to a classic dramatic shape without the need to bowdlerize the facts or pump up the melodrama. I then read Kevin's script. Despite some wonderful writing, I saw several unexplored opportunities to better reveal the inner lives of the characters, the kind of moments that might give the movie the breath of life rather than the musty smell of textbook history. We were in the middle of the first season of *thirtysomething* when I told Marshall about the offer. He could see the excitement in my eyes. "Go," he said. "We'll survive." And so I called Jeff and said yes. Next, I called Freddie to set a meeting with Kevin to talk about a rewrite.

"Good luck, kid," was all he said.

It's not uncommon for a director to leave his mark on a script. These collaborations can be hugely gratifying. I would have them in years to come with such gifted writers as Stephen Gaghan, John Logan, Charles Randolph, Paul Attanasio, Steve Knight, Geoff Fletcher, and Tom Stoppard. When they are working well, they're an opportunity for two creative voices to challenge each other, subjecting each scene or story problem to a litmus test of authenticity in search of a solution that's neither one artist's nor the other's—not a compromise but a new idea that each writer can endorse with equal fervor.

Kevin didn't feel that way. "The script is perfect," he said as we huddled in a booth in the penumbral Formosa Cafe, a refuge for day drinkers on Santa Monica Boulevard. It was hard to see Kevin in the shadows. He wore black leathers and his shoulder-length hair fell across his face as he leaned over the table, mumbling softly and sipping Bushmills. This was a new situation for me. I'd been in Kevin's position before, having worked as a writer for other directors before being given the chance to direct. Since then, I'd had nothing but happy experiences—with a gifted writing staff on *thirtysomething*, and most recently with Tim and Denise on *About Last Night*. Not knowing quite how to respond to Kevin's pronouncement, I chose to ignore it. This was nothing more than the common defensiveness of a writer protecting his creation, I thought, and pressed on. I went through the script, page by page, offering suggestions, respectfully but firmly signaling my intention to make manifest the relationships that were latent in his script. Kevin didn't say much as I went on and on. After an uncomfortable couple of hours, he stood up and said, "I'll get back to you." Moments later I heard his Harley roar to life and fade into the afternoon traffic.

His rewrite arrived eight weeks later. As best as I could tell, he had polished two or three scenes and reordered the action in the second act. I called him.

"Kevin," I said, "this isn't how it's going to work. The studio isn't going to make your script as it is."

After a long silence, he said, "That's their problem."

"No, Kevin. It's actually your problem. But if that's the way you want to play it . . ."

Click.

My next call was to Jeff. "You do it," he said.

And so, I got to work. When I handed in my draft, I'd changed the title to *Glory*. The studio made encouraging noises, but they weren't ready to commit to a start date. I racked my brain trying to come up with a way to get them off the dime. Cast a movie star! Of course, but who? Tom Cruise was the latest phenomenon, but he wasn't available. Tim Hutton would be great, but he'd lined up two gigs in a row. As I canvassed agents and casting directors for an inspiring idea, I heard about a reenactment of the Battle of Gettysburg in commemoration of its 125th anniversary. There would be twenty thousand men in arms in full uniform, with authentic weapons and tactics.

"We've got to be there," I told Freddie.

"Let me see what I can do," he said.

Three weeks later, on July 1, 1988, we found ourselves in the middle of a remarkable scene: cannons blasting, cavalry charging, long lines of troops in uniform advancing in rank amid clouds of black powder. It's a rare moment when a director sees his vision appear in the flesh, but what I beheld on that field exceeded anything I could have imagined. There would be many more such times to come, but that was the moment I sensed we were in pursuit of something extraordinary. Freddie had persuaded the studio to give us $25,000 for film and equipment. I'd called in a favor from my friend Dan Lerner, a gifted cameraman, to come join us. The reenactors insisted we wear wool Union Army uniforms in the one-hundred-degree heat. I was worried Freddie might feel out of place so far from Beverly Hills, but he didn't seem to mind as he schlepped heavy film cannisters in the ninety-eight percent humidity.

"Finally, I'm going to film school!" he beamed, as his Gucci loafers stepped in a pile of horseshit.

We shot every roll of film we could afford—thirty thousand feet—including a staged cavalry charge Freddie finagled by bribing the regimental commander with a case of Gatorade. Having used up all the money the studio had given us, we had nothing left to pay an editor. My friend Steve Rosenblum had cut my student film at AFI and was still working as an assistant editor. I had been furious when the studio hadn't let me hire him to edit *About Last Night*. My chagrin about that didn't stop me from imposing on him to help. Each night we would sneak into another director's cutting room after everyone had gone home, eventually emerging with a seven-minute piece accompanied by Ennio Morricone's elegiac "Gabriel's Oboe" from his score to *The Mission*. We showed it to the studio in their new screening room. To see it projected on a beautiful screen, seventy feet across and thirty feet high, was emotional. A year later, a few of the images we shot during those three days made it into the final cut. When the lights came up, the executives sat in stunned and delighted silence, Jeff most of all. It was no longer just a development deal; we had started making the movie, except nobody had quite given us permission. This was 1988. We had created a sizzle reel.

I'd like to say the rest came easily, but in fact the months that followed were more torturous than anything I had ever experienced. There were many reasons for this. The studio may have liked our reel, but the degree of their commitment—by which I mean the budget—was far from determined. Freddie's crafty genius was to sell the studio on the notion we would be making *Platoon* in the Civil War, which is to say a small, low-budget movie with a little bit of action. This bit of flimflam, of which Freddie was a consummate master, is known as "getting the studio pregnant," the rationale being that once you can get them to start spending money, it's hard for them to stop because they would have to admit they've wasted it. Think of it as the producer's equivalent of the military's "mission creep" in 1960s Southeast Asia, and you'll get the idea. But that fight was yet to be fought and the green light of a "go" movie was still as distant as the glow on Gatsby's dock. First, we had to cast the movie.

No matter how impressed the studio was by the script or by the footage we'd shown them, they agreed to go forward for only one reason: Matthew Broderick agreed to play Robert Gould Shaw. This might seem bizarre given that Matthew's stardom in Hollywood's estimation had come only recently because of *Ferris Bueller's Day Off*, a delightful John Hughes movie but as different in tone from *Glory* as any two movies could be. Also, that Matthew's box-office appeal, such as it might be, was probably limited to teenage girls. But this is often how studios think. They needed a marquee name, as it was explained to me, "to protect their downside." This isn't to take anything away from Matthew's ability. I had seen his charming performances in *Torch Song Trilogy* and on Broadway in Neil Simon's *Brighton Beach Memoirs*. I considered him an extremely talented actor and could certainly imagine him doing the part. He was also roughly the same age as Shaw, and even bore a passing resemblance.

The problem was that the studio actually *told* Matthew they were only making the movie because of him. This was a horrible thing to do to a young actor. To have such a huge psychological burden placed on his shoulders was the opposite of how he should have been made to approach a difficult part in an arguably risky movie. Hollywood lore is full of stories of self-destructive young actors who have crumpled beneath such psychic responsibility. Matthew already carried quite a heavy karmic burden for someone his age. The year before, while driving with Jennifer Grey in Ireland en route to pick up his mother at the airport, he had veered into the wrong lane and hit an oncoming car head-on, killing its driver and passenger. Matthew, himself, had suffered serious injuries. Resilient and mentally tough, he had gotten through it; still, it's hard to imagine the lingering price he must have paid.

Now finding himself about to make an ambitious movie, Matthew felt he needed help. Unfortunately, he didn't think I was the person who could give it to him. I can understand why he was wary of me from the start. He had won a Tony at twenty-one and was accustomed to rarified New York circles. To that way of thinking I was a lightweight. I'd only made one feature—a romantic comedy set in Chicago's bar scene. Most of all, I was a TV guy: *thirtysomething*, despite its success, was an intimate, whiny talkfest. What did I know about filmmaking on an epic scale? Admittedly, I had done little to suggest I could handle the logistics, the stars, or the spectacle. And while I have no idea who was whispering in Matthew's ear, I know enough about the legions of ass-kissers and ego-strokers who attach themselves to a rising star that I can imagine what he was being told: *You should be working with Spielberg! You need a big director. You need to be protected!*

Before going any further in describing what was to become a nightmare from which there seemed no waking, I need to say that as a principal player in the drama as well as its narrator I am entering murky waters. There were things I said and did over the next months that I regret, and I'll do my best to include them, but nothing I might have done could possibly rival Matthew's role in the theater of cruelty that was about to begin. It's important to say I no longer bear him any ill will. For many years I did, but he has long since apologized for his behavior and I forgave him. Even while having compassion for Matthew's predicament, I still intend to give an unvarnished account of the shit he pulled. It is also a Rubicon for this book. If I intend to write about what it's really like to make movies, I might as well suck it up and tell it like it is, even at the risk of causing some hurt. Fear always leads to bad choices, especially when you're young. Given the kind of actor horror stories I have since heard from other directors, I've come to realize that my story was more commonplace than I thought. As Bill Goldman once wrote, "Life is pain, highness. Anybody who says differently is trying to sell you something."

A short time after Matthew agreed to do the movie, he suddenly announced he was quitting. I couldn't have known there were other forces influencing him, one of whom was his mother, Patsy, who had read the script and hated it. At this point Patsy was still offstage, her unseen hand unknown to all. Matthew and I hadn't even met in person yet. He was in Manhattan, and I was with my wife and son in a little cabin at nine thousand feet in Crested Butte, Colorado, that we had bought with proceeds from the sale of Liberty's first screenplay. (It also happened to have been her first and *only* screenplay, despite my many entreaties to her to write another. For some reason, her commitment to political activism and raising our two children outweighed the allure of the movie business. Go figure.)

My only means of communication with Matthew was an ancient radiophone I had inherited from the previous owner. As with a walkie-talkie, it was necessary to hold down the PTT (push to talk) button and then say "Over" when you wanted the other party to speak. It was also a party line so our conversation could be listened to by anyone on the mountain—not the most conducive way to bond with a reluctant star. The connection was crackly and sporadic, and it always seemed at its worst when we'd speak. One day it broke down altogether and I had to snowshoe two miles down the mountain in a blizzard to a pay phone to hear Jeff tell me Matthew was quitting.

"You've got to talk to him! We've already been spending money!" His voice tended to climb to a higher register when he got anxious.

"Calm down, Jeff. What happened?"

"He's trashing the script. Says it needs a complete rewrite!"

"Okay, I'll call him."

"We're already spending *money*!"

"You said that. I'll call him."

Apparently, Jeff had just had the shit kicked out of him over the phone by Mike Ovitz, the ostensibly Zen but in actuality cruel master of the universe and CAA cofounder who happened to represent Matthew. This being one of the biggest movies Jeff had green-lit, he wasn't sure how to respond when told he'd better make Matthew happy or Ovitz would see to it that he got fired.

"Calm down, Jeff. He's just trying to see how far he can bully you."

"I know, I know. But you'll call him, right?"

It wouldn't be the last time I felt compassion for my friend. Jeff was only beginning to understand that even studio heads were sometimes forced to endure the indignities of the universe, or in this case of the powerful nation-state that was CAA. I also knew that Freddie was jobbing him about our budget, which my AFI classmate, our line producer, Pieter Jan Brugge was already estimating to be at least double what the studio believed. It would soon become apparent that Jeff's fate and mine were linked. We would succeed or we would both be going over the falls in the same barrel.

I called Matthew. The radiophone was working again.

"Hi, Matthew, I hear you want to talk about the script. *Over.*"

"Yeah, well, I have a lot of notes . . ."

He neglected to say "over." In fact, in all our conversations on the radiophone, he petulantly refused to say it, so I never quite knew when he was done talking and it was time for me to PTT.

"Let me hear your notes. I really want to know what you're thinking. *Over.*"

Four seasons with an ensemble of articulate stage actors on *thirtysomething* had prepared me for such sessions. The most important thing I'd learned about listening to the ideas of anxious actors was to try to understand the note behind the note. As Matthew went through the script, his thoughts were all about his character—no surprises there—but there was something unspoken, something he didn't want to get into. And no matter how I tried to pry it loose, he remained vague and taciturn. As I understood them, his notes weren't extensive, and they felt doable. It certainly didn't sound like he was trashing the script. I told him I'd dig into the scenes and send him pages. He seemed satisfied and clearly wanted to get off the phone. I said, "Over and out," and we hung up.

He was back in the movie. For now.

Thus reassured, the studio gave us the go-ahead to begin prep in earnest. This meant scouting locations and hiring crew members, including a designer and DP. As far as casting, they made it known that as long as Matthew was on board, I was free to fill the "other roles" (their words). Meaning: the Black actors.

Denzel Washington was at the top of my list. His performance on Broadway in *A Soldier's Play* and on film as Steven Biko in *Cry Freedom* had blown me away. We'd met briefly on the CBS-Radford lot when we were both shooting TV shows, although he claimed not to remember. I'd heard he was unhappy doing *St. Elsewhere* and very much wanted to do *Glory*, but he was cagey when we talked about it. When we offered him the part of Private Silas Trip, his representatives insisted on a higher fee than was in our budget, but the studio refused to up our offer. I threw a tantrum. The studio said no. I harangued Jeff. He said the budget was hemorrhaging. Freddie knew how much I wanted Denzel and, bless him, gave up $50,000 of his own fee to have him in the movie. He couldn't have known that casting Denzel would change his life and mine.

Morgan Freeman had made a strong impression on me as the terrifying pimp in *Street Smart*, so I didn't know what to expect when we met. He walked into my little office, sat down, and gave me the warm, open smile that was to become his signature over the course of an extraordinary career. "You got me," was all he said.

Thus began one of the most rewarding relationships I'd yet had with an actor, mostly because I hardly had to say a word. His performance as Sergeant Major John Rawlins was spectacular from the first shot. Morgan had gone through tough times earlier in his career. He was quite open about it, and even more vocal about the serenity he'd found in sobriety. His kind, steadying presence was something I came to rely on when things got tough.

Casting is second only to the script. The phrase "the die is cast" pertains to directors as much as it does to George Washington on the banks of the Delaware. It doesn't matter where you put the camera, no movie is better than the worst actor in it. Mary Colquhoun, formerly the casting director for Joe Papp's Public Theater, was as relentless as she was gifted. One evening after an exhausting day of seeing actors in Manhattan, she announced that if we hurried, we could make it to the senior showcase of graduating actors at Juilliard. There was someone she wanted me to see. I groaned a bit but knew better than to try her famous temper. We fought our way uptown in a torrential storm and found seats in the back row of the Peter Jay Sharp Theatre at Lincoln Center. Andre Braugher was nothing less than a revelation. I'd never seen such power and command in a young actor. His parents had wanted him to become an engineer but everybody in that theater could tell his destiny was elsewhere. It made no difference that he'd never been on a movie set before. We cast him the next day as Corporal Thomas Searles.

Jihmi Kennedy was a graduate of the University of North Carolina School of the Arts. A well-trained actor, for years he had only managed to find work as a day player on TV series, yet I sensed in him none of the telltale hunger of someone looking for his big break. Jihmi's audition was earnest and heartbreaking. As we got to know each other, I learned he was deeply religious. Faith would become a central underpinning of the movie. Jihmi's shone like a beacon. He became Private Jupiter Sharts, the fourth soldier in the tent.

I was a huge fan of *The Princess Bride*. That Cary Elwes could be both satirical and heroic took great skill. But I felt it was unlikely he would accept a smaller supporting role. Having starred in movies, another actor might have bridled at the notion. But like so many others, Cary sensed something larger at play in making *Glory*. He wanted to be a part of it. Against the advice of his agents, he cut his fee and came on board as Major Cabot Forbes.

With the cast set, the time had come for the production to move to Georgia and for us to begin building Fort Wagner. That meant starting to spend real money, the kind that gives studio heads sleepless nights. I was standing on a beach in Jekyll Island, along with an ornithologist from the Audubon Society, two members of the Georgia Coastal Regional Commission, the head of the Georgia State Film Commission, and three officers from Army Corps of Engineers, all stakeholders in the preservation of the coastline. The army corps was worried about the impact of construction on the tidal plain, the Audubon Society was concerned about disrupting the nesting terns, the coastal commission was responsible for the health of the fragile dunes, and the film commission was afraid we'd move to South Carolina if we couldn't figure out a way to please everyone and still build a massive earthen fortification worthy of the vainglorious final assault. The look in Pieter Jan Brugge's eyes confirmed that things weren't going well. They resembled the meter of a runaway cab with dollar signs scrolling higher by the minute.

Out of nowhere, a production assistant came sprinting toward us across the dunes. When he caught his breath, he announced that Jeff Sagansky had called the production office to say it was an emergency and that I was to call him back immediately. This was 1989, remember. There were no cell phones. Part of the location manager's job was carrying a roll of dimes for pay phones, but there were no pay phones on the beach and the production office was miles away. I had no choice but to take off across the dunes; there was only one emergency that would prompt that kind of call. Matthew was unhappy again.

"He says you didn't respond to his notes!" Jeff pleaded.

"Of course I did . . ."

"Well, he sent the script to Horton Foote, who says it has all kinds of problems."

"Maybe we should start considering other actors for the part," I said. "Kevin Bacon is available."

"Matthew is already pay-or-play. You've got to call him."

"I'll call him."

I knew that Matthew and the heralded screenwriter of *To Kill a Mockingbird* were close. Matthew had acted in Foote's *The Widow Claire* off-Broadway and then starred in the film adaptation of his play *1918*. He was also currently dating Foote's daughter, Daisy. *That* close. (Horton Foote was also a third cousin of Shelby Foote, whose Civil War histories I so admired.) I called Matthew, asking if Horton Foote wanted to talk to me about the script. Matthew hedged and changed the subject. Again, I tried to get him to articulate his problems with the script. He kept mentioning Emerson. I knew that Ralph Waldo Emerson had been the soul of the abolitionist movement in which Shaw was raised, but I still couldn't understand what Matthew was getting at.

"Fly down this week and let's get into it," I said.

"I'm not sure when I'm coming down," he said. "I've got a lot going on up here."

It was dawning on me that Matthew didn't like confrontation. By the end of the call, it was clear he wasn't walking off the movie. We'd have several more of these long, awkward, circular conversations, but what I hoped would be a substantive opportunity to hear him out always seemed to dissipate into something vague and purposeless. Later, I'd hear how unhappy he was with the call. Still, I imagined once we got to the starting gate, he would find his footing. I'd seen it happen before with actors whose anxiety would rise the closer we got to shooting, and then disappear the minute the cameras started to roll.

Meanwhile, rehearsals with Denzel, Morgan, Jihmi, and Andre had begun. It's possible that four other actors might have had the kind of chemistry they did, but I doubt it. It was mesmerizing. Everybody had something to contribute to the scenes. I had sent them copies of a book that moved me, a collection of excerpts from slave diaries and oral histories called *Bullwhip Days*. Morgan, who would someday buy the plantation on which his family had been slaves, was a repository of stories, some moving, others chilling. As we began to do improvisations, Jihmi stayed in character the whole time. Andre was tentative at first, but gradually began to feel safe. Watching his creation of the character of Searles was dazzling. Denzel was taciturn. I sensed him feeling his way toward Trip. He wasn't yet ready to take the plunge.

One scene we worked on was the impromptu prayer meeting the enlisted men hold on the eve of going into battle. Nothing Kevin nor I could have written came close to what the actors discovered when they began to explore it. I had seen Morgan preach in *The Gospel at Colonus* at the Brooklyn Academy of Music. He could thunder like hellfire and just as quickly murmur words as comforting as a soothing balm. Jihmi attended the local Baptist church on his days off. One day I went with him, and I watched people rolling in the aisles and talking in tongues. Jihmi invested the character of Sharts with his own pure, simple belief. I knew Denzel's father was a Pentecostal preacher who ran two churches. But when it came his turn during rehearsal to testify, he stuck to the script, often mumbling, revealing little of what was going on inside. At first, I was confused and even a bit anxious, yet the other actors didn't seem to mind. This, I would come to understand, was Denzel's process. He was preparing, and in the meantime, he was simply incapable of doing anything inauthentic. What he'd be like on the day, I'd have to wait and see.

· This was only the first intimation that I was in the presence of something beyond my understanding. Any thought of overdetermining, of "directing" the actors' performances, was foolish. They were hearing music I couldn't even imagine. Yet during each session, a transcendent moment, usually unwritten, would occur. It was at once thrilling and daunting, like realizing you are on a runaway train to an unknown destination. The best thing I could do, I realized, was shut up and hold on tight.

Any worries I might have had about being a white kid presuming to tell Black men about their experience had vanished by the end of the first rehearsal. If a line in the script didn't work, they massaged it, or instinctively came up with a better one. Dialogue I feared might be clichéd made them laugh. The racial slurs they came up with were much worse than anything I had dared write. The voices of their parents and grandparents, of ancestors they'd never met, were so available to them, they fell into their rhythms with good humor and without the slightest self-consciousness—just as I might have done if imitating my immigrant grandfather. I scribbled notes constantly, stealing bits of behavior from an improv that I could repurpose while shooting. When I did have an idea about a scene, their attitude was unflaggingly receptive and generous. Why I was surprised by this reveals the depth of my own anxiety and prejudice. I count those days in a dingy rehearsal room as the true beginning of my career as a film director. I would lie in bed at night in my hotel room listening to the container ships chugging upstream on the Savannah River and marvel at my good fortune.

But as the saying goes, you never hear the bullet that hits you. If I was wrong in fearing my relationship with the Black actors could be fraught, I was even more wrong in assuming it would eventually work out with Matthew. Because the next day I got a message that "Bo" Goldman had called. Bo was the Oscar-winning screenwriter of *One Flew Over the Cuckoo's Nest*. He'd won another for *Melvin and Howard*. He told me Matthew had sent him the script and asked him to rewrite it. Was this something I endorsed? I was speechless. It didn't take him long to figure out what was going on.

"Don't worry," he said. "I've been there. I'll let him know I'm too busy."

After my inadequate words of gratitude, he added: "Really like the script. Great project. Good luck with it."

I called Jeff. Did he know anything about this?

"Yeah, I heard about it. Don't worry, we can't afford him."

"But—"

"You've got something else to worry about," he said. "Matthew says he needs his mother to come down there and work with you on the script."

"His *mother*?"

"She wants to meet with you about the script. Apparently she's some kind of writer."

"His *MOTHER*?!"

"Ovitz insists we fly her to Savannah every weekend on a private jet."

"That's not in our budget!" I was shrieking now.

"We'll cover it."

It was hard not to point out that he was able to find money for this folly while we were being pressured to find budget cuts everywhere.

"Apparently she's been sick," he went on. "Ovitz says she won't fly commercial. She'll be there on Saturday."

"My wife and kid are coming in this weekend. I haven't seen them in two months."

"I'm really sorry, man." Translation: "I'm giving in to Ovitz."

When Patricia Broderick arrived that weekend, I kissed my three-year-old son and my unhappy wife and headed back to the office. The weeks to come were the most stressful of my life. Principal photography was closing in, the budget was skyrocketing, the studio was hammering us for cuts, and I had stopped sleeping.

"Patsy," as she was called, was a brilliant woman, a painter and playwright of some success but never with the recognition she felt was her due. We met— Matthew, Patsy, and I—in my office for hours on end going through the script, page by page. Although I'm sure she was capable of warmth and charm, I was never treated to that side of her. From the moment we met she was contemptuous, demeaning, and volatile. As Matthew sat in opaque silence, I was forced to defend, in excruciating detail, my rationale for every line in every scene. Patsy knew an enormous amount about the Transcendentalists but not so much about screenwriting. She insisted on elongating the first act to include a scene at Brook Farm, the utopian community that was the incubator of abolitionism, of which Shaw's parents were founding members. Also, that Shaw's dialogue should include long passages of . . . wait for it . . . Emerson! (At least now I understood why Matthew kept bringing him up in our calls.)

She also maintained we needed to add Shaw reading from Harriet Beecher Stowe's antislavery polemic *Uncle Tom's Cabin*, watch him training troops in front of the admiring young ladies of Boston, see him attend a famous speech by Frederick Douglass, and best of all, play a long scene in which he is convinced to take command of the regiment by . . . you guessed it . . . his mother. It wasn't as if I didn't know the contextual history Patsy was referring to; I just believed it had no place in the movie. I had studied Shaw's letters at the Houghton Library at Harvard and gone over the script with Shelby Foote. I was proud of having his blessing.

One of the many ironies of the sad saga with Patsy is that I had known her late husband, James, quite well. A wonderful actor and an amiable pro, he had starred in *Family*, where we had worked together happily. He had died of cancer only a few years before, at age fifty-five. Clearly my friendship with Matthew's father had done nothing to endear me to his mother. Patsy was relentless in her criticism, and I fought her at every turn, doing my best to ignore her profanity and insults. One of her choicer comments was to describe my writing as "limp as a penis." I'd read *Beowulf* in college. In it, Grendel's mother is described as "a monstrous hellbride, brooding on her wrongs," and "ferocious in defense of her child, a swampthing from hell." Like Grendel's mother, Patsy clearly believed her son to be in imminent danger and had come to defend him with no holds barred. At times she would go too far, and I would respond in kind. Yet if I got visibly angry, which I regrettably did at times, she would burst into tears or say she had to go lie down. I didn't know how to react.

Jeff had mentioned, in passing, that Patsy had been sick, but it wasn't until several weeks later that my assistant found out she had survived lung cancer and triple-bypass surgery only a few years before. I was fighting with a sick woman! This at least explained some of her extreme behavior, yet did it mean I had to allow her to savage the script? In retrospect, I can see we were both desperate. Had I understood it then, I might have been more compassionate, but empathy is more elusive when you're young, and can seem like a disadvantage when life is coming at you hard and you're convinced your ship, laden with treasure, is in danger of sinking any second.

It must have been excruciating for Matthew. He was in an impossible position, too, obviously concerned for his mother's health and only a few years past his father's death, not to mention the trauma of his car accident. Yet he hardly said a word. He already had no respect for me. Seeing me go toe-to-toe with his mother could only have made him hate me more. Curiously enough, Patsy had little to say about the roles of the Black soldiers, yet she took great offense when I suggested that enlarging Matthew's part would risk turning the film into a white-savior narrative. By the time shooting was to begin, I had agreed to some of her well-chosen additions to Shaw's letters (including one Emerson quote), a few expository scenes in the first act, and precious few changes to the rest of the script.

The next day I received word that Kweisi Mfume, head of the Congressional Black Caucus, wanted to come see me. I tried to imagine his purpose. Could there be some objection to the story? The last thing I wanted this movie to become was a political lightning rod. He arrived in the evening, a soft-spoken man, gracious and good-natured. The moment we sat down he came to the point.

"The thing that's most important to us in your presentation of the Fifty-Fourth Massachusetts," he said, "is that Black culture not be portrayed as a monolith."

Relief spread through my adrenals. I told him the four Black principals were portrayed as coming from all corners of the Black experience—one a runaway slave, one an educated man raised in the north, one a religious man having arrived via the Underground Railroad, and one a freed slave. Not only that, I said, but the "dress extras"—fifty men who had come from all parts of the country to train in marching drills, weapons, and the manual of arms—were lawyers, history teachers, ex-military, and current soldiers who had taken leave from their families and their jobs to take part in the movie. A couple were aspiring actors. One was a retired air force colonel. Another was the current sergeant major of the army. Living in tents, enduring ugly weather, and cooking their own food, we couldn't be making the movie without them. He grinned, tucked his napkin in his lap, and asked if the restaurant served she-crab soup.

Another word about the extras. Most of them were reenactors—among them were men I had met during the week I spent filming at Gettysburg. They liked to call themselves "living historians." Not only did they live in conditions that were substandard for any normal production, but they also taught me what I needed to know about tactics, drills, fighting techniques, and period language. Increasingly, the lead actors came to rely on them as invaluable sources of research for their performances.

I had run out the clock by the time of Representative Mfume's visit. It was time to start shooting. Having endured the trials of the past months, I was excited to begin. When I did, the day after the congressman left, it couldn't have gone worse.

This wasn't just the usual first-day jitters; everything looked wrong when I looked through the lens. I told myself it was because we were shooting the expository scenes Patsy had insisted be included and I was predisposed to hate them, but that night when we looked at dailies, they were more dreadful than I anticipated. The lighting was too bright, the costumes were too new, and Matthew seemed uncomfortable in his role.

Just as we did on *thirtysomething*, everyone would take to a cramped room after shooting to watch dailies, where we would huddle together, eating dinner in the dark on paper plates held precariously in our laps.

I glanced over and saw Steve Rosenblum, on board this time as my editor, sitting with Norman Garwood, our production designer. Both were wearing sunglasses—a not very subtle expression of their displeasure with the look of the film. Freddie looked ashen. The movie sucked. I cried myself to sleep.

But a few horrible days later a major storm system descended on us; it turned out to be the best thing that could have happened. We were shooting the regiment's arrival at their Readville training camp. I watched as the bedraggled men marched in, ankle-deep in mud, shoulders hunched and miserable in their sopping-wet rags. In the gray, clinging fog it looked just like the research photographs Norman had shown me when we first conceived the look of the movie. I went to Freddie Francis, our esteemed cinematographer, and as we stood in the rain, I admitted I was unhappy about our first week's work. I gestured to the scene unfolding before us.

"This is the movie I want to make," I said. "What if we were to shoot it today just as it is, without lights?"

"Well, why didn't you say so, dear boy?"

It was the moment everything began to turn around.

The next day it was time to shoot the first tent scene. I said good morning to Morgan, Jihmi, and Andre as they walked onto the set, ready to rehearse. Denzel was nowhere in sight. After a few minutes I began to get edgy. The AD told me he was still in makeup. Ten minutes later I was getting angry. We were on a very tight schedule. Finally, he appeared with his head shaved. We'd never discussed it. But the moment he began to rehearse, I stared, open-mouthed, at the utter transformation that had taken place. Overnight he had become Trip. Volatile. Funny. Angry. Mesmeric. The next night as we watched dailies, despite the wonderful, specific work by the other actors in the scene it was impossible to take your eyes off Denzel.

"Jesus Christ," Freddie exclaimed, "the kid carries his own lights!"

That night I still couldn't sleep, but it wasn't anxiety that kept me awake. I had been in the presence of greatness. I'd never seen an actor command the focus by doing so little. It wouldn't be the last time I felt that way working with Denzel, neither on this movie nor the others we were to make in years to come. But another thing entirely was happening in that tent in addition to his revelatory work. I was beginning to sense the spirit of something much larger than any of us. I had never considered myself a particularly spiritual person, and initially I had no language to describe what I was seeing and feeling. Scene after scene were revealed to be more impactful and resonant than I had imagined, as the actors discovered implications and nuance I hadn't considered even when they were words I had written. I came to believe they were in a state of grace. I realize how grandiose that sounds, but there was rapture in them as they honored the souls of men who had gone before them. The more work I watched, the less I had to say. I was putting into practice the humbling lesson I'd first learned in our rehearsals: sometimes shutting up is the best direction of all.

It wasn't just Denzel whose work astonished me. Andre had never been in front of a camera. It usually takes a certain amount of experience before an actor can blot out the presence of the five or six or fifty people staring at him from close distance. On the first scene we shot outside the tent, the operator told me he couldn't hold focus because Andre had played the scene from someplace other than the one at which he'd rehearsed.

"Andre," I called from behind the camera. "You've got to play closer to your mark."

He looked confused. "What's a mark?"

After explaining the purpose of focus marks, I remembered something Nina Foch had taught us—that if an actor knows his action going into a scene, he'll never have to look down, and if he plays the same action every take, he'll land there every time. Andre's concentration was so intense he never missed another mark for the rest of the film, even when surrounded by gunfire and explosions.

Morgan never wanted to talk much about his scenes. Yet he always managed to make known how he wanted me to stage them. One night we were shooting the moment when Shaw comes to Morgan's character, Rawlins, and asks for his help. As we rehearsed, I noticed that Morgan never once looked Matthew in the eye. Just as I was about to move the camera to catch his look, I realized that he was making a point of *not* looking at him—not out of defiance, but as a Black man who had lived a lifetime wary of being punished for being "uppity," he couldn't risk being confrontational with his white superior. To watch him struggle with the dilemma of how to make it known to Shaw that the men need good shoes, and yet never meet his gaze, is a lesson in subtlety. Finally, as Shaw is walking away, Rawlins can no longer contain himself. "Shoes," he says, still looking straight ahead, ". . . the men need shoes." In that moment a bond is formed between them, and for that, Shaw later names him the first Black noncommissioned officer.

Brad Pitt said something to me years later about Morgan after working with him on *Seven*.

"He's the master," Brad said. "The thing about Morgan is you never see him move."

A movie tells you what it wants to be. With each scene the four costars played, it became undeniable that they, not Shaw, were the beating heart of the story. This is not to take anything away from Matthew. Once we began shooting, he gave himself over completely to the role and his performance was pitch perfect. There was something meta in a young movie star watching as it's revealed that the focus of a story isn't exclusively his. He couldn't help but notice as I began to write additional material featuring the others —in fact, he supported it: Rawlins receiving the promotion aboard the barge; Sharts learning to load his rifle more quickly and later using it to save his life; Searles saving Trip's life during the skirmish and Trip later helping him stand upright before the final charge; Trip's conversation with Shaw when he tells him, "I won't carry your flag."

We had only been filming for a few weeks when the time came to shoot the whipping scene. Denzel and I hadn't talked about it much; in fact we hadn't talked much at all. Like the character he was playing, he remained very much apart from the rest of the cast and crew. It wouldn't be until later, after the movie was finished, that our friendship would take root. On the morning we were to shoot the scene, I watched as the makeup department expertly applied keloid scars to his back—the cruel signature of whippings Trip had received before he ran away and came north. The prop department had fashioned a whip out of soft chamois. I asked them to show me what it felt like. It stung just enough to let you know you were being hit. John Finn was playing Sergeant Major Mulcahy, the man who would do the whipping, and he was anxious about the scene. The vestiges of slavery could still be felt in Savannah. No more than a mile from us were caves dug deep into the slimy walls of the harbor, dungeons really, in which newly arrived slaves had been kept in chains until sold.

It was upsetting to watch Denzel frog-marched, manacled hand and foot, onto the parade ground to the tattoo on the little drummer boy's snare. I had the grips lay enough dolly track to allow for a push-in on his face. It didn't take directorial genius to know the money shot would be a big close-up. But the way a single tear came to be one of the iconic images of the movie, not to mention of Denzel's career, is as good an illustration of the silent collaboration between an actor and director as any I have known. Nothing is more arresting than watching a transition play out on an actor's face. It's not about the tear—the magic is seeing emotion happen in real time. We cry because he's trying not to. Even though it's not our story, we weep for ourselves.

One thing I knew for sure, Denzel wouldn't want to do this shot more than a couple of times. Once we felt no wobble in the long tracking move or buzzed the focus of his close-up, it would be time to shoot coverage. After the most rudimentary rehearsal of Denzel's position, I called "Action." The scene went off without a hitch. The shirt was ripped off his back revealing the scars, John stepped back, raised his arm, and brought down the whip. Once, twice, three times. Denzel reacted as I imagined he would, taking each lash stoically, denying, as best he could, any sign of what—in real life—would have been horrific pain. I gave a silent signal to the key grip that it was time to push in. The camera crept forward until it ended on a perfect close-up of Denzel's face, beautiful in its defiance. His performance was very good. That was no surprise—I'm not sure there's ever been a single foot of film I've shot with Denzel that wasn't very good. But we did the shot again anyway—as a safety mostly. We were on a very long lens, the possibility for focus error was high; this wasn't a scene anybody wanted to have to reshoot. At the end of the second take, the operator signaled that we were good. It would have been easy to move on to the reaction shots.

But something told me there was more to be mined.

I told Denzel we needed to adjust something at camera and that we would do the scene only once more. Then I took John Finn aside and told him not to stop whipping until I said cut. He gave me a dark look but nodded grimly. I walked back to camera, made sure the dolly grip would again wait for my signal before pushing in, and called action. Just as he had done on previous takes, John ripped Denzel's shirt away and began to mete out the lashes.

Once. Twice. Three times.

In the prior takes, this would have been the moment for the camera to begin dollying in. But I waited. John raised the whip and brought it down again.

Four lashes.

Five.

Six.

On the earlier takes, Denzel had absolutely refused to acknowledge the pain and humiliation of the moment. He would take any punishment that could be meted out. He would show nothing. He was in control.

Seven.

Eight.

But now that control had been taken away. There he stood, helpless—the actor as well as the character—just as thousands of others had stood there before, abused, powerless, and alone. How long would this go on? he must have wondered. Without entirely understanding what I was doing, I had re-created the circumstances of over a hundred years before. By exerting my dominion over him, I was unconsciously shaming him.

Was it manipulative? Was I violating his trust? Was he furious? Yes to all, and yet not at all. Though I hadn't told Denzel the plan, I somehow knew he wouldn't break character. The shame and mortification were real now. It only made him fight harder, refusing to break. I stared at the monitor, watching him struggle. His face twitched. I signaled the dolly grip to push in. As immersed as Denzel was in the moment, with the duality of consciousness reserved for only the greatest actors, he could sense the camera drawing near, digging deeper.

That a single tear appeared and slid down his face, catching the light at the perfect moment, is the magic of movies. But something else was happening at that moment, something that transcended actors and directors, dollies and lenses. We had summoned ghosts. We all felt them among us. If you listen closely, you can hear Cary Elwes weeping off camera.

After I called "Cut," I waited a moment before approaching Denzel. I put my arm on his shoulder, but he shrugged it off and moved away. Later that day, as we were shooting a scene with Matthew and Cary, he stopped by the set wearing his Yankees hat and joking with the crew. When I met his eye, he grinned. He knew what he had done. Much later, I asked how he'd prepared for the scene.

"I was alone in a little room, waiting," he said. "And I felt the spirit. So I said a prayer, 'Be with me.' "

This is vintage Denzel. Deep, abiding faith tempered by an impenetrable and at times inexplicable banked rage. Sometimes on set you can feel the anger simmering just below the surface. In those first days of working together, I worried it was personal. In fact, it was anything but. Once released from the demands of a scene, he could be great fun. I don't know anyone, comedians included, who can make me laugh like he does. One thing about movie stars is a certain air of "Fuck it." They accept your adoration but never ask for it. As needy as they can appear, the best ones don't really care what you think of them. They're not apathetic or rebellious, just self-contained. They can often be mistaken as being oppositional, but it's not so much that as it is an unerring instinct not to have their imagination limited in any way, a ferocious insistence to remain open to the improvisation of life. That's what's so challenging about directing them; you never know what they're going to do next, and neither does the audience. As for Denzel, I've noticed how acting can sometimes bore him when he's not being challenged. There have been times I've wondered if he'd just as soon be doing something else. He never watches himself in dailies. Once he's done it on the day, it's done forever. I know there are movies he's made that he's never seen. I'm pretty sure he'd hate me presuming to demystify his process any more than I already have, but the odds are he won't read this, either.

The prayer meeting—known as "the Shout"—wasn't supposed to be shot for weeks, but a sudden schedule change obliged us to get it without any warning or preparation. I hadn't come up with a tune for the men to sing nor had the composer's team had time to build a click track. We didn't even have a pitch pipe. In such circumstances there's only one thing to do: fake it.

By this point in the production, the *dress extras* had become the de facto face of the regiment, a kind of mute chorus always to be found strategically placed around the principals. Their esprit de corps was remarkable, uncomplaining whether trudging through fetid swamps, being knocked around in hand-to-hand combat, or making up profane marching songs as they tried to keep dry in one of the wettest Georgia springs on record. I'll refrain from quoting some of their more profanity-laced ditties, most of them referencing the asshole director who was forcing them to stand for hours in the pouring rain, each verse ending with a dirty rhyme for "Zwick." But it was this irreverent tune that became the basis for one of the most moving moments in the film. All it took was a quick rewrite from the blasphemous to the biblical—"Fucking rain . . . rain, rain, rain" became "Oh, my Lord . . . Lord, Lord, Lord . . ." and voilà, a spiritual was born.

We shot all night long in a freezing drizzle. If you look closely, you can see the condensation of the men's breath as they huddle together to keep warm.

Jihmi was to be the first to testify. His words in the scene, as with the other actors, were mostly his own. With his shining face lit from within, his eyes focused heavenward, he set the tone with a simple, unadorned speech. Morgan was up next. When he'd preached in *The Gospel at Colonus*, it was an artfully written, rehearsed performance. He'd had no time to prepare for this night, yet the speech he improvised was magnificent. And when he reached its epiphany with a beatific smile and began to clap in double-time you could feel the spirit rising to his call.

Then it was Denzel's turn. I had no idea what he was going to say. Despite his background in his father's church, he'd never really taken part in our improvs for the scene. But as he stood before the other actors, feeling their love and encouragement, his alienation became his subject and his truth.

The Shout is my favorite scene in the movie. I like to think it not only captures the belief and sacrifice of the characters, but also the commitment of those who made it.

When the time came to shoot the final battle, I knew we had a logistical challenge. I had watched Kurosawa's *Ran* a dozen times and been overwhelmed by its extraordinary scope and spectacle. I also knew it was accomplished on a very limited budget and realized there are remarkably few shots with hundreds of extras. The rest of the time he fills the frame, crowding it left to right and top to bottom. We were scheduled to shoot on the beach for two weeks, yet I could only afford the large corps of seven hundred extras for three days. By ripping off Kurosawa's methodology, I contrived to capture at least one big image of each significant moment of the battle using the entire contingent and then go back and shoot it all again with a smaller group. When it's cut together, the larger image stays in the audience's mind as long as they're never allowed to see blank space at the peripheries of the frame.

This kind of directorial sleight of hand has now been rendered obsolete by the dominance of CG, and sometimes I can't help but feel something ineffable has been lost in the absence of real time and scale. These days you can fill the frame with as many Orcs or Elves as you wish, but the minute an audience senses fabrication or falseness, they retreat to an intellectual appreciation of what's happening rather than remaining emotionally connected.

As I scouted the beach with Dan Lerner, who I'd asked to be my second unit director, we weren't at all sure we'd be able to accomplish the work we had storyboarded in the time allowed. Then he turned to me and said, "You know what would make this really spectacular?"

"Don't say it."

"But can you imagine the rockets and the explosions against the night sky?"

I knew he was right, of course. But we were already way over schedule and over budget and under tremendous pressure to cut costs. I called Jeff.

"You're fucking kidding me," he said. Or words to that effect.

"Think of it, Jeff. It's the finale! The moment the whole film has been building to."

"But . . ."

"Colored rockets streaking against the sky. Huge fireballs lighting up the night."

"But . . ."

"What if I figured out a way to add a transition so we'd only have to shoot part of it at night?"

He was silent for a second.

"I'll get back to you."

I'm not sure he ever officially said yes, but he conspicuously never said no. It's not clear he even told his bosses what we were planning until it was too late to stop us. He must have withstood a world of second-guessing from the financial guys. He was putting his job on the line for us, and I knew it.

I won't try to articulate the challenges of shooting that sequence. There were too many—from an unexpected high tide that almost swallowed a $300,000 camera car (a track vehicle with a crane attached) to the windblown sand that abraded our faces raw. Yet they were exceeded by the marvels: a close-up of Matthew looking out to sea, a gorgeous piece of internal acting, silently reconciling himself to his destiny before setting his horse free; the faces of the four costars as they stood

shoulder to shoulder before Andre stepped forward and offered to pick up the
flag should it fall. It all exceeded my most secret dreams, especially the timeless
iconography of Black men in blue suits against the pristine white beach as they
filed through the ranks of cheering white soldiers toward an almost certain death.
Kevin Jarre (remember him?) had long since become a cheerleader for the film. I
invited him to Georgia and cast him in a pivotal role. It was he who, as the Union
soldier who earlier taunted the Black soldiers with racist epithets, now called out,
"Give 'em hell, Fifty-Fourth!"

I t's hard to believe *Glory* was the first feature that my friend Steve Rosenblum
ever edited. He received an Oscar nomination for it and has cut just about
everything I've done since. It's not entirely clear why I'd asked Steve to cut my
student film in the first place—he'd once had a summer job syncing dailies for an
industrial film company but that was the extent of his training. I couldn't have
known he would turn out to be one of the most gifted editors of his generation,
but I must have intuited something of his genius. To Steve, there's no such thing

as an "editor's assembly." He believes the process is dialogical—that cutting the film is a conversation, an exchange between the way I had shot it and the way he sees fit to cut it. He feels it's important that he shows me the film in ways I might never have considered. He's fierce in his convictions, occasionally willful and contrary, but always willing to submit to my prerogative as the director once he's had his say.

As Steve and I assembled the first cut, it was clear to us both that the Shout scene—originally scripted to precede the regiment's first skirmish—should play in the penultimate moment, just prior to their final assault. To hear the men of the regiment declare their faith and brotherhood on the eve of what they know may be a fatal task amplifies their sacrifice and deepens our understanding of what we are about to witness.

After ten weeks in the cutting room, I showed the film to the studio. As the screening began, I realized I hadn't told them I had cut the entire first reel, eliminating all the expository scenes of young Shaw among the abolitionists, training his troops, submitting to his mother's entreaties. Instead, the movie began with Shaw marching toward Antietam, his first engagement. As we heard his first letter, studied his innocent face, and sensed his insecurity, we learned everything we needed to know about who he is and what he is about to encounter. Having shed the dead weight of the original opening, the narrative moved apace toward its ineluctable end—with Matthew and Denzel lying side by side in a shallow grave.

Sitting in the darkness before the house lights came up, I could hear sniffling in the room. Jeff and the rest of the executives were generous with their praise. They knew they had something to be proud of, but typically enough they were cautious about embracing it uncritically until they knew how an audience would respond. They decided to preview the movie without changes and chose a theater somewhere in Orange County; I was so anxious driving there I got lost, missed the turnoff and barely arrived in time. The audience response was as enthusiastic as any screening I've had since. The focus group that followed was a love fest. As we stood outside the theater, Jeff was beaming. He put his arm around my shoulders and said, "Matthew heard we were screening the movie. He wants to see it before you lock picture."

"He's not a producer."

"We're going to need him to do press for the movie's release."

"Fine. Have him come to L.A. I'll show it to him on the dubbing stage. It's a gorgeous screen."

"He's in Toronto rehearsing for his next movie."

"So, we'll dupe a print and send it to him."

"He wants you to bring it there."

"That's ridiculous. First of all, I'm working with James Horner on the score. And second of all, no."

"I need you to do this. For me."

"You mean Ovitz needs you to do this." I sighed. Jeff had stuck his neck out for the movie when we needed it most. If this was so important to him, I could swallow a bit more of whatever dignity I had left and take the movie to Toronto.

I took the red-eye and stumbled into the hotel for a quick shower. In the elevator on the way down I ran into Dustin Hoffman. He and Sean Connery were starring with Matthew in *Family Business*, to be directed by Sidney Lumet. Dustin was very chatty—we had reconciled after our bust-up on *Drawing Fire*. He smiled mischievously and said, "I heard you were coming." Before I could glean his sub-text, the elevator doors opened. There was Matthew. And Patsy. I shouldn't have been surprised.

After a few forced pleasantries, we walked across the street to a brand-new eight-hundred-seat theater. As the lights dimmed, I began to sweat. Jet lag? PTSD? Oh my God, I realized, they didn't know I had cut the entire first reel, or that I had also excised an unnecessary subplot—dear to Patsy—about a ro-mantic evening Shaw spends in Beaufort, South Carolina, with Charlotte Forten, a beautiful social worker, whom he unconsciously offends when he refers to her mixed race.

The movie played beautifully on the huge screen. While watching it I entertained the fantasy that Matthew and Patsy would love what they saw and that all would be forgiven and forgotten. That was before the lights came up and they walked out without a word or a backward glance. I flew back to L.A. and was hard at work on the ADR (automated dialogue replacement) stage when the phone rang. It was Mike Ovitz.

"Matthew wants to do a cut of the movie."

I started to laugh.

"What's so funny?"

"No."

"What do you mean, 'no'?"

"What part of 'no' don't you understand?"

He hung up on me. Jeff called minutes later.

"What did you say to Ovitz?"

"I said no."

"That's what I thought you'd say."

"I have final cut, Jeff."

He took a deep breath.

"Then that's what I'll tell Ovitz."

Which he did. It was Jeff's finest hour.

I went back to working with James Horner on the score. *Glory* was the first of several films he and I were to do together. His combination of mastery and sensitivity was exactly right. How to give a musical voice to a story? This is the challenge presented to a composer when he first looks at an unfinished film. Inevitably there are certain mundane tasks to be addressed: a transition to be smoothed by a musical sleight of hand, a sequence that can be better knitted together to help underline a theme or a relationship. Not until that mysterious process begins— when the composer sits alone at his keyboard, and out of the absolute stillness dares move his fingers across the same twelve keys that have been struck by composers for hundreds of years—does a kind of alchemy occur, some magical process of passion, pain, instinct, and craft crystallizes as a musical phrase emerges that manages to express something far beyond the limitation of words, or a melody seems to materialize from the deepest part of an actor's soul.

I had always imagined using the sound of boy sopranos in *Glory*; to me, the innocence in their voices evoked the purity of the men's belief. James agreed and we began inquiring about English boys' choruses. It was Freddie Fields who came up with the idea of the Boys Choir of Harlem. The studio was suddenly feeling bullish about the movie's prospects, so we were able to convince them to fly eighty boys and their director, Walter J. Turnbull, out to L.A. for the session. For many of them it was their first time on a plane.

We recorded the score over three days on the famous Lionel Newman stage at MGM. The sound of a hundred-piece orchestra topped off by a chorus of angelic voices endowed the images with a grace and tragedy no dialogue could ever express. Neither before nor since have I seen a room full of jaded Hollywood session musicians in tears. Word spread on the lot, and other directors began dropping in. At one point, while trading on the privilege of sitting among the orchestra, I happened to glance back toward the engineer's booth and, at various times, saw that Paul Mazursky, Bob Zemeckis, and Steven Spielberg had stopped by to observe. It felt like my bar mitzvah. In some sense, I suppose it was.

Hovering over me throughout the process of making *Glory* was someone I had neither seen nor spoken to in two decades. Yet his investment in me was at the heart of the movie. His name was Jamie McClendon (Mr. McClendon, as we called him then). He was my homeroom advisor in high school, from freshman year through graduation. The only Black teacher in an all-white school, he taught American history, more than a little aware that his radical views were out of step with his surroundings. After receiving his doctorate in urban studies at the University of Chicago under Richard Wade, a pioneer in the field, Jamie was initially unable to get a teaching job in suburban Chicago. For years he worked at a meatpacking plant, then at a wire mill, until finally being hired to teach in the Waukegan, Illinois, schools. The year before I arrived at New Trier, a well-regarded public high school in Winnetka, he had just begun teaching there.

It was 1966. I arrived for my first day of high school—sheltered and not yet fifteen—and found my way to my homeroom to discover a ripped, barrel-chested Black man with a shaved head calmly smoking a pipe and taking attendance. Each morning for the next four years, Mr. McClendon would sit at that desk facing fifteen bleary-eyed, suburban white boys and discuss the news of the day. I remember him telling us about his grandparents, who had descended from slaves. This would inevitably lead to a heated discourse about civil rights and the need for critical thinking and revisionist history.

Each year as America slid deeper into chaos, we sat in our homeroom and tried to make sense of it all. The war in Vietnam was escalating, RFK and Martin Luther King Jr. were assassinated, there were riots downtown at the Democratic convention in Grant Park, and through it all, Jamie McClendon would challenge us with his withering sense of humor and radical view of American history. He could be impatient with the naivete and entitlement of the faces before him, and he relished confronting us with our ignorance and our privilege, but he always encouraged us to push back, and he enjoyed it when we would take him on.

As if this weren't enough to "raise our consciousness," he created a program called Summer Seminar in which white and Black students would learn about the city and one another, whether by building a playground in Uptown, spending time at Operation Breadbasket (a national organization to improve the economic condition of Black communities), or sitting in on the Chicago City Council. He even arranged for us to spend a day in the courtroom of the Chicago Seven trial. He was also the freshman wrestling coach and mercilessly hounded me to join the team, goading me that I was too much of a wimp to make it through a season. He knew just how to push my buttons and eventually, if only to make him shut up, I joined. I hated every sweaty moment: working out in a plastic suit to make weight, running stadiums until I puked. I lost every match, but when I considered quitting, he pushed me even harder. After the last match of the season—when I managed to eke out a draw—he took me aside and shook my hand. It was my Rocky moment.

One of my favorite places growing up was the Chicago Historical Society. It featured magnificent dioramas of the Fort Dearborn Massacre and the Great Chicago Fire (complete with battery-powered flames and a tiny version of Mrs. O'Leary's cow). I asked the studio if we could hold the Chicago premiere in the Society's theater as a fundraiser. I had ulterior motives. My family all lived in the city, and I looked forward to giving them an early look at the movie. Most of all, though, I knew that Jamie, although retired, still lived in the area. I hadn't seen or spoken to him in twenty years, but I sent an invitation to the last address I had. I never heard back. The screening was followed by a lovely reception. As I embraced my family I couldn't help glancing around to see if he was there. He wasn't. As the crowd thinned and we all got ready to go to dinner, I noticed a shiny bald head standing at the edge of the room. He was smaller in stature than I remembered. His once-powerful physique had shrunk with age—or maybe his presence had just loomed much larger in memory. As he moved out into the light and walked toward me, I could see his face was wet with tears. He hugged me fiercely, his grip still that of a wrestling coach. That embrace meant more to me than all the other attention the movie received.

Photo by David Glenn Smith

Glory opened on December 15, 1989. It was nominated for best picture by the Hollywood Foreign Press, and I was nominated for best director. Denzel won the Golden Globe for best supporting actor. He also won the Oscar, as did Freddie Francis for best cinematography, and Don Mitchell for best sound. Steve Rosenblum was nominated for editing, and Norman Garwood and Garrett Lewis for art direction.

When the movie was being released, I had several bad fights with the studio because they refused to advertise in Black media. It pained me to see the movie promoted only as part of official white culture. It's not uncommon these days for people to ask me if I thought a white director would still be allowed to make it. I'd like to think so, but just as likely not. In a climate of such overzealous sensitivity, there might even be pushback against any emphasis on Robert Gould Shaw's role in the story for fear that it might seem a white-savior narrative. This would be as much of a left-wing canard as the banning of books about slavery and critical race theory is a reactionary one on the right. The issue of cultural appropriation is real, but so was the history of the 54th Massachusetts.

That the movie has now been taught for years in schools is one of the things that makes me most proud. After all this time, I have come to understand that there are four ways to measure a movie's success and the first three don't count. Box office is a false accounting, critics no longer matter, and awards are forgotten within days.

Time is the only measure.

EIGHT HELPFUL HINTS
FOR YOUNG DIRECTORS

Which I'm too old to remember, myself.

1. **EVERY SHOT IS OPENING NIGHT**

   In the theater you have months to rehearse. On set you have minutes. If something goes wrong, you can't put a sign on the screen that says "It wasn't my fault."

2. **THE PERFECT IS THE ENEMY OF THE GOOD**

   On Tuesday you fall behind. On Wednesday you forget a shot. Friday you lose the light. Multiply those three compromises times eight weeks of shooting. That's twenty-four moments in the finished film at which you'll cringe.

3. **IT'S YOUR PARTY—BE A GOOD HOST**

   Learn everybody's name. Say "please" and "thank you." Make it feel like a democracy even though it isn't. The truth is, you want what you want because you want it.

4. **WHEN IN DOUBT, TAKE A NAP**

   In your chair. In the back of the prop truck. In your trailer. Wear good shoes and change your socks at lunch. Stay away from craft services. And drink lots of water. What can I say? Your mom was right.

5. **FALL IN LOVE WITH THE ACTORS**

   But don't mistake it as being real. Transfer your fascination with them to the screen. And don't sleep with them, though they are shiny and alluring.

6. **BE MERCILESS TO THE SCRIPT**

   Even if you've written it yourself. Great actors will inevitably tell you there are too many words. Or simply, "I can act this." No words necessary. They may not speak the same language as you, but their stomach brains are remarkable.

7. IT'S POSSIBLE TO MAKE A BAD MOVIE OUT OF A GOOD SCRIPT

But impossible to make a good movie from a bad script. Hitchcock claimed three things make a great movie: a great script, a great script, and a great script.

8. IF AT FIRST . . .

The best thing about directing is that you don't always have to get it right on the first take unlike, say, brain surgery.

CHAPTER SIX

The Nobility of Failure

Leaving Normal, 1991

I was on top of the world. *Glory* had won three Oscars. *thirtysomething* was still piling up Emmy wins. I was wined, dined, and opined. The phone rang constantly. Offers abounded. What could possibly go wrong?

The answer: everything. I should have been exultant, yet I was depressed. I tried meditating. Began doing yoga. Even tried shaving off my beard. (Everyone agreed that was a big mistake.) Listless and lost, I went into therapy and discovered I was recklessly in pursuit of success at the expense of all else. I was determined to change. To seek meaning in my work. And then Ridley Scott sent me a script.

It was called *Thelma & Louise*: a lively, subversive take on women's rage and revenge, written by Callie Khouri. I liked it and discussed it with my therapist.

"Is this the kind of story you want to tell?" he asked.

I waffled. "It's wildly entertaining," I said, "but does it have depth?"

He did what all shrinks do when the patient poses a rhetorical question. Nothing.

I passed.

The question "Who am I?" arises for a director at several points during their career. You ask yourself, *Am I working in a service industry or in the personal expression business?* Your answer determines every choice you make and may change from film to film or even from moment to moment.

Not long after passing to Ridley Scott, Sydney Pollack sent me a new script he had developed to produce: a charming tale of two women in search of themselves by Ed Solomon, writer of *Bill & Ted's Excellent Adventure*. A gentle and witty road movie where the journey is the destination, *Leaving Normal* was a story of female bonding.

"We'll get two amazing actresses," said Sydney.

We sent it to Cher, who loved it. Then to Holly Hunter, who loved Cher. Then to the studio, who loved Cher, Holly, Sydney, me, and the script. Everybody loved everybody.

A week later Cher dropped out—no explanation given. We'd had what I thought was a convivial dinner. She showed me her Malibu mansion; I laughed at her anecdotes. Was it a mistake to say I'd loved Sonny and Cher while in middle school? Next, I heard that Jessica Lange was interested. I was excited, having admired her work for years. I planned to fly to Florida where she was shooting *Cape Fear*. I invited Holly to join me. After a pleasant dinner, they read a few scenes together. On the page the words were lively, but when read they seemed flat. I suggested a few adjustments, trying to inject a bit more levity, but it didn't help, and I didn't feel comfortable pushing it further.

On the long plane ride home, Holly asked how dare I not cast Jessica Lange. This devolved into a fight, and we hardly spoke for the rest of the flight. By the time we landed in L.A., Holly was out.

Undaunted, I pressed on. Who needs movie stars? I'll cast great actresses! Christine Lahti and Meg Tilly are funny and soulful, and my brilliant direction will make it work!

Christine, Meg, and I start rehearsing and get along fabulously. Christine was droll and inventive on-screen and just as much fun off. Meg had exactly the right blend of sweetness and otherness. It was a joy.

Only . . . after the first two weeks' shooting, when I looked at a few scenes cut together, it just sort of sat there. Steve Rosenblum was unavailable. (He was enmeshed in cutting *Jack the Bear* for Marshall—for which I have never forgiven him.) The editor I was working with, Victor Du Bois, was very talented but I was uneasy. Was there something intrinsically off in the script? Was it my work?

We were shooting in Hyder, Alaska, the northernmost ice-free port in the U.S., and a rough town. One night the locals blew up the new customs shed when the IRS tried to impose a tax on cheap booze driven across the Canadian border. It was midsummer 1990. The sun was up twenty hours a day. I lay awake, fighting panic in the endless half-light. I knew I should call the studio, tell them it wasn't going well, possibly even suggest pulling the plug. Instead, I soldiered on, trying to reconcile the unholy cocktail of ego, denial, and fear roiling in my gut.

Thelma & Louise had just come out in May and was a big hit. For three more months I resolutely cheered on the actors and crew on set. But once we were in my L.A. cutting room, no matter how hard we worked, there was something intractably pleasant and inoffensively nice about the movie that resisted our efforts to bring it to life. Sensing my despair, Sydney joined me in the cutting room. At times he was angry, however much he tried not to show it. After a couple of days working together, he too was defeated. His disappointment in me was obvious, even though it was he who had developed the script.

At the first preview, the audience's response was muted. Our numbers were barely acceptable. The moderator of the focus group asked how many of them would recommend this movie to a friend. A few raised their hands; the rest sat on them.

Steve Rosenblum was waiting for me in the lobby when I walked out, shaken. "Don't worry, pal," he said. "You're going to get to make lots of other movies."

I wanted to murder him; it's a feeling I often have about Steve while working together when he persists in telling me a hard truth.

There's always some magical thinking when a movie opens: "Maybe it'll be a sleeper! A critical darling!" But you can tell by the oversized smiles on the faces of the marketing executives that they're just trying to make you feel better. They've been here before.

On the opening day for *Leaving Normal*, I stopped by a theater in Santa Monica to see how the audience of the four o'clock show would react. They didn't. Then again, there wasn't much of an audience. I walked outside to check the size of the audience lining up for the six o'clock show. There wasn't one. Not a soul in sight. It looked like a neutron bomb had been dropped. Tumbleweeds were blowing across the Third Street Promenade.

I looked around and saw smoke rising over downtown, to the east. When I got in the car and turned on the radio, I heard about Rodney King. The L.A. riots had begun. That night, everyone in America was home watching TV.

The next morning, the reviews called it "a pale version of *Thelma & Louise*." The movie played for one weekend and then disappeared without a trace. In the office on Monday, the phone hardly rang. In fact, it wouldn't do so again for months. I was in what the agents charmingly refer to as "movie jail."

You never forget your first flop. It's the moment it dawns on you that you've been on a tightrope all along. In certain ways, my childhood was lived on a tightrope. No, that's being overdramatic—it was my father who lived on the tightrope while my mother, sisters, and I were down in the cheap seats, looking up, wondering when he would next fall off. I watched Allen Zwick go bankrupt not once, not twice, but three times. A gifted entrepreneur, he was even more gifted when you consider he was a high-functioning alcoholic. He was at various times a dress manufacturer, mortgage banker, retailer, and video store owner who somehow managed to juggle a house in the suburbs, piano lessons, summer camp, riding lessons, and all the trimmings while avoiding creditors, dodging phone calls and the IRS. He also had a lifelong love affair with the smell of a new car. After the Mercedes was repossessed (or was it the Caddy?), he'd convince another gullible dealer to lease him a Jaguar that same afternoon, drive out to "the club," and over a few drinks manage to schmooze his rich doubles partners into investing in yet another pipe dream.

I evoke these painful memories because they reveal the shaky psychological baggage I brought with me into a business based on boom or bust. On the surface, my path into this life was conventional. My mother loved the theater. Though her closest brush with the limelight was as assistant director of the class play in high school, she still followed Broadway openings avidly and often took me to see the bus-and-truck companies when they reached Chicago. It was a point of pride for her to know who had studied at the Actors' Studio, who preferred Meisner, and which actress was a Strasburg disciple. Long before the days of IMDb she could rattle off an actor's film credits in chronological order. She also had a habit, charming in retrospect but cringy to a fifteen-year-old, of referring to certain luminaries by their nicknames. Elia Kazan was "Gadge," Lauren Bacall was "Slim," and so on. As much as it might have embarrassed me at the time, I can now appreciate her desire to be "on the inside." Because I share it.

My father, on the other hand, was drawn to the showy side of the biz. Whenever a new movie would be released, he insisted on seeing it the weekend it opened. Generally, it would be one of the muscular tales so popular in the early 1960s. Some of my fondest memories are of ditching school and sitting beside him at a two o'clock matinee in a downtown movie palace to watch *The Guns of Navarone*, *The Great Escape*, or *The Magnificent Seven*. To this day, I still love those films, just as I admire their gifted journeymen directors—J. Lee Thompson and John Sturges, and others like them.

Tellingly, on the wall of my father's crowded little office behind the wrap desk of his crowning achievement—a lovely men's and women's clothing store called London Corner Ltd. (no relationship to London, not on a corner, and definitely unlimited)—he'd hung a signed, framed Hollywood headshot of Jane Morgan, a sexy pop singer of the fifties and sixties. *To Allen, with love*, it read. My guess is she'd come into the store while touring the Midwest in dinner theatre and given it to him. As best I could tell, this was the closest he'd ever come to a glamorous star. Yet as a thirteen-year-old I wondered why he'd hung her photograph so prominently among the stacks of accounts receivable. Did he really know her? More than know her? Why had she signed it "with love"? And how did my mother feel about Jane's breasts spilling out of the low-cut dress and her come-hither smile there beside the kids' drawings and family pictures?

I call attention to this possibly innocent, even trivial detail because, taken in a larger context—especially his flagrant affairs and my parents' subsequent, messy divorce—it offers a darker explanation of my attraction to the movie business and its resemblance to my childhood. (Full disclosure: I have a few pictures of myself with various stars in my office—outnumbered by family photos, I hasten to add.) My relationship with my father was agonizing at times. Allen Zwick was a classic narcissist: charming, charismatic, handsome, seductive, and self-absorbed. He burned very bright and lived to be the center of attention. I couldn't help but notice how people were drawn to him, because I was, too. Toward me, he was alternatively affectionate, casually indifferent, and occasionally depreciating. There was something unattainable about his attention, even his love. That I should choose a life pursuing intimate relationships with movie stars is almost comic in its Freudian implications. It's possible it accounts for a certain love-hate relationship I've always had with them. When your job is presenting them as the gods and goddesses the audience desires, it's easy to fall in love with your own creations. But having elicited the occasional great performance from a movie star, my relationships with them—intense and deeply personal for weeks and months at a time—have often proven disappointing. Yet I remain a moth irresistibly drawn to their bright flame.

Liberty compares me to Charlie Brown and the football. "*This* one is different," I tell her as I plunge headlong into the passionate exploration of a character with an eager actress. "*This* is a real friendship," I insist after a long, wine-soaked *bro* dinner with an actor on location. "I can't wait for you to get to know him. You'll love him!" I tell her in a late-night call from my hotel room. "We'll have him and his wife over for dinner after wrap!" Only to be left wondering, not long after the movie's opening and even attendant award nominations, why a phone call isn't returned, or years later, why a script isn't read or responded to.

Much of this is my doing. It is clearly my own inhibition (read, self-loathing) that keeps me from making the kind of extraordinary gesture that might sustain, or reboot, such relationships. Perhaps more to the point, it is the fear that such a gesture will be rejected, or even worse, ignored. Because, let's face it, a certain amount of initiative is necessary with a movie star, not only because their dance

cards are full and their lives so complex, but because stars are accustomed to receiving. With so much energy directed toward them every moment, there just isn't
the need to initiate. The legacy of growing up in the specter of my father's public failure and humiliation is perhaps the most telling of all. With every business
debacle—each larger than the one before—his place in my personal pantheon
diminished. No longer the life of the party as much as the subject of embarrassed
whispers and sidelong glances, as his jokes grew louder and his drinking reached
critical mass, so did my shame. It's not clear what was more painful: the spectacle
of his downfall or my secret, forbidden satisfaction at watching it happen.

"Shame is a heartless beast. It hounds you when you are most vulnerable,
taunts you with ancient versions of yourself: the child, the gawky adolescent."
I found these words in a notebook from my first time in movie jail (although I
neglected to include the attribution). The appalling public spectacle of my father, drunk and belligerent, berating a waiter in a restaurant, or sitting by a curb
after cracking up his car and claiming it wasn't his fault, or stumbling home contrite and crawling into my bed because my mother had locked the door to their
bedroom and telling me he loved me, his mumbled kisses reeking of gin—these
were my formative experiences in shame. Shame is always there when I sit down
to write, chuckling derisively, or standing behind me on the set, its hand on my
shoulder, just waiting for any sign of weakness as its cue to pounce.

Before the train wreck that was *Leaving Normal*, having made two very successful movies and a hit TV show to boot, I felt as if I'd finally been invited into
the club—in this case a metaphorical club, but nonetheless clubby—chatting with
Spielberg and Scorsese at parties, dinners with the Hankses or the Washingtons.
I was nevertheless incapable of escaping the gnawing fear that it could all come
crashing down at any moment—a waking nightmare my first flop seemed to con-
firm. After all, in a town rife with Schadenfreude, it wasn't hard to interpret the
subtly consoling glances. To hell with Samuel Beckett's "Fail again. Fail better."
It's one thing to read that phrase in the dorm and quite another to live it in the
lobby of CAA.

My experience with *Leaving Normal* was only my first inkling of the most important lesson I still needed to learn: that a director's career is a distance event, not a sprint. A quick glance at an experienced director's IMDb page reveals a run of great success—if he's lucky—leavened by just as much time in the wilderness. Or as Preston Sturges put it, "A hit is something you do between flops." As hard as it is to break in, it's just as hard to stay relevant. It's never a question of *if* you're going to get knocked down, but *when*. And most of all, how long it takes you to get up. The best hitters in baseball have lifetime batting averages below .333. That means they've grounded out, struck out, flied out, two out of three times. The key to hitting is to forget your previous at bat. Easier said than done. Just as there's a real phenomenon of getting "hot," so is the chill that accompanies failure.

It took quite a while to deal with my sudden fall from grace. After many tears, several sleepless nights, and lots of therapy, I finally managed to suck it up and get another movie going. There was a project I'd been working on that I really liked. It was a long shot, but utterly original: the story of a production where everything goes wrong. Set in the sixteenth century in a theatrical world with a striking resemblance to Hollywood, William Shakespeare is a struggling writer-director making a tragic love story . . .

CHAPTER SEVEN

Julia, Harvey, and the Bard

Shakespeare in Love, 1991–1998

According to Heisenberg's uncertainty principle, one cannot measure the position and the speed of a particle with absolute precision. This also applies to a movie in development. There are just too many variables that determine when and how it makes it into the theaters. It might come down to a studio head's desire to imitate another movie's recent success, or his sudden reluctance to replicate another movie's failure. Just as likely, that same studio head will be fired before your movie's ready to go. As a result, we end up hedging our bets by working on several projects at once.

One afternoon in 1991 while escaping the madness of the *thirtysomething* production offices, I met a talented writer named Marc Norman, whose office was down the hall. We began talking stories, as writers do. Marc pitched me an idea about young William Shakespeare and the writing of *Romeo and Juliet*. His clever conceit was to imagine the Elizabethan theater as the Hollywood of its day, with young Will Shakespeare as just another struggling writer-director having to cater to the public's appetite for innocuous, pleasing fare, deal with treacherous producers caring only about commercial success, mollify temperamental actors, struggle with writer's block, and survive the plague. In other words, the usual.

I prevailed upon Universal to hire Marc to write a script. His first draft did a good job of shaping the overall premise—Shakespeare's love affair with a young actress becomes the inspiration for the play as well as drama in its own right; life becomes art and art becomes life. As well written as it was, the script lacked the wit, whimsy, and insight of Shakespearian comedy. Having once directed a tiny college production of *Rosencrantz and Guildenstern Are Dead*, I knew of only one writer in the world whose verbal virtuosity, humor, and plotting acumen could reach such a high bar. Unfortunately, he wasn't interested in being the second writer on anything, or so I was told by Tom Pollock, then chairman of Universal, when I suggested we get Tom Stoppard to do a rewrite. Years before, Pollock had been my first lawyer—he took me on as a client after seeing my AFI student film—so I made a personal plea. Let me go to England and try.

I arrived in London in the spring of 1991. With some reluctance, Stoppard had agreed to hear my entreaty. Arriving at his Chelsea apartment, rather than an intimidating presence, I found him to be generous and welcoming. In fact, he was the most gracious, well-mannered, self-deprecating, world-renowned genius I had ever met. Also, the only one of that description, before or since. As an English major in college, I had been obliged to defend my senior thesis in front of several big-shot professors, among them Harry Levin, an acclaimed Shakespeare scholar of his day. I was infinitely more anxious about this conversation. Fighting flop sweat and jet lag, I launched into my pitch. This wasn't just an excuse for a knockabout comedy, I said, it was an opportunity to talk about transmutation, the process by which the chaff of life is turned magically into the gold of art. I suggested several structural revisions, a few gags, and ended with a bald-faced plea: here was an opportunity for him to show his classical mastery—already well-known to theater afficionados—to movie audiences the world over. After I finished my overheated supplication, he was very quiet. He turned to look out over Chelsea Harbour for a moment and it's possible I heard him humming to himself. Then he looked back at me, smiled pleasantly, and said, "Shall we go for tea?"

© James F. Hunkin / National Portrait Gallery, London

I wish I could recall everything we talked about that afternoon. I suspect I'd been working hard to impress him with my repertoire of erudite literary references before he kindly put me at ease by asking about my life in Hollywood. I must have mentioned the disastrous reception to my most recent film because the conversation took a personal turn, especially about the importance of failure. He talked about his early struggles, fleeing Czechoslovakia to Singapore at age two, how his father died in a Japanese prisoner-of-war camp, about arriving in England with his mother at eight, and how studying Shakespeare had been intrinsic to his love of language. I remember he referred to himself as a "bounced Czech," a line he threw away with typically casual brilliance.

After tea we took a long walk, stopped in a secondhand bookstore where he picked up several musty volumes on English country gardens and one about A. E. Housman (both would figure centrally in later plays), and then it was time to say goodbye. As we went our separate ways, I realized he'd given no indication whether he was interested in signing on. It's not as if I didn't care, but sitting there talking about life and career with a childhood idol who'd been kind enough to act interested in what I had to say restored some inner confidence that had been rocked by my recent failure. I returned to L.A. with renewed hope and energy.

And then Tom said yes. Well, not exactly yes. Yes, if the studio was willing to pay him a million dollars. Which they weren't. Until Julia Roberts entered the picture, that is.

Someone, possibly her manager or agent, had gotten wind of the project and intimated to Universal that Julia might be interested in starring in a period rom-com, possibly this one. The mere possibility of having the "Pretty Woman" wearing a corseted gown was exciting enough to get the studio to cough up the dough. Ten weeks later I was back in London, where a xeroxed copy of Stoppard's first draft was waiting in my very fancy hotel room.

There's something about opening a new script that's fraught with tension, especially if it's one for which you have high hopes. As I stared at it, unopened on the bed, I remembered how a veteran director once described the moment. "You only get to see a new lover naked once," he'd said. Putting aside any sexual connotations for the moment, I knew that this first reading would be my only experience akin to the audience's. Most times when reading a new script, I will fall asleep midway through, narcotized with disappointment, my hopes dashed by the unfortunate reality of wooden characters, bad dialogue, predictable plotting, or all three. Sydney used to say you can open a script to any page, and within a few lines know whether it's worth reading. What he was getting at is that a writer's quality is indelibly encoded in the DNA of every scene.

From the first page of Tom's first draft, it was immediately clear it was one he was born to write. I read it as if in a trance, the scenes flying past. No sooner had I finished it than I went back and read it again, catching laugh-out-loud jokes, puns, and double entendres I had missed the first time through, not to mention a few academic references so recherché they would have required several hours poring through the *Variorum Shakespeare* to decipher. By the time I finished, it was 4 a.m. L.A. time. I hadn't slept much on the plane, but I was too turned on to sleep. I knew in my heart this script would change my life. I took a long walk on Hampstead Heath, hoping to tire myself out, and I remember thinking this was the movie I'd waited my whole life to direct. I might have done better had I remembered Gloucester's words as he wandered blindly on another heath, crying out, "As flies to wanton boys are we to the gods; They kill us for their sport."

I stayed in England for a few days, meeting with Tom for a couple of hours in the afternoons. He appeared to be interested enough in my thoughts on his draft and was unfailingly patient, but he was also an eminent playwright accustomed to absolute control of the text and wasn't about to suffer fools. My enthusiasm seemed to amuse him at least, and he indulged me more than I deserved. There were times I overstepped, though, and he let me know it in a manner that was no less devastating for being done so politely. Sometimes I didn't realize one of his barbs had drawn blood until long after the session was over. One day I'd been holding forth at length, no doubt too stridently, on the importance of a particular story point—it doesn't matter which one—and when I finished, he gave me a be-atific smile, and with his charming, inimitable lisp, tartly observed, "Well, Ed, you say it so much better than I could."

See what I mean?

There's one contribution to Tom's wonderful work for which I will claim a small part. In his early drafts the lovers' attraction was exquisitely soulful and wildly romantic, but oddly chaste. It seemed such an obvious point and I remember trying to think of how to put it decorously, until one day after circling the subject for a while I finally blurted out that Romeo and Juliet was a play about two kids discovering sex who brought ruin upon their families and themselves because they were in such a daze from constant fucking they were incapable of thinking about the consequences and shouldn't we see them spending more time in bed?

Tom seemed taken aback for a moment, and then he cocked his head to the side and said, "Oh. Right."

Tom's next draft was waiting for me when I got back to the States, and I couldn't have loved it more. The studio felt the same and arranged for me to meet with Julia right away. Our first meeting was, as most tend to be between a director and a movie star, tentative, polite, and utterly false. There are all sorts of reasons for this. The movie star doesn't want to appear too needy but can't help wanting to know she's wanted. The director wants the movie star to know how much he wants her but doesn't want to sacrifice what little dignity he hopes to maintain once he has her in the movie. Each of them wants the meeting to go well and so it does, but little of consequence is really discussed and even less is revealed. Meanwhile, the actor knows it really doesn't matter if the director wants her or not; she's already been told by her representatives that the movie is hers if she wants it, but that doesn't stop her resorting to her default mode, which is to say, pleasant, pliable, and seductive. Meanwhile, the director knows it's entirely possible that the best performance the actor will give is the one she's in the process of giving during the meeting, and he won't know her true nature until it's far too late to do anything about it, yet he too is giving a performance: abnegating his natural anxiety, fear, and dread for that of the patient, kind, and supportive surrogate dad.

A few days later Julia said yes, and as the agents, lawyers, and business affairs executives prepared to do battle over her deal, I got back on a plane for London to begin prep. The next six weeks were dreamlike. Working at Pinewood Studios with gifted designers, costumers, and prop masters whose lives had been devoted to Shakespearian production was humbling and thrilling. An exact replica of the Globe Theatre was to be the centerpiece of a warren of streets and alleys that were to comprise an Elizabethan bankside. Every day I'd marvel at the speed with which the enormous set rose.

I then came home for one last trip to be with my family before returning to London for casting, rehearsals, and the final frenzied weeks before shooting began. Julia would be coming with me to England this time. I had scheduled chemistry readings for her with a wonderful crop of actors I'd met who were vying to play Shakespeare. It was on the morning of our departure that things began to get weird. The plan was for a car to pick me up, then we'd pick up Julia en route to LAX. But an hour before the car arrived, I received a cryptic message from her assistant; Julia was staying at an undisclosed location (no one was to know it), and the driver would pick me up as planned and only then would we be informed where to find her. It seemed Julia's personal life, already a constant subject of tabloid drama, had gone off the rails.

I'm obliged to evoke a few details, not as gossip, but rather because they directly figure in the travesty that followed. Apparently, days before she was to marry Kiefer Sutherland, her costar in *Flatliners*, Julia had more or less left him at the altar. The address to which we were directed was the home of Jason Patric, Kiefer's friend and costar in *The Lost Boys*, with whom Julia was currently shacking up. She ran out to meet us, glancing around furtively for lurking paparazzi, jumped in the car, and off we went to the airport.

In those days, the first-class cabin of the British Airways direct flight to London was very intimate. Rather than sleeping pods, seats were arranged in adjacent pairs. When laid flat, the effect was perilously close to that of a double bed. Julia and I didn't know each other well, but this arrangement had every indication of changing that in a hurry. Over dinner and a couple of glasses of wine we chatted about friends we had in common, our childhood love of movies, our experiences in Hollywood. It was the kind of conversation that touches gingerly on more personal subjects but then dances away as you both wait to see who will be the first to volunteer an embarrassing detail or reveal a secret.

It didn't take Julia long. I dozed off and awoke to find two famously brown eyes staring at me from only inches away. Suddenly I was back at summer camp with my bunk squeezed in beside a fellow camper who in this case just happened to be a world-famous movie star. I can't remember how the conversation took the turn it did, a night flight across the ocean carries its own romance and we were both headed off on an adventure. Julia was obviously too excited to sleep; she was a twenty-three-year-old girl riding a whirlwind. She wanted to talk about her life, and I was her anointed confidant. It wasn't an entirely unfamiliar role for me. As a director, I'd been privy to some very private confessions, but the speed at which her intimacy tipped into the red zone took me by surprise. She began, innocently enough, by talking about why she loved the script, how it captured the madness of falling in love, but she soon moved on from literary criticism to self-revealment, talking about the almost trance-like abandon of giving oneself over to a new lover, how that was the very excitement at the core of her acting.

"It's one of the reasons I love making movies," she whispered. "I know some people might not understand or approve, but I can't help falling in love with my costars. You understand, don't you?"

I nodded. Another important part of directing is nodding.

She went on, whispering in the dark about being in love with love. She talked about past costars who had become much more, Kiefer, Dylan McDermott, and Liam Neeson. Why was she telling me all this? I wondered. What was it she needed me to know? I couldn't help but notice she didn't seem to fall in love with her directors. Despite a momentary frisson of rejection based on ego alone, this was a good thing given that I was in love with Liberty and wished to stay married.

I soon realized Julia wasn't really talking to me anymore but had drifted into a kind of soliloquy. Was she trying her hand at a Shakespearian convention? It was mesmerizing and at the same time oddly terrifying. I couldn't help but recall one of my favorite lines from a Fitzgerald short story about a young flapper.

"Lola Shisbe had never wrecked a railroad in her life. But she was just sixteen and you had only to look at her to know that her destructive period was going to begin any day now."

And then Julia got to the punch line.

"I've decided who should play Shakespeare," she said.

I cut in, starting to list all the brilliant actors I had read who were scheduled to meet her in the coming days. But Julia was on a roll.

"There's really only one actor who can do it," she gushed.

I closed my eyes in dread. "Who?"

"Daniel, of course!"

She was referring to Daniel Day Lewis, who had won the Academy Award for Best Actor the year before. "He's brilliant, he's handsome and intense. And so funny!" she said. "Did you see his performance in *A Room with a View*? He's done Shakespeare too. Don't you think he'd be perfect?!"

I took a deep, cleansing breath. "I can't argue with you, Julia. But I met with Dan last month. He's committed to do *In the Name of the Father* with Jim Sheridan. Jim directed him in *My Left Foot*. They're very close. He calls Jim his best mate."

"I know," she said, brushing my objection aside. "I can get him to do it."

There was something in the way she said it—it was the same tone of voice I would recognize years later when, while giving her Oscar acceptance speech for *Erin Brockovich* she refused to be played offstage, looking down at Bill Conti in the orchestra pit and ordering him to sit down: " 'cause I may never be here again, Mr. Stick Man!"

I looked at Julia. Her face seemed to morph. Her smile was still dazzling, the very smile that had landed her at the top of the Hollywood food chain, but it had suddenly taken on a vaguely feral quality. I couldn't speak.

I have no memory of the rest of the flight. It was one of those moments in the life of a director where you are reminded that control is an illusion, that there are certain forces of nature, the weather for instance, that will not heel to your command. As we deplaned and I followed meekly behind Julia as she sailed, impervious, through the swarming paparazzi who had somehow been notified of her arrival, I understood that she was going to be a force to be reckoned with. Despite my many entreaties, she was already on her cell phone asking her assistant for two dozen roses to be sent to Daniel, along with a card that read "Be my Romeo."

The Halcyon Hotel in Holland Park was once West London's version of the Chateau Marmont: home to high-profile trysts, celebrities in residence, and touring rock stars from both sides of the Atlantic. Comprising two interconnected Belle Époque town houses, it was by far the most glamorous place I had ever stayed. After being shown to my gorgeous suite, I promptly fell asleep with my clothes on. Hours later I awoke jet-lagged, dehydrated, and disoriented in the darkness.

I sat up and tried to regroup. Julia's fascination with Daniel was understandable. There's often a mirroring effect in Hollywood romances. Acclaimed everywhere as the "it" girl, she naturally felt her costar should be the world's greatest actor. There was something poignant that a young woman every man desired was trying to find someone she herself desired. She had said it herself: part of what animated her best work was love. Who was I to deny her this fantasy? It would all work out eventually; once she learned Daniel was truly not available, she would get past the disappointment and open herself to the parade of brilliant English actors lining up to play opposite her. This wasn't the first time I had dealt with a difficult actor. And *Glory* had worked out, hadn't it?

I was feeling better already, especially after devouring the £35 club sandwich from room service. I called home and told Liberty about my flight with Julia. Having spent the night back in Santa Monica taking care of our six-month-old daughter, who had come down with the flu, she seemed insensitive to my predicament. "I'm so sorry you had to spend the night in first class with a gorgeous twenty-three-year-old movie star talking about her love life," she said. "Is your suite nice?"

That night, I introduced Julia to Tom at dinner at the Savoy Grill. It was a festive occasion with a champagne toast to the success of the film. Julia gushed about the script and couldn't have been more enthusiastic. I did notice her checking her phone quite often but thought nothing of it. Then, just as the waiter brought the dessert menus, she received a message and leapt to her feet, grabbed her purse, made a quick garbled apology about having forgotten plans to see an old friend, and hurried away. Tom looked slightly confused by her sudden hasty exit. I on the other hand smelled disaster. He sensed my chagrin, shook his head knowingly, and simply said, "Actresses."

Casting was scheduled to begin the next morning at 10 a.m. By ten fifteen, a few actors were waiting. By ten forty-five, the bar of the Halcyon looked like the greenroom of a play on the West End, filled with well-heeled studs who'd attended the same drama school, acted together at the National Theatre, and competed for the same roles throughout their careers. By eleven, I was sweating. And then the phone rang.

"It's Julia . . . he-he . . ."

"Hi, Julia. Where are you?"

"I'm in my room . . . he-he . . ."

"We're all downstairs. There are actors waiting."

"I'm really sorry, you'd better come upstairs. . . ."

"What?"

"Room thirty-four . . . I'll explain."

I climbed the ornate stairs and knocked.

"Come in."

I stepped into the most majestic hotel suite I'd ever seen. Ornate chandeliers, gold flocked wallpaper, overstuffed furniture, and a raised four-poster bed fit for a queen.

Or in this case, Julia Roberts.

Julia was flushed and giggly, her smile even bigger than the night before. She preceded to tell me that Daniel had agreed to do our movie and I should cancel today's casting.

I was speechless. I tried not to envision what had happened after she left the restaurant and ran off into the night. Had she really managed to beguile him in that Olympian hotel room? I'll never know. What else could I do but walk back downstairs and inform a group of surly, brilliant British stage actors that the American movie starlet wasn't feeling well after her flight and abjectly beg their forgiveness? I went back up to my room and sat on the bed, immobilized. What was wrong with this picture? I should have been triumphant. Instead, I sensed disaster.

Hours later, the phone rang. It was Daniel. "Hey, can you meet me at the pub across the street?" he asked.

I put on my coat and trudged across to the little place where we had met for a drink weeks before when I'd asked him about being in the movie. Daniel had already ordered me a pint of Guinness.

He looked at me with a sheepish grin. "I can't do your movie, you know."

"Of course not."

"I told you I'd promised my mate, Jim Sheridan, I'd do his film."

"I remember."

After a few pleasantries, Daniel left, leaving me with the tab in more ways than one. I finished my beer and plodded back across the street, mumbling to myself, "It will all work out. Every movie encounters a bump in the road. And I have so many wonderful actors lined up for Julia to meet. She is a pro. She loves the script." Back in my room, I didn't have the heart to call her myself. I asked the beleaguered casting director to call Julia's assistant and let them know casting would start up again the next day at 10 a.m.

Julia's smile was nowhere in sight when she came downstairs the next morning. Eyes red-rimmed, hair unkempt, she looked like she hadn't slept all night. I tried my best to act like it was business as usual, but my transparent cheerleading couldn't elicit more than a wan smile. I can't imagine a worse state of mind for an actress to read with other actors, especially for a romantic comedy. I should have canceled the session, but our prep schedule was terrifyingly tight.

My favorite among all the actors I wanted Julia to meet was Ralph Fiennes. Not only was his work onstage nothing short of magnificent (he would win a Tony for *Hamlet* in 1995) but he also had the driest, keenest wit I'd encountered since . . . well, since Tom Stoppard. In addition to great warmth and charm, he projected intelligence and had a face that photographed beautifully.

After some awkward chitchat, he and Julia opened their scripts. It would be the first time I was to hear her in the role, and I was more than a little curious. Ralph's reading was every bit as good as I remembered, but Julia was hardly there at all. I initially wondered if, like Denzel, she was the type of actor whose first readings are often restrained. But this was something else. Even as Ralph did his best to elicit the famous smile, Julia barely acknowledged him. I'm not suggesting she was deliberately sabotaging, but it was a disaster nonetheless. I tried to catch Ralph's eye to apologize as he left but he couldn't get out of there fast enough. After he was gone, I turned to Julia, awaiting her reaction.

"He isn't funny," is all she said.

The rest of that day and every day in the week that followed went just as badly. I no longer have my cast lists, but among the yet to be discovered young actors we saw I remember Hugh Grant, Russell Crowe, Rupert Graves, Rupert Everett, Colin Firth, Sean Bean, Tim Roth, and Jeremy Northam. Julia found fault with all of them: one was stiff, another wasn't romantic, and none of them, no matter how gifted, funny, or handsome, were as "right" as Daniel—which stands to reason because they *weren't* Daniel. To this day, Russell Crowe berates me for not having cast him in a role he desperately wanted. Mark Rylance must have been the only actor in England we didn't audition because he had recently taken over the new Globe and refused to come in, sending word that he was offended by our portrayal of Shakespeare.

After two weeks of casting, there was only one actor with whom Julia was willing to move to the next step. His name was Paul McGann. We arranged a full screen test at Pinewood. That morning, Julia emerged from makeup, looking radiant in full period costume. But once she began to say the words, something was off. There was no magic. The problem wasn't the script. Or Paul McGann. It was

Julia. Ostensibly, she had been working for weeks with tapes sent to her by Joan Washington, the illustrious dialect coach. But from the moment she began acting it was clear she hadn't been working on the accent.

Adopting a dialect can be tricky. It involves overlaying a left-brain process (language) on what is essentially a right-brain exercise (acting). Only after hours and hours of repetition does it become second nature. Until then, it has the unsettling effect of dimming an actor's essence; the performance flattens out and becomes all about the dialect rather than the acting. Years later, when Leonardo DiCaprio assumed a "Rhodesian" accent in *Blood Diamond*, I watched as he devoted hours a day for weeks on end to tapes of native speakers made for him by Tim Monich, a disciple of Edith Skinner who'd spent a decade on the faculty at Julliard. Even after we began filming, Leo would speak in character. As odd as it sometimes seemed listening to him chat at the craft services table in a foreign accent, he was right in believing it was the only way he could be entirely comfortable and convincing on-screen.

As I watched Julia's performance, I imagined the hard work it would take for her to get there. Sensing her discomfort, I tried to be encouraging, but she must have intuited my unease, and I made the tragic mistake of underestimating her insecurity. Having only recently been catapulted to the dizzying heights atop the Hollywood food chain, she must have been terrified to fail. But I would never get to talk her off the ledge. The next morning when I called her room, I was told she had checked out.

I made several calls trying to track her down—to her assistant, to her agent—but nobody seemed to think anything was amiss. It wasn't until late that afternoon that I reached Julia's manager, who informed me Julia had flown back to the U.S. and that she was leaving the project. I called Tom Pollock, who by now had been told what was going on.

"She can't do this!" I screeched. "We made her deal! She's been on the movie for months. We've secured locations, built sets, made costumes . . ."

"I realize that," he said.

"We've spent millions of dollars . . ."

"Six million, to be exact."

"You've got to hold her feet to the fire, Tom."

"I plan to," he promised. "She's probably just scared. How many times did Matthew Broderick walk off *Glory*? She's an emotional twenty-three-year-old."

"You're right," I sighed.

"Just give me a little time to get into it," he said. "And relax. You've been working seven days a week. Take the day off and enjoy yourself. I'll be back to you soon. And don't worry, this will all work out."

It didn't work out. Whether because Universal had other projects in mind for her, or some agenda to which I wasn't privy, Tom chickened out. He ordered the production to be shut down. The next day I stood there and watched as the Globe Theatre was destroyed along with my dreams of grandeur.

I've never spoken to Julia again. Instead, I've observed her career from afar, watching as her work has grown in depth and stature. I bear her no ill will. She was a frightened young person looking for love.

Saul Zaentz, the legendary producer, once told me he'd lived through 1967's Summer of Love in Haight-Ashbury, read the *Kama Sutra* cover to cover, and believed he knew everything there was to know about getting fucked. Then he came to Hollywood.

But this is only half the story. It is at this point in the saga that a villain worthy of Shakespeare's pen makes his grand entrance on the Elizabethan stage.

I had heard of Harvey Weinstein, but it was 1994 and he had not yet achieved his full eminence. Two years had passed since Julia Roberts walked off *Shakespeare in Love*, and having gone off and made *Legends of the Fall*, I was in New York City doing press screenings when my agent, Jeff Berg, called to say that Harvey had heard about the western epic and asked to see it.

My phone rang at eleven that night as I was finishing dinner with friends downtown. Harvey had just watched the movie and somehow managed to track me down. I could hear James Horner's end credits in the background as Harvey went on and on. It was the best movie he'd seen all year; I was going to win the Oscar for best director, and could I please, please, please come to Tribeca and talk to him. "Now?" I asked. "Right now!" he exclaimed. Ever a sucker for praise, and with an agenda of my own, I said yes.

Harvey Weinstein's depredations are public record, but little has been said about his extraordinary displays of enthusiasm and powers of persuasion. At the risk of wearing out a metaphor, Richard III's seductive prowess comes to mind.

"You're a genius!" he told me. "What do you want to do next? I'll finance it, whatever it is!"

"There's a movie I almost made called *Shakespeare in Love*."

"Let me read it! Who wrote it?"

"Tom Stoppard."

"My hero!"

I sent over the script the next day. He called two hours later to say he loved it, and that his next call would be to Tom Pollock to see if he could get the rights in turnaround. Unfortunately, when Tom mentioned the $6 million in sunk costs, Harvey's enthusiasm withered and that was the last I heard from him for a few years.

But Harvey had helped in one significant way. His unbridled zeal helped sustain my belief in the project and, given the success of *Legends of the Fall*, I decided it might be a good moment to see if anybody else in town was willing to step up. Over the ensuing three years I must have shown the script, often more than once, to every studio and independent financier with two nickels to rub together. All said no. At various times I finagled different pairings of actors to play Romeo and Juliet: among them, Kenneth Branagh and Winona Ryder, Stephen Dillane and Emily Watson, Jude Law and Somebody I Can't Remember. None of them elicited enough interest for someone to write a check for the $6 million in sunk costs before proceeding. Mel Gibson read the script, showed interest for a while, then danced away. So did Johnny Depp.

After each attempt fizzled, I'd go off and work on something else. *My So-Called Life* was on the air from 1994 to 1995. *Courage Under Fire* was released in 1996. In 1997, I was scouting locations in NYC for *The Siege* when I saw an announcement in the trades that Harvey Weinstein and Miramax had acquired the rights to *Shakespeare in Love* and intended to make it the following year. How perfect (and how very Harvey, as I would soon learn) that neither he, nor anyone else, had seen fit to tell the contractual producer, aka me.

There's a story I've heard a couple of times—it may be apocryphal—about how Harvey's interest was rekindled in the project enough to pursue the rights. It seems there was a moment in which Winona Ryder and Gwyneth Paltrow were best friends, and that while staying at Winona's house, Gwyneth happened upon the *Shakespeare in Love* script I had sent to Winona. And that Gwyneth, having made six or seven movies for Miramax while becoming Harvey's go-to movie star and resident muse, told him she wanted to do it.

Whatever happened prior, what's certain is that Harvey learned that Universal wanted the rights to *King Kong,* and he called Tom Pollock, offering to make a trade. What other terms may have been part of the deal I don't know, but it was done quickly. When Jeff Berg called and asked Harvey what my role would be in a movie I'd developed and nursed for six years, Harvey said I was being cut out of the process. He said I had been paid during the term of my deal with Universal and he had no obligation to include me. My next call was to Bert Fields, the same litigator who represented Dustin Hoffman and had long ago said Tri-Star wasn't paying his client enough to do *Drawing Fire.* Equally respected and feared throughout town, Bert sent Miramax a legal letter. And that's when Harvey's threats began.

"You think you can sue me, you prick? You don't know who you're dealing with. I'm going to ruin you!"

It was midnight. I was in a hotel room across the street from Michael Reese Hospital in Chicago, where my father was dying. "Hello, Harvey," I said.

"I'm going to make sure you never work again!"

"It's late, Harvey. My father is sick. It's not a good time."

"Oh, you're *sensitive*! I've hurt your *feelings . . .*"

"Fuck you."

"I'll kill your whole family, you little fuck."

"Nice talking to you, Harvey. See you in court."

More than twenty years later, having learned the extent of his sexual depreda-tions, I can't help but think of the full force of Harvey's malignant energy focused onto a young girl alone and terrified in his hotel room. There's no way I could have known the extent of his evil, yet I'd like to think there was something more than the righteousness of my cause that drove me to fight back as hard as I did. In the fifteenth century, the Borgias were lecherous, treacherous monsters. But also patrons of the arts with exquisite taste. Aggression and intimidation are useful in a business with as little governance as Hollywood, and they served Harvey well for years. Until he was called out at last. And rightly punished.

This wasn't the only late-night call. I started recording them and forwarding them to the lawyers. Apparently, Harvey didn't believe I would go through with a lawsuit, so he was surprised when we threatened to enjoin his production and he was served a subpoena to be deposed. He called Jeff Berg the next day and begged to meet. The suite where we convened at the Peninsula hotel has since become infamous. I'm happy to say Harvey was not in his bathrobe when we walked in. But it was an unrecognizable Harvey, nonetheless, meek and abjectly contrite.

"I'm sorry for everything, Ed. You're a brilliant artist. You know how much I respect you."

I said nothing. Jeff spoke up on my behalf. "And is this how you treat artists you respect?"

"I know, I know," Harvey said. "I get carried away. I'm sorry. I'm so, so sorry."

As he repeated "I'm sorry, I'm so sorry," something monstrous happened. His eyes began to fill with tears.

"I can't help it. I do bad things."

It was as good a performative apology as I had ever seen. Big crocodile tears dripped down his face. I wouldn't have been surprised if he'd fallen to his knees. Had it not been for the unhinged, threatening calls I might even have believed it. I couldn't help but imagine how many others had been susceptible to his act. Instead, I just shook my head, fighting the impulse to laugh.

"This movie would never have existed had it not been for you, Ed. What can I do to make it up to you? I've just acquired the rights to *Rent*, would you like to direct it? We have a great script of Elmore Leonard's *La Brava*. You'd be great for it."

"How about *Shakespeare in Love*?" I said.

"But you're already in prep for *The Siege*. My deal with Universal is that *Shakespeare in Love* must go into production this year."

It wasn't a long meeting. Among the many things Harvey promised was to include my central role as producer in all press releases and to feature me in every major interview about the genesis of the movie. In exchange, Marshall, though my longtime producing partner at our company Bedford Falls, nobly agreed to have his producer credit replaced by Donna Gigliotti and David Parfitt. The presentation credit for Bedford Falls would remain. In later years I read that Harvey claims to have fired me. What's more likely is that he was lying about his deadline from Universal to put the film into production.

Back in New York for final prep on *The Siege*, I met with Paul Webster at Miramax to discuss directors for *Shakespeare in Love*. I'd seen John Madden's theater work at Yale and very much liked *Mrs. Brown*, the film he'd done with Billy Connolly and Judy Dench. I gave John my blessing—not that I had any real influence. Things went south when I sent Gwyneth a letter asking if she'd be interested in the part in *The Siege* eventually played by Annette Bening. At that point Miramax had no production date set and I assumed she could do both films. Nevertheless, Harvey went apeshit, and the threats began anew. From that moment on, I was excluded from all press, including the production notes, and wasn't sent dailies of casting as we'd agreed.

Not that I would have been able to concentrate. I'd begun shooting *The Siege* and had more than my share of problems making a huge action movie on the streets of New York. I managed to put all the drama with Harvey out of my mind until we heard he was again threatening to remove my credit. Another call from Bert Fields solved that. It was only upon watching the final cut in a preview that I saw Harvey had placed our Bedford Falls presentation credit over the shot of a foot stepping in a pile of horseshit. Classy move.

In France, there are pigs who root around in the muck and mire for treasured truffles. They have a remarkable nose for what is valuable, but at the end of the day they're still pigs. It wasn't until years later that we found out Harvey had given himself a first-dollar gross position in the profit stream of *Shakespeare in Love*, thus denying thousands to all the other participants. Had we known, that alone would have been cause for yet another lawsuit. Meanwhile, for the president of a studio to have given himself a producer credit created a firestorm within the industry that resulted in what has come to be known as "the Harvey Rule," which stipulates that to earn the PGA (Producers Guild of America) credit, a producer must have performed some real role in making the movie. I'm proud to point out that Marshall, a former president of the PGA, was among those who created that rule.

There's no reason to go into the infamous Oscar campaign smack-down between "our" film and *Saving Private Ryan*. It's been well documented by others. I do have two other significant memories, though, each from an awards ceremony. One was rewarding, though I received no award, and the other was traumatic when I did.

The first took place at the Golden Globes, always a weird and wonderful night—weird because it's an illegitimate, corrupt, and biddable institution, wonderful because they serve booze at your table for hours and the food never arrives, and everybody is so shit-faced by the time the awards are handed out that the winners can be counted on to give crazy, epically cringy acceptance speeches. But when Tom Stoppard stepped onstage to accept his award for best screenplay, his first words were, "Sorry, Harvey. I first want to thank Ed Zwick."

I realize just how petty it is that this pleased me so much. But it was the first and only time my contribution had ever been publicly acknowledged, and it meant something to me. Thanks, Tom.

The second was at the Oscars. Before the ceremony begins, the producers of nominated movies can often be seen huddling together in the lobby making a plan. In this case, Harvey was elsewhere. If by chance we won, we agreed that Donna Gigliotti would speak first, then David Parfitt, then me. No one was eager to be treated to another heartfelt acceptance speech in which Harvey thanked his parents, his wife and children, his brother, every employee at Universal and Miramax, the cast and crew—everyone but the other producers responsible for making the movie.

We did win. A close examination of my body language onstage when it was my turn to speak shows me inching toward the mic, knowing it is my turn after David finishes.

Suddenly, though, I realize the fix is in. Donna knows what side her bread is buttered on and takes the mic from David and hands it to Harvey rather than to me. Unnerved, I allow myself to be hip-checked aside as Harvey waddles toward the mic. As I stand there, the rictus of a frozen grin immobilizing my face, listening to Harvey's prepared, saccharine, self-serving acceptance, it occurs to me to shove him over the edge of the stage into the orchestra pit. Faced with the choice between an act of violence before a worldwide audience of 100 million movie fans or false modesty, I make the wrong choice. I close my eyes, not at all present in the moment, recalling instead the joy I felt first imagining the film, the exaltation I was going to get to direct it, and the crushing disappointment when I realized I wasn't. What I'm most afraid of, I realize, is that this might have been the best work I would ever do and that I may never be up here again.

In film school we were all contemptuous of awards. As we got older, it turned out we were not so averse to winning them. Back then, we believed that institutions have never been reliable judges of art. How can a comedy about a sixteenth-century playwright be compared to a drama about the men who died on Omaha Beach? I look out into the audience and see Steven Spielberg. He's sitting in an aisle seat so he'd be ready to come onstage if his name was called. He is stone-faced and looks upset. His marvelous film has just lost.

Does that make him a loser?

In some essential way we are all losers in Hollywood. It's hard to think of any other bond that distinguishes us as a community. In each of us there is something unfulfilled, some ache or deficiency of character that leads us to fill a hole in our heart with the love of strangers. Or awards. Like the Scarecrow in *The Wizard of*

Oz, we imagine that what is broken can somehow be fixed by a . . . by a . . . by an Oscar.

The faces of my children suddenly swim into my thoughts. It occurs to me that they are staying up very late to watch me and that it is a school night. Tomorrow, in fact, is my day to drive carpool. I'm tempted to leave right after the ceremony. Uncharacteristically, Liberty, who looks radiant in her Elizabethan gown, wants to attend the after-parties. My sisters have flown in to be with me. We go to the Governors Ball. By two in the morning, after a glass of champagne or three, my sour mood has lifted.

It occurs to me I just won an Oscar.

THE COST OF DOING BUSINESS (IN TEN PARTS)

Everyone tells stories; I happen to collect the indignities.

1. A FAIRY TALE

A writer-director friend was known for making gritty films. A big movie star, known for his pop taste, begged him to do a CG children's movie. On the first day of shooting the actor rewrote every word. It only got worse. Apparently neither had ever heard the tale of the scorpion and the frog. The movie died too.

2. THE STRUGGLE

The actor had a bad reputation. The director's peers advised him to go another way, but the actor was so right for the part the director cast him. On the first day, they got into an ugly public fight. Neither backed down. When the director saw dailies, the actor was brilliant. They fought every day. Then made two more movies together.

3. MENTORS

A famous actor begged to work with the hot young writer-director. He then rewrote her script, told her where to put the camera, recut the movie, and then blamed its failure on her. The director never made another feature; the actor won a lifetime achievement award.

4. THE COST OF DOING BUSINESS

Every morning the actress would panic. The director spent hours talking her off the ledge. It's to be expected that an actress shows her anxiety while the director must hide hers. For her work, the actress won an Oscar; the director became addicted to Xanax.

5. KICK THE DOG

The movie star arrived to find his trailer parked farther from the set than his costar. He refused to get dressed until that was remedied. It wasted an hour of shooting time. The producer abjectly apologized to the actor for the delay and then at wrap berated the director for going into overtime.

6. **A HELPING HAND**

The headstrong young actor wouldn't take direction. His costar, a brilliant actress, sensed disaster and begged him to help her run lines each morning, during which she would subtly direct their scenes. The stellar reviews credited the director with eliciting great performances from both.

7. **EGO UNCHAINED**

In prep the actor made the director watch him try on forty-eight pairs of pants. Then he essentially directed himself, often making the director sit and watch. He even insisted the studio fly the DP from L.A. to NYC to light his TV interviews. No one ever said no to him. Except the audience when the movie bombed.

8. **TOUGH LOVE**

At lunch on the first day of shooting, the director was tearing his hair out at the ingenue's performance. On the first day of shooting he took her aside. "How much are you making for this movie?" he asked. Convinced she was getting fired, she whimpered, "A hundred K." "Well, you've earned all of it," he said. "Now stop acting."

9. **THE PRO**

"Which line would you like me to cry on?" the actress asked. "Uh . . . how about the second-to-last one?" the director asked. "Which is better lit, my right or left?" she asked. "The right," he admitted. And that's exactly how she did it. All four takes.

10. **NEVER ASSUME**

While staging a scene, I suggested to the movie star it would be natural if he were to be doing the dishes. During rehearsal he seemed uncomfortable and asked if he could stir some soup instead. It dawned on me he'd never done dishes in his life.

CHAPTER EIGHT

The Griefs of a Man's Life

Legends of the Fall and *My So-Called Life*, 1993–1994

I came of age when movies were the only game in town. There were three channels on TV mostly showing crap, one football game broadcast on Sunday, one on Monday night, and no cable, YouTube, Netflix, Amazon, Hulu, Instagram, iMessage, or TikTok. Movies were ephemeral. My relationship with them was passionate. You only saw them once—unless you stayed in the theater, as I often did, and watched them a second time. There was no hope of renting them or streaming them or pausing them to look at your texts or check your email. If you were lucky, you'd catch one by chance on late-night TV. After going to a movie, you stayed up late drinking coffee with your date or getting high with your pals and talking about it all night long. Movies defined us. They mirrored us and inspired us.

I remember one late-night dorm-room conversation, where my friends and I decided there were only two kinds of movies: forgettable or memorable. The longer I've been in the business, the more I realize we were onto something. What we were getting at was the difference between entertainment and culture. Because, let's face it, today is all about mindless entertainment. It's disposable and distractible. It allows us to escape our social conscience, fills the gaps in the boredom we so deeply fear, takes our minds off the struggles of everyday life, shields us from the awareness of the pain and suffering of the world.

Here is a partial list of the movies I watched in 1979:

Apocalypse Now

Midnight Express

The Tin Drum

Straight Time

Kramer vs. Kramer

The China Syndrome

The Deer Hunter

And Justice for All

Being There

Mad Max

Manhattan

Wise Blood

Heaven Can Wait

The Marriage of Maria Braun

By every measure, these were memorable films, the kind I aspired to make. That same year, my girlfriend, Lucy Bingham, turned me on to *Legends of the Fall*, a novella by Jim Harrison published in its entirety in *Esquire*, at the time the longest piece of fiction ever included in a periodical. Having just graduated from film school and dreaming of the movies I might someday direct, I bought the hardcover edition and wrote notes in the margins on how I'd adapt it, if ever I got the chance.

I had no idea how one acquired the film rights to a book, but eventually I managed to contact the book's agent—Bob Dattila, a jovial, crafty, and effective schmoozer—and asked if the rights were available. They weren't. But Bob went out of his way to be kind to an earnest, broke twenty-six-year-old. He explained that by selling the rights each year to such Montana pals as Tom McGuane, Jack Nicholson, and Peter Fonda, Jim had been able to afford writing the erudite poetry that had led him to be named a Yale Younger Poet, to win a Guggenheim, and to carry on a Rabelaisian lifestyle notable for a consumption of food and drink that would become his signature and his demise.

Encouraged by Bob's kindness, I would call every year to check on the availability of the rights. It wasn't until after the release of *About Last Night*, seven years later, that I was in the position to make a serious offer. Bob informed me that the rights, which had most recently been controlled by "a commercial director in NYC," were due to lapse that very month. I immediately called Jeff Sagansky and asked if Tri-Star would make an offer. Aware of my fervor, Bob drove a hard bargain, insisting the studio "perfect" the rights, which is to say, buy them in perpetuity. Knowing how long it might take to get the movie going, I was perfectly happy to act as a shill to induce the studio to make such a big play.

Once I'd secured the rights, I set out to find the perfect writer. Alvin Sargent was my all-time favorite screenwriter (and pretty much everyone else's). Having begun his career in television, writing for such esteemed shows as *Naked City* and *Route 66*, he had gone on to be credited for *Paper Moon*, *Straight Time*, and legendarily uncredited for his work on *Kramer vs. Kramer*, *The Way We Were*, and *All the President's Men*. Alvin was also famously supportive of young filmmakers. After reading Jim's novella and sitting together for a couple of meetings, he agreed to take on the project. After some hesitation, the studio stepped up to pay his hefty fee.

While Marshall and I began shooting the first season of *thirtysomething*, Alvin went off to wrangle with an adaptation. One thing about Alvin—he was maddeningly slow. After almost a year of struggle, undone by the amount of time covered by the narrative, the number of characters, and the complexity of its subplots, he admitted he hadn't been able to figure out how to do it, and graciously withdrew. At that time, I was so overwhelmed making the TV show, and simultaneously beginning prep on *Glory*, I knew *Legends* would have to wait.

One day in 1989, something odd was happening in the *thirtysomething* offices. The female assistants kept disappearing. I'd walk into the bullpen and find it empty. One by one, women were making up excuses to visit the sound-stage. It seems word had spread that a "dreamy" actor was working that day on an episode for the third season. His name was Brad Pitt; he had been cast as a day player with one line. In the episode, while confronting their diminished sex life, Hope and Michael come home early from an evening out to discover the babysitter in flagrante delicto with her boyfriend, played by Brad. His line, spoken when he looks up and sees the grown-ups standing there, is, "Hey . . ."

Apparently, it was enough to set hearts aflutter. I couldn't have known then that Brad and I were fated to meet again.

I left Marshall holding the bag with *thirtysomething* and set off for Savannah to shoot *Glory*. When I returned four months later, I was determined to rekindle the development of *Legends of the Fall*. Even as Steve Rosenblum and I hunkered down in the cutting room on a first cut of *Glory*, I was looking for a writer to replace Alvin. Bill Wittliff was a giant of Texas culture. Screenwriter, photographer, book publisher, novelist, sketch artist, archivist, preservationist, champion of the arts, man of letters—I had admired his work on such films as *Raggedy Man, The Black Stallion*, and especially his adaptation for television of Larry McMurtry's *Lonesome Dove*. I wasn't surprised that Bill knew Jim's novella. He quickly agreed to take the job and suggested I come to Texas to talk about it.

I had never been to Austin before. When Bill picked me up at the airport, he described it as "an island in a dry sea of rattlers." As we drove into the hill country toward his ranch, he asked if I'd had breakfast. When I said no, he gave me a big grin and suggested we stop someplace along the way. The steak and eggs in the little diner was epic. As I recall, Bill had seconds. Eventually we got back on the road and arrived at his place—several hundred acres of live oaks and brown hills—where Bill had carefully excavated ancient Comanche hunting grounds, dug his own bass ponds for fly-fishing, and restored a nineteenth-century stone hacienda. After a good morning's work, he asked if I was hungry. Before I could answer we were back in his truck and heading for "some local barbecue." Little did I know that the City Market in Luling, where I had two helpings of a mixed grill of beef brisket and ribs, was almost as famous as the Alamo.

That afternoon, after my comical introduction to fly-fishing, Bill and I got back to work. Sitting in the stone-cooled shadows of his vast living room, surrounded by Native artifacts—arrowheads, pottery, baskets—I felt like I had gone back in time. And when I awoke from a drooly nap, Bill said he'd drive me to the hotel. As he dropped me off and got back in his car, he rolled down the window and said: "I'll pick y'up around eight. There's a place in town with the best rib eye in Texas!"

Somehow managing to get out of Austin without a coronary event, I returned to L.A. and dove back into the TV show. After all the smoke-filled battlefields, exploding cannonballs, and hundreds of uniformed extras in full-throated charge of *Glory*, it was especially pleasant to get back to the intimate scene work of *thirtysomething*. But I lost track of Bill, and almost a year had passed before I realized I hadn't heard from him.

As I suspected, he was having similar trouble to Alvin with the book. After some friendly persuasion, he agreed to send me his first draft. I returned to Austin and, meeting him at another of his favorite restaurants (it may have been possible in those days to find a fresh vegetable in Texas, but it definitely wasn't a priority for Bill), we sat down to talk about his draft. I went to some length to note the parts of the script that were working well. But likable and talented as he was, Bill wasn't particularly flexible about rewriting. This isn't to suggest he was curmudgeonly or unyielding, he was just one of those writers with a fierce belief in his words and the willingness to fight for them. I knew, based on Bill's response, that this hadn't been an easy assignment and he had any number of justifications for the choices he'd made. The problem was, I didn't agree with them. After a few days of wrangling and more cholesterol, Bill promised to do his best to incorporate my thoughts.

Months later, when the script arrived, he had indeed tried to respond to my notes, but rather than solve its problems, Bill's solutions had created others. After two drafts it was time to show the studio where we were. They felt as I did. Also, by this time the studio management had changed. Jeff Sagansky had left to buy companies around the world and flip them for big bucks. Mike Medavoy, formerly a big-deal agent, had taken over Tri-Star, and after several frustrating meetings—constructive criticism not being Mike's strong suit—it was clear he wasn't willing to invest in another writer. For the moment at least, the project was dead in the water.

thirtysomething ended, the enjoyable and disheartening experience that was *Leaving Normal* played out, and then I was in London to start constructing the House of Pain that was *Shakespeare in Love*. Returning from London after it all fell apart, tail between my legs, I moped around the now-ghostly *thirtysomething* offices, occasionally wandering down to the soundstages to watch our sets being torn down. After having observed a similar demolition of the Shakespeare sets, this was becoming an unhappy ritual. And so, when Stacy Snider, who had recently taken a job serving under Medavoy, called to resurrect *Legends*, I couldn't have been more grateful.

To do the rewrite on Bill Wittliff's script, I turned to Susan Shilliday. I suppose it stands to reason that it might have been easier to create an unalloyed professional relationship uncluttered by the thorny dynamics of marriage, but Marshall's spouse loved Jim Harrison's novella and we had developed a happy creative rapport when I would direct her writing on *thirtysomething*. Working together, we came up with a new outline that we hoped would address the problems of the earlier drafts. Eight short weeks later Susan handed in a masterful script. The key had been for us to re-imagine the story in the idiom of oral history. It is a story told by One Stab as he sits before a campfire, and in the vein of the great epic sagas of earlier times, his narrative hurtles forward from event to event, choosing behavior over psychological explanation. The script also returned to Jim's original text in one crucial way; by using a rotating epistolary device, we learn of the characters' inner lives not so much from their speeches as from their letters. When the studio read the new draft, the winds shifted dramatically and for the first time they began to talk about casting.

Long before Robert Duvall starred in *Lonesome Dove* he had been good friends with Bill Wittliff. He also knew the novel quite well. When Medavoy sent him the script, he attached himself to play William Ludlow. The focus then shifted to casting Tristan. Medavoy was intent on getting Tom Cruise and had CAA send him the script. Cruise read it and invited me to come to Wyoming, where he was in the middle of filming *Far and Away*. I had met Tom only once, when he had accompanied his old friend Emilio Estevez on a visit to the *About Last Night* set to see Demi Moore, Emilio's girlfriend at the time.

I flew into Casper, rented a car, and headed west. It's always an awkward moment when one director visits another's set. Everyone is nice and welcoming, but there's the inevitable sidelong glance from a crew member, possibly someone who recognizes you, as if to say, *What the hell is* he *doing here?* But Ron Howard, whose reputation as the nicest man in Hollywood is deserved, greeted me warmly and we chatted, as directors invariably do, about actors. Ron is such a nice man I doubt he would have said anything critical even if he'd felt it, which he obviously didn't. He corroborated what I had heard many times before; Tom Cruise was a director's dream. As I was to learn in years to come, that is entirely true. It is also, however, a bit more complicated—but I'll get around to that eventually. Tom came out of his trailer to greet me, as gracious and enthusiastic then as he will forever be.

"Do you ride?" he asked.

"Sure."

"Then let's go!"

Moments later I found myself galloping, no, check that, *racing* hell-bent-for-leather across the sagebrush-covered plains. The horses on the set of a western are famously fast, reliable, trained to respond to the slightest command—imagine a Ferrari with the suspension of a Cadillac. Nevertheless, as we hurtled across unfamiliar ground, one misstep into a gopher hole and I would have been catapulted into Idaho. I wondered if this was some kind of test, but it soon became apparent it wasn't about me at all. Tom's unbridled glee, his absolute absorption in the moment, was infectious. His need for speed was metabolic, as if only extreme motion could match the rpms of his internal engine.

After an hour or so of riding, or in my case holding on for dear life, we retired to his trailer. The word doesn't do it justice. Larger than certain apartments I'd lived in, complete with a Jacuzzi, a queen-size bed, and full kitchen, I tried to be nonchalant about the trailer and not gawk overtly as we chatted. We never got to talking about the *Legends* script—I quickly realized this was more of a meet-and-greet than a meeting—but Tom seemed interested in the few thoughts about the movie I slipped in and asked if we could meet again when he returned to L.A. in a couple of weeks. Leaving, I ran into Nicole Kidman and said a brief hello (we'd had lunch years before when she first arrived in L.A.), got back in my rental car, and headed for the airport. I was home in time for dinner with absolutely no way to gauge the level of Tom's interest.

We met again a few weeks later. This time, Tom had some penetrating and helpful things to say about the script. But after an hour or so, he asked about Tristan's ethics—to which I responded that he essentially had none, and that was at the heart of the character. It was then I realized he would never do the movie. I'm told his question had something to do with Scientology, but if it did it was the only time over the course of making movies together that it ever found its way into a creative conversation. In any case, Tom eventually demurred. We wouldn't see each other again for ten years—when we did, it would be one of the most gratifying experiences of my career—but for now, my hunt for Tristan continued.

With Tom out of the picture, Medavoy's enthusiasm quickly cooled. It turned positively cold when Robert Duvall jumped ship to sign on to another movie. Lily Kilvert, our production designer, was called back from a preliminary scouting trip, and Pat Crowley, the line producer we'd hired to do a budget, was let go. With no cash flow and no cast, the movie was once again in limbo.

Richard Kramer, a friend and collaborator throughout my career, knows I don't do well being idle. He claims I once said, "Work is something I do so I don't have nothing to do." He may have a point. Even as we were making *Legends*, Marshall and I developed a new TV show, one that we had promised ABC so they would let us out of our commitment to keep doing *thirtysomething*.

While writing for an adolescent girl character on *Family* named Buddy, whenever I'd come up with what I considered to be authentic teenage dialogue—which is to say oppositional and disagreeable, if not downright rebellious—I would receive notes from the network in the margins of my script with the initials "N.O.B.," meaning "Not Our Buddy." I vowed that someday I'd get to write truthfully about adolescence. Similarly, Marshall had once written a pilot for Showtime called *Secret Seventeen* that the network ultimately rejected, considering its portrayal of teenagers inflammatory. But by the time we asked Winnie Holzman—one of our talented writers on *thirtysomething*—to develop the show with us that became *My So-Called Life*, the network claimed to be open to depicting young women as they never had before.

After researching for a time by teaching middle school, Winnie found her way into the show by writing an entire diary in the voice of Angela Chase. That voice not only became the signature of the show, it presented a protagonist at once so undeniably lovable and tormented that the network had no choice but to let us make it.

Claire Danes was not yet fourteen when we met her. Our brilliant, ever-resourceful casting director, Linda Lowy, had seen her in a small role on *Law & Order* and insisted we fly her out from New York. Claire was with her parents, lovely people somewhat daunted by their daughter's genius and self-possession. When Claire finished her audition, we were stunned. There are certain actors so preternaturally gifted it takes your breath away; what they know simply can't be taught. That same week we had met Alicia Silverstone, a talented and appealing actress who would go on to do *Clueless* and several TV series. But Alicia was a sophisticated sixteen-year-old, and Claire, in addition to being the age of the character as written, was . . . well . . . Claire.

ABC/Mark Seliger

Given the shooting demands of a one-hour show, no one had ever dared cast someone as young as her in a lead role. One of the reasons, we realized, was that California has appropriately strict child labor laws governing the number of hours a minor can work during a day and how much time must be spent in school. Nonetheless, we felt we had no choice; that's how much we wanted Claire.

To make it work obliged us to reconceive the show, and like many such compromises in a TV series, it turned out to be a blessing in disguise. Winnie was able to endow the supporting characters—Angela's friends and parents—with substantial subplots. Angela's love interest Jordan Catalano (the sublime and inscrutable Jared Leto, actually twenty-one at the time), developed an unexpected camaraderie with Angela's neighbor and wannabe boyfriend, the geeky, lovable Brian Krakow; meanwhile, Angela's new best friend, Rayanne, and her former best friend, Sharon, forged a relationship of their own; while in the background, the trouble in Angela's parents' marriage cast an unexpectedly dark shadow over Angela's world.

When we read Winnie's description of Ricky Vasquez—a gay fifteen-year-old Puerto Rican—we couldn't imagine finding him. And then Wilson Cruz walked into our office. It wasn't just Wilson's gifts as an actor that so brightened the ensemble, it was his charisma. As Winnie came to know him well, she realized the circumstances of Wilson's personal life were not just a living mirror to the storyline she'd imagined—he was indeed the first openly gay actor to play an openly gay character in a leading television role—but also a source for an even deeper exploration of a kid in a tough situation at home.

Given the impact the show has had over the years it's hard to believe we only made nineteen episodes. Our collaboration with Winnie was intense and just as intensely gratifying. Although we worked closely with her on the stories, only writing and directing occasionally, Winnie's was the true voice of the show. Scott Winant, our co-executive producer, not only directed the pilot but gave the show its unique visual language. There was only one additional writer who made a substantial contribution: Jason Katims. Jason was a struggling playwright in New York when I first read his work at the Louisville One-Act Festival. We brought him to L.A. for his maiden job in TV, and though Winnie would have liked to write every word,

Jason's talent was undeniable and he contributed to several scripts. It was to be the first of our many happy collaborations together—not to mention Jason's illustrious career on his own with *Friday Night Lights, Parenthood*, and many other shows.

Despite rave reviews, Emmy nominations for writing, directing, and best actress for Claire, never has a show been so tortured by a network's lack of confidence: six episodes one year, six the following season, seven more after a long hiatus. It was the death of a thousand cuts. Despite the executives' admission of how much the show meant to their daughters, and a rabidly devoted fan base, they refused to see the culture as it was changing around them.

"We can't program a show about teenagers," they said. "They're just not an important market for our advertisers."

There's a famous, possibly apocryphal, conversation between Louis B. Mayer and Irving Thalberg that's always been dear to my heart. Mayer told Thalberg he wanted to buy the rights to *Gone with the Wind* for MGM.

"Forget it, L.B.," said Thalberg. "No Civil War movie ever made a nickel."

My point being, Claire Danes became the star we always knew she would be (as did Jared), and it wasn't more than a year later, when MTV ran a *My So-Called Life* marathon, showing episodes back-to-back for what seemed like months, that the show took off and finally found the audience it deserved. It's entirely possible those nineteen episodes will be the thing most remembered among all we've done. Ironic, yes. Still, as Angela would say, "We had a time."

I had never given up hope on getting *Legends* made and was always looking for the right actor to play Tristan. In the years since his fleeting appearance on *thirtysomething*, Brad Pitt's career had gained traction. I made a point of following each thing he did and watched his craft grow from movie to movie. Yet even after starring in Robert Redford's *A River Runs Through It* and then his memorable shirtless appearance in *Thelma & Louise*—with special mention to Geena Davis's $6,700 orgasm—I was still unable to persuade Medavoy that Brad could carry our movie. Nevertheless, I asked his agents if he'd like to meet. Sitting with him in my office only confirmed my instincts. It's not enough that a movie star be handsome; good-looking actors are a dime a dozen. And it's not just the way light and shadow plays on someone's bone structure. It's the unnamable thing behind their eyes suggesting a fascinating inner life, whether they have one or not, that somehow emanates. We don't know what's going on inside their heads, but we desperately *want to*, and often that's enough. Brad also had a genuine passion for the script and a strong attraction to the character. Growing up in rural Missouri, he had known men like Tristan, he said. When he left the meeting, I felt I had found the right actor. I was more determined than ever to push it over the line.

In his years as a talent agent one of Medavoy's clients had been Sir Anthony Hopkins. When I prevailed upon Medavoy to get a script to him, I couldn't have known that the acclaimed classical actor from the National Theatre had always wanted to do a western. When I met him, he regaled me with imitations of the great cowboy stars of his childhood. He did a perfect Lee J. Cobb in *How the West Was Won*, a spot-on John Wayne in *Red River*, and a brilliant Jimmy Stewart in *The Man Who Shot Liberty Valence*. He could talk avidly about everything from John Ford's Cavalry Trilogy to Sam Peckinpah's *The Wild Bunch*. He insisted I call him "Tony" and committed to the movie. Medavoy at last had the international marquee name he needed to keep the foreign distributors happy. He gave *Legends* the green light. After fifteen years of dreaming about it, we were a go.

Marshall (who was producing with me) and I invited Jim Harrison to a celebratory dinner before we were to head up to Canada to begin prep. I would have other meals with Jim over the years—one a memorable feast at Babbo with more courses, more wine, and more iced vodka than a normal human should consume in a month—but this moment had special significance. It had been a long time coming for Jim and me both. We'd corresponded but never met; I knew he'd become blind in one eye in childhood, but I wasn't prepared for his voice, oddly high-pitched for such a bear of a man—the phrase "high hilarity" comes to mind. He was a remarkable storyteller in person as well as on the page. He told us about his ancestors from the Upper Peninsula of Michigan, and the Union uniform that hung in the barn, worn by a relative who had been wounded at Gettysburg.

He also described the origins of *Legends of the Fall*, about finding a trove of letters in an old chest of drawers in an attic, and that on reading them he had fallen into
a deep sleep and the story had come to him in its entirety, that he had woken up and
written it down for twelve hours without pausing to eat—which, for Jim, was perhaps
the most remarkable part of the story. "Automatic writing like Coleridge and 'Kubla
Khan,'" he said, his laughter ringing through the restaurant, causing other diners
to put down their forks and stare. I learned later that he had once written his own
adaptation of the novella, but typically he was much too polite to bring it up. Jim was
known for his generosity to other writers, some of whom he mentored throughout
his life. He was also notably gracious about the departures of plot we had undertaken
in our screenplay, even going out of his way to say, "A book is a book, and a movie is
a movie." As he stood up from the table, I could see he was unsteady as he hobbled
toward the men's room. "Gout," whispered Jenno Topping, at the time an aspiring
producer who had joined us at dinner. "He doesn't like people to know." It would be
a few years before Jenno would begin her prodigious rise as a producer—I'm guessing she was angling to get Jim to write something for her. Jim was always generous
to bright young people, from poets to panhandlers. Tom McGuane once described
him as "a genius with a genius for friendship. A country boy who'd been touched."

Image by Andy Anderson

Long after the movie was released, I'd hear from Jim now and then, mostly to suggest another of his stories he thought would make a good movie. Although there were several that would have served, I never felt about any of them as I had about *Legends*. And though I was invited, I was never able to join him on one of his famous eating tours through the French countryside; thirty-seven-course lunches in Burgundy with innumerable raw cheeses, slabs of foie gras, toasted sweetbread, and fried duck bacon. It's possible I might not have survived it.

I did get to go fly-fishing with him once. It was on the Yellowstone near his summer home in Livingston, Montana. He wasn't talking much that day, uncharacteristic for Jim. But I remember him looking out past the rippling waters toward the majestic Gallatins rising in the distance, then shaking his head and saying almost to himself: "Right here. Right here."

As we got closer to production, the budget began to climb. Medavoy, already edgy about its commercial prospects, became even more so. Only weeks before shooting he demanded we cut $2 million from below-the-line, an arbitrary and unreasonable request this close to our start date. After we told him it couldn't be done, he persisted. When it reached a stalemate, he insisted that unless Brad and I give back half our fees, he would shut us down. I called Brad to see how he felt. Neither of us was making a killing on the movie, but like me Brad was so emotionally invested that he agreed. Our agents negotiated a caveat in our deals: should the movie do well at the box office, we would get paid double. It turned out to be one of the best bets either of us ever made.

We were only four weeks from shooting and still hadn't found our Susannah. We read many wonderful actresses, but none of them had the combination of vivacity and sadness—in other words, manic depression—that foretold her tragic end. It was during one of these readings that Brad met Gwyneth Paltrow. Though she was too young for the part, there was more than movie chemistry in the room as they read. When I saw them together months later at our premiere, I wasn't surprised.

Mary Colquhoun, our casting director, called as I was about to leave for location in Calgary. She urged me to see an HBO movie called *Stalin*, starring Robert
Duvall and a relatively unknown actress named Julia Ormand. As always, Mary
was right. I showed the movie to Brad, and he liked Julia too. That night we were
on a red-eye to New York. Julia flew over from London to meet us in an empty
warehouse for a hastily arranged screen test. John Toll, our DP, was unavailable
but he prevailed upon his friend the magnificent Allen Daviau to shoot it. After
Brad and Julia did the first scene, he and I exchanged a look; we had found her.

Days before shooting, we held a table read. Given the script's dependence
on narration and visuals, it didn't play very well in the sterile conference room.
I could see Brad's growing discomfort as it went on. Hours afterward, his agent
called the studio to say Brad wanted to quit and would reimburse the cost of prep.
Fine, said the studio lawyers, all he had to do was write a check for $2 million.
Marshall spent some time talking to Brad and it was never mentioned again, but it
was the first augury of the deeper springs of emotion roiling inside Brad. He seems
easygoing at first, but he can be volatile when riled, as I was to be reminded more
than once as shooting began and we took each other's measure.

It was the wettest summer in Alberta history, which turned our beautiful
location into a hellscape of mud that stalled five-ton trucks, ruined actors' costumes, and played hell with our schedule. It also brought forth the most beautiful
cloud-scudded skies and sunsets of heart-stopping beauty. Lily Kilvert, John Toll,
and I had come up with an audacious plan. We would build a practical house on
location in sight of the Rockies—a radical decision because it obliged us to travel
much farther to get to the set. But the benefits far outweighed the cost. Every day
we had the flexibility to move outside at will, to break a big scene in the middle,
race out to shoot exteriors during magic hour or to capture an incoming storm or
an awe-inspiring sunset, then return the next day to finish the scene we had interrupted. It's exactly how John Ford shot his great westerns. The evening the three
Ludlow brothers set off to war was shot over the course of three magic hours.

It wasn't the only reason John won the Oscar that year; his interiors were
just as breathtaking. It's impossible to overstate the influence of a director of

photography, especially on a young director early in his career. John Toll had spent twenty-five years working his way up from first assistant to camera operator to DP, serving under such greats as John Alonzo, Jordan Cronenweth, and Conrad Hall. Though *Legends* was only his second feature, his experience and knowledge was encyclopedic, and his sympathetic understanding of the story and characters rivaled mine.

After only two weeks of shooting, we had our first disaster. The weekly cost report revealed an overage of a million dollars in costumes alone. It turned out Deborah Scott, our gifted costume designer (we'd worked together on *About Last Night*), had run into terrible trouble sourcing the period costumes and had racked up ungodly hours of overtime to have them made in England. Medavoy went ballistic; this amount of weekly overages, if continued, suggested a runaway production like *Heaven's Gate*, the 1980 Michael Cimino western that had almost bankrupted United Artists. No matter how sincerely we assured him this was a onetime aberration, Medavoy decided he had had enough and issued an ultimatum. Cut ten pages from the script or he wouldn't allow us to go to Jamaica at the end of production for the scenes depicting Tristan's travels.

Those scenes were as essential to the movie as any dialogue, and I couldn't countenance losing them. I enlisted Marshall in a devious scheme. I told him to wake Medavoy up the next morning at home at 5 a.m. L.A. time and tell him I was refusing to come out of my trailer, that those were my favorite scenes, and I was in there weeping and disconsolate. He was to say I had locked myself in and the cast and crew were standing around, listening to me sobbing. When Medavoy heard this, he panicked as I knew he would. He insisted that Marshall persuade me to go back to work by saying he would come to Calgary to figure things out. Somehow, magically, Marshall managed to get me back to work! When Medavoy showed up on location a week later, Marshall offered to take him out riding and explore the location, neglecting to mention the regular afternoon thunderstorm was coming in. When they straggled back to the set two hours later, Medavoy was a wreck, teeth chattering, clothes soaked and mud-splattered, his expensive Italian loafers ruined. He was driven back to his hotel, two hours away, and returned to L.A.

the next morning without ever having his conversation with me. Tristan's travels to Borneo, Africa, and Jamaica remain some of my favorite scenes in the movie.

While staying in an old-fashioned cattleman's hotel in Calgary, I was given a room on the same floor as the actors on what was called the "concierge" level. I discovered this meant breakfast was served every morning in a little nook on the same floor, sparing the movie stars the indignity of going down to the dining room and mingling with the real people. Sir Anthony Hopkins ("Call me Tony") and I were always the first ones awake. We would sit quietly, respecting each other's privacy as we prepared for the day's work. Every now and then I would sneak a glance at his script and notice "N.A.R." scribbled beside a scene. Finally, I got up the nerve to ask what it signified.

"Oh," he chuckled. "No acting required."

One day my father came to visit. He and my mother had divorced more than twenty years before, and between then and 1983 he and I had been cordial but wary. My mother's tragic death that year had brought us back into relationship—something that would have appealed to her keen sense of irony. An even more comic wrinkle was his new business venture, a video store in downtown Chicago called Video Schmideo that he opened after hitting me up for a loan of $10,000. There, he would boast to all who would listen about his son, the big-deal movie director. Whether this intimate affiliation with the movie business helped sales is hard to say. More likely his profits were supplemented by the porn he sold in the back room for cash-only in order to hide the dough from the IRS. On the wall behind the counter hung a glossy of my father with Roger Ebert, arms slung around each other's shoulders, one with a thumbs-up, the other a thumbs-down. Roger had become my dad's drinking buddy, and in the cool dark of Billy Goat Tavern, they would spend many a long, hot Chicago evening. To Roger's credit, their friendship never seemed to affect his critical judgment. As brilliant a critic as I've ever known, he was quite kind to me about certain films and blistering on others. Every now and then a young actress I'd meet in L.A. would mention having met my father on the obligatory pub crawl all actors take while shooting on location in Chicago.

"He is so sweet," they would invariably say. "And so proud of you."

True enough, I'd say to myself, wondering how long it took before he tried to charm her back to his apartment.

We had been shooting in Calgary for several weeks when Allen Zwick walked onto the set wearing jeans and a denim shirt. It was the first time I'd ever seen him wearing jeans. He was always fastidious about his dress, and I had to smile thinking of him buying this outfit in order to dress the part for a visit to the set of a western. At some point between setups, Tony came to sit in his chair near us. I introduced them and they chatted innocently. Inevitably, I was called away by the AD to check something about the next shot. Mere minutes later, as I headed back to where I'd left them, I heard what I thought was shouting. Hurrying around the corner I saw it was Allen crying out, "Schmuck! Schmuck!"

Courtesy of the author

He was imitating Sir Anthony's performance as the ventriloquist in William Goldman's *Magic*. I stood frozen, mortified, wishing only for a chasm to open in the earth and swallow me whole. Also, my father, if possible. My father, who throughout my childhood had invariably found a thousand ways to embarrass me—loudly razzing someone on the tennis court, jumping into the pool at the club with his clothes on—had managed to do it again. Though Tony was laughing politely, I mumbled something about wanting to show my father the inside of the Ludlow house and hurried him away. Later that afternoon after Allen had gone back to the hotel, I told Tony I hoped he hadn't been offended by my father's fanboy enthusiasms.

"Oh, dear boy, no," he said. "He was perfectly charming."

His English manners were so good, it was hard to know whether to believe him or if he was just trying to make me feel better. What I do know is that it was the last time I saw my father before his death three years later.

Another visitor on the *Legends* set was Liberty's father, Ray Godshall, a handsome man with a close resemblance to Robert Ryan. He was a kind of Updike character; a Bucks County "gentleman farmer" who also owned a car dealership, he had always dreamed of being an artist and was also a talented painter. Eternally boyish, he was still playing tennis in his nineties when he felt some tightness in his chest and drove himself to the hospital to have a second stent put in. It had become a tradition that Ray would visit me on location and I'd find a small role for him in the film. This wasn't only to butter up my wife; it was enlightened self-interest. Casting directors always complain how hard it is to find an older man with the innate dignity not to look upon a few lines with Brad Pitt as the biggest moment in their career, and then overplay their part, or worse, freeze in terror. Over the years Ray played a senator in *Special Bulletin*, an abolitionist in *Glory*, a surgeon in *Courage Under Fire*, a Senator again in *The Siege*, and an arms dealer in *The Last Samurai*. His steadying presence was something I always looked forward to amid the chaos of production. From the moment he realized his daughter was in a happy marriage, he'd been unqualified in his embrace of me, even taking secret delight in the scruffy, subversive, left-wing Jewish interloper who had invaded his ordered WASP world. Given my contentious relationship with my own father, it's not hard to understand how much his unalloyed support and love meant to me. Long after his death in 2012, I can't help but identify the parts he would have played in each movie I've done since.

As the shoot continued, Brad's anxiety about the movie never quite went away. Sometimes, no matter how experienced or sensitive you are as a director, things just aren't working. You think the actor is being oppositional, while he finds you dictatorial. Some actors have problems with authority, but just as many directors are threatened when intelligent actors ask challenging questions that reveal their lack of preparation. Both are right and both are wrong.

There are all sorts of reasons an actor might pick a fight. Most likely he's afraid. Insecurity manifests as arrogance and fear precipitates bad behavior—on the director's part as well as the actor's. Brad would get edgy whenever he was about to shoot a scene that required him to display deep emotion. It was here that his ideas about Tristan differed from mine. Brad had grown up with men who held their emotions in check; I believed the point of the novel was that a man's life was the sum of his griefs. Steve Rosenblum had been complaining in dailies that he was having trouble cutting scenes where Brad's stoicism appeared more blank than internal. I agreed. Yet the more I pushed Brad to reveal himself, the more he resisted. There's a bright line between strong direction and dominance, especially when a male director is directing a male star. At times it risks becoming what a shrink and friend once called "an issue of phallic identity"—in other words, dick-measuring. A strong director working with a strong actor can be like two dancers who are both trying to lead. But such tension can also yield very good work. George Clooney and David O. Russell got into a fistfight on *Three Kings*. Each claims the other started it. Was it worth it? It was a great movie.

So, I kept pushing and Brad pushed back. One afternoon I started giving him direction out loud in front of the crew—a stupid, shaming provocation—and Brad came back at me, also out loud, telling me to back off. The considered move would have been to tell the crew to take five and for the two of us to talk it out. But I was feeling bloody-minded, and not about to relent. I was angry at Brad for not trusting me to influence his performance. Also for the reluctance he'd shown after the first table read. Who knows, I might even have been acting out my own inability to be vulnerable. But Brad wasn't about to give in without a fight. In his defense, I was pushing him to do something he felt was either wrong for the character, or more "emo" than he wanted to appear on-screen. I don't know who yelled first, who swore, or who threw the first chair. But when we looked up, the crew had disappeared. And this wasn't the last time it happened. Eventually the crew grew accustomed to our dustups and would walk away and let us have it out. "We hate it when the parents fight," said one.

Yet, after each blowup, we'd make up, and mean it. It was never personal. Brad is a forthright, straightforward person, fun to be with and capable of great joy. He was never anything less than fully committed to doing his best. I, on the other hand, am a movie director masquerading as a rational human being. I present myself as a mensch, a thoughtful, collegial guy who wants everybody's opinion while in fact I am Ahab in a baseball cap. I want it done exactly as I asked and I want it *now*. Now, meaning before we lose the light, or the storm hits, or another plane passes overhead, or the studio shuts us down for going into overtime, now, because I'm only going to get to shoot this movie once, because this shot will most likely be in the movie and I'm going to have to look at it a thousand times in the cutting room and the previews and in the premiere and live with it for the rest of my life. Because in the insane intensity of this moment, it feels like my entire career depends on it, that I will have another flop and might never work again unless I get this take right. Scratch the surface of any director worth his DGA card and you will find a roiling madman, his inner son of a bitch held tightly in check but capable of emerging at any moment like the monster bursting out of Kane's chest in *Alien*. Some of us use self-effacing charm to hide the depth of our ambition, rage, and exalted self-regard. Some sublimate it by being passive-aggressive—like William Wyler sitting behind the camera and after each take only saying "Again," or David Fincher making Jake Gyllenhaal walk through a doorway a million times. Others, I'm told, are sadists for whom the opportunity to order hundreds of people to jump at their beck and call is a thrill bordering on the sexual. When my six-year-old daughter was asked in kindergarten what her father did for a living, she answered, "He yells at people."

When all was said and done, the movie Brad and I made reflected the depth of our passion. Was it worth it? I'd have to say yes.

Directing an ensemble brings its unique challenges. In this case, the four leads came from as diverse a set of backgrounds and training as can be imagined. Henry Thomas, playing Samuel, the youngest of the Ludlow brothers, had grown up on film sets since starring in *E.T.* Brad had made his way from dressing up as the chicken mascot for an El Pollo Loco restaurant to this moment of stardom. Aidan Quinn, playing oldest brother Alfred, was a prized product of Chicago's independent theater scene, while Tony Hopkins, playing the father, had emerged as one of Britain's National Theatre's many gifts to the movies. At times I felt like one of those interpreters at the UN who wear the headphones, except I was translating English to English. Invariably, one actor needed multiple takes while another lost his spontaneity. Thus, the less well-trained actor gets the attention while the grown-ups are short-changed. Ludwig Erhard defined the art of compromise as dividing a cake so that everyone believes he's gotten the largest piece. Directing an ensemble is like that.

Aiden's role as Alfred could have turned out to be thankless. Instead, he found great dignity and heart in the character and proved himself a strong foil to Brad's wildness. Aidan is the kind of actor whose manner is so easy and whose work is so consistently crisp and thoughtful that he was easily ignored by a director beset by crises everywhere. Without Aidan's grounded ballast, Brad's character would have had nothing to bump up against.

As we waited for the lights to go down for our first preview, Steve Rosenblum and I were confident we had a good movie. Then again, every movie is perfect. Until we show it, that is. The minute we do, it's never quite as perfect as we thought. And it's no longer ours. This is as it should be. A movie is made to be seen by the public. Still, the preview process is barbaric. Painful as it is, the audience always knows if something isn't working, even if they can't articulate why. My intentions don't matter; the urgent question becomes: Can I see what they're seeing? To make changes according to the idiocies of ten people in a focus group is folly, and the studio inevitably weaponizes test results and research to serve their own agenda. "Studio opinions," a producer once instructed me, "are like assholes. Everybody has one and is one."

Still, learning to interpret why the butts are shifting in their seats is a necessary skill; I can always tell when the first act is dragging, or the audience is confused about a plot point. I do wish I'd kept some of the outrageous preview cards written by audience members still sitting in their seats immediately after a test screening. After a showing of *Trial by Fire* in Phoenix, Arizona—an open-carry state where I watched in horror as audience members passed through a metal detector and were made to surrender guns, knives, and brass knuckles—one citizen-critic summed up his reaction to our movie about the death penalty this way: "All talk, no titty."

In the second reel of our first *Legends of the Fall* preview, when Tristan and Susannah meet late at night in Ludlow's study and kiss, we could hear the audience going south. It was as if they were all screaming, "Don't do it, Brad . . . If you kiss your brother's girlfriend, we'll hate you for the rest of the movie!" Steve turned to me and said, "Oops." We went back to the cutting room that night. By trimming no more than ten seconds, we utterly changed the audience's attitude toward the protagonist. Once Tristan and Susannah are shown as being *tempted* to kiss but manage to restrain themselves, they keep the audience's trust. It seemed to me more of a distinction than a difference, but when we previewed the following week with this as the only change, the audience's embrace of the movie was unequivocal. The scores were through the roof. Ten weeks to do a first cut, ten seconds to do the final.

For the score, I worked with James Horner again. We talked a great deal about the atavistic nature of the film—the dark and bloody heart that Tristan cuts out of his brother and brings home; Tristan and Susannah's love that's both overwhelming and destructive, and the struggle of three brothers for their father's blessing. We also talked about the melodies of the "old" place (Cornwall, England) from which the Ludlows had come; and the sounds of the "new" place (Montana), whose native rhythms and wildness had come to represent family and the ties that bind. All I can say is that somehow James managed to distill those lofty conversations into a score that is at once brooding and lush, redolent of both love and loss, and that touches that secret place of awe I had experienced only once before—on my first reading of *Legends of the Fall*.

When I showed Brad the final film, he wasn't pleased. He felt I'd underplayed his character's madness. I had in fact cut only a single shot from the scene where Tristan is raging with fever, screaming as the waves wash over him on the schooner. But it was a shot he dearly loved, and it would have been little enough to leave it in, and I should have. Apologies, Brad. He was also unhappy when *People* named him "Sexiest Man of the Year"—something for which I take neither credit nor blame.

Despite Brad's reservations, expectations for the film built steadily in the lead-up to its release. There's a mysterious phenomenon in Hollywood. Somehow, long before a movie is released, word begins to spread that it's going to make a splash. A sound mixer tells his cousin who just happens to work for a PR firm, or someone's assistant plays tennis with another assistant who works at *Variety*; but no matter how it happens, it's as if there's a mitochondrion under Wilshire Boulevard with tendrils spreading throughout the halls of the agencies and studios. Soon after our preview, I began to get weird calls. Would I mind if Warren Beatty came by the cutting room? He's casting a new movie and has heard about Brad's performance. Could Mel Gibson stop by? He's directing his first movie (*Braveheart*) and wanted to see John Toll's work. (Mel ended up hiring John, Steve Rosenblum, *and* James Horner—all three were nominated for Oscars; John won his second in a row.) There's an unspoken code among directors, a kind of honor among thieves, that we make ourselves available to each other, and most important, we tell each other the truth.

"I know why you're calling," I said to Sydney Pollack. He had heard about Julia Ormand and was looking to cast the lead in his remake of a Billy Wilder movie. "She's not Sabrina. She's a fine actress but there's a shadow side to her that comes through. That's why I cast her as the suicidal Susannah. She's just not Audrey Hepburn."

He thanked me and cast her anyway. Let's just say only Audrey Hepburn was Audrey Hepburn.

After Brad and I were both nominated (and lost) at the Golden Globes, and despite John Toll's Oscar and the unexpected commercial success of *Legends* and the subsequent doubling of mine and Brad's fees, Brad and I didn't speak for a year. I was sad that he was unhappy. I liked him. Despite our differences we had both given our all to the movie.

Months later, when the studio asked me to do the "director's commentary," I asked if Brad would be doing one. They said he was considering it. I called Brad and suggested we do the commentary together. We decided to have dinner first. Afterward, we smoked a joint and talked for hours. We were so high we barely got to the recording session; if you listen closely, you can hear us giggling.

Later, walking to our cars, Brad sighed. "Man I didn't know what I was doing half the time on set. "Brad," I said, "I don't know what I'm doing *most* of the time on set." We hugged. It was a nice moment. We've never worked together again.

NINE REFLECTIONS ON A CAREER AT THE MIDPOINT

What I've learned, what I've forgotten

1. **THE SCHMOOZE**

   It was 1993, and I was on a dubbing stage recently vacated by a successful director. He had left his appointment book behind. Every page noted a movie star's birthday, anniversary, favorite flowers, restaurants, and executives' children's names. He understood that artists are very good at receiving. And schmoozing works.

2. **HIERARCHY**

   It took a while to learn I already had the authority and there was no need to yell. There's too much noise on a set anyway. "If you must shout," says Lily Kilvert, my savvy production designer, "you're only allowed to shout up, never down." Which is to say, always at a studio executive, but never at a PA.

3. **BETWEEN ME AND THEE**

   Something intimate was lost when they invented the video tap—a video monitor that allows the director to see what the camera sees. Proximity to the actors kept their work three-dimensional. The monitor turns it into a performance. Don't become passive as if you're watching TV. Intercede.

4. **TECHNOLOGY**

   When scientists discovered how to put paint in tubes, it allowed painters to work in natural light and brought forth Impressionism. With the invention of digital, we can shoot endlessly without stopping to reload and actors can do take after take. But are the movies appreciably better these days?

5. **INFINITE JEST**

   The conundrum of shooting digital is that you have infinite choices. How do you know when you have the performance? Is another take worth falling behind schedule? Overshooting is the director's equivalent of overacting.

6. THE TAKEAWAY

Every great film has at least one indelible image. If you try to plan it, it seems labored. If the apogee is well structured, the image will appear. Don't overthink it. Steph Curry doesn't have time to mull it over before he shoots a three.

7. THE LAWS OF PHYSICS

When computer graphics took hold, the mantra became "Because you can do it, do it." A camera move can defy the laws of physics. Instead of two hundred Orcs, you can have two million. Without a reality principle, the audience distances themselves. The minute they know it's fake, they start checking their text messages.

8. CAUGHT

I learned the painful lesson to wait a few seconds after saying "Cut!" before giving direction. Too often the soundman hadn't yet turned off the machine and for months to come I was tortured by the sound of my wheedling, fatuous voice saying, "That was great, but let's go again, and this time . . ."

9. WHY DIRECTORS ARE SO WEIRD

Everybody else on the crew goes from one director's set to another. A director, meanwhile, lives in a lonely world of his own devising, reinventing filmmaking according to his unique obsessions, eccentricities, and fetishes. Actors who become good directors have been around. And paid attention.

CHAPTER NINE

Heroes

Courage Under Fire, 1996

After traveling the world together for the release of *Glory*, whatever reticence that had existed between me and Denzel faded away. Shared success can have that effect, but I like to think there is more to our friendship than that. We were about the same age, both raising young families, both trying to maintain marriages while balancing the demands and pleasures of blossoming careers. After winning the Oscar, Denzel was a shooting star. In short order he did *Malcolm X*, *Philadelphia*, and *Crimson Tide*. I rebounded after my time in the wilderness with *Legends of the Fall* and *My So-Called Life*. We even ended up renting little houses next to each other in Malibu where I got to know Pauletta and their kids. One day while playing father-son touch football in the sand with John David Washington, fourteen, and Jesse Zwick, twelve, I made the mistake of trying to cover John David too closely. He didn't mean to break my foot, but he was a little tank and already a serious athlete—he would go on to become the leading rusher in the history of Morehouse College. I was in a walking cast for six weeks. Ten years later John David calls and wants to come see me. He wants to talk about his career. He talks about his father. There are things about him he doesn't understand. I do my best to answer his questions, but mostly I listen. He's a great kid, soon to be a movie star himself. I'd like to think that Jesse could talk to Marshall about me. Maybe he already has. To some degree, every father is unknown to his son.

One day in 1995 my assistant told me there was a call from someone I didn't know named Joe Singer. Joe was a familiar Hollywood archetype. He'd arrived via New York—Wall Street, or so he said—with no background to speak of in film. But what he lacked in experience he made up for in chutzpah. A fast talker with a smooth line of patter, he told me he had a script that Denzel wanted to do. What he didn't tell me was that he'd already called Denzel and told him I wanted to direct it. By the time Denzel and I made plans to meet for lunch, it had the makings of a done deal.

Except Denzel had no intention of doing the movie. *Courage Under Fire* was written by Patrick Sheane Duncan, an accomplished screenwriter and Vietnam vet. It was the story of a lieutenant colonel tank commander responsible for an incident of friendly fire in the Gulf War who is asked to investigate the first Medal of Honor to be awarded to a woman for bravery in combat. Within minutes of sitting down, Denzel didn't hold back his critique of the screenplay—the lead character was mopey, his investigation was passive, his marriage didn't feel real. I couldn't disagree with anything he said. While the *Rashomon* storytelling device was compelling, looking at the incident through the varied perspectives of the soldiers, the characterizations were two-dimensional and flat. There was no point trying to convince Denzel of its merits. One lesson I had learned was that the most disastrous thing you can do is try to "handle" a movie star. After years spent having smoke blown up his ass, no one has a more finely tuned bullshit detector. That doesn't mean you need to be unnecessarily confrontational, but telling the truth tends to work better than prevarication.

"So why do you want to do it?" he asked.

"I don't yet," I said, "but I think there's a way to make it into an interesting character study."

I went on to talk about a new psychological phenomenon I'd been reading about called PTSD. More and more research was being published about the trauma experienced by veterans in the Gulf War. Shellshock was nothing new, but the journal articles I'd read described something less obvious and more pernicious. By the time I finished my long-winded disquisition, Denzel put down his fork.

"I'll do it," he said.

I couldn't help but laugh. The funny thing was, I honestly had no expectation of convincing him. I wasn't selling or pitching, just speaking passionately about something that interested me. I was overjoyed at the thought of making another movie with him. Now all we had to do was make a deal.

This was to be the first film for a new division of 20th Century Fox, called Fox 2000. It was run by Laura Ziskin, a talented producer and executive. Laura was enthusiastic about the movie and so was her boss, Peter Chernin. I can't remember what Denzel's representatives were asking for as his fee, but it was many millions. The studio made a generous offer, Denzel's reps countered, and the two sides were soon gridlocked, a million dollars apart. Apparently, Rupert Murdoch was less than thrilled about the movie's politics and insisted on holding the line. I tried to weigh in, cajoling both the studio and Denzel's wonderful, longtime agent, Ed Limato. I didn't try to reach Denzel; he was in South Africa with Nelson Mandela, with whom he had remained close after making *Cry Freedom*. The truth is it didn't feel right trying to convince him to take less. He knew his worth. Finally, when it appeared the deal was going south, I made a last, overheated plea to Laura and Peter. They agreed to try again with Rupert. The next day, Fox agreed to pay Denzel an additional million dollars, and hours later he announced he was making a million-dollar contribution to Mandela's Children's Fund. In other words, Rupert Murdoch had just given a million dollars to the ANC. I could hear Denzel laughing ten thousand miles away.

Susan Shilliday came on and nailed a rewrite of the script, and I offered Meg Ryan the part of the heroic chopper pilot whose Medal of Honor Denzel's character is investigating. Like everyone, I'd been enchanted by Meg's work as a comedienne, but I'd also been intrigued when she ventured out of her comfort zone in movies like *Promised Land, Flesh and Bone*, and the strong but unfortunately titled *When a Man Loves a Woman*. After a great meeting, she said yes to playing Captain Karen Walden. I cast Matt Damon, Seth Gilliam, Tim Guinee, and Lou Diamond Phillips as her army medevac helicopter crew. Scott Glenn also did great work as an investigative journalist pressing Denzel's character for the truth. It bears repeating: No film is any better than its supporting cast. When they're boldly drawn and capable of holding the screen, their strong, distinctive voices and oppositional points of view highlight the lead actors the way great orchestration of a musical score can support its central themes.

Meg had never fired a weapon before, but she gamely joined the boys on a "confidence course," a training ground made up of obstacles and moving targets designed to promote what the military calls "confidence in self and team." I asked Lon Bender, our sound designer, to put together a track of gunfire and rotor noise. When we did improvs to create the kind of banter and camaraderie the group would have developed, everything took on new energy and urgency because they were forced to raise their voices above the din. Later, while rehearsing a gun battle, Meg came up with what I consider to be one of the best lines in the movie. I immediately put it in the script. In a single sentence she epitomizes her dilemma and her fortitude. Although gravely wounded, she keeps fighting. When it looks like she might not be able to carry on, Matt Damon's character tries to get her to lie down.

"Are you sure you can do this?" he asks.

She stares at him and growls, "I had a baby, asshole."

Denzel's scenes would be with each crew member individually; he was their interrogator. I decided there was more to be gained by not letting them get to know each other, hoping their scenes would carry the electricity of a first meeting. Besides, I knew Denzel wouldn't want to rehearse, anyway. Instead, we did research together. We went on night maneuvers with the 11th Armored Cavalry at Fort Irwin in the Mojave Desert. Months later, when Denzel climbed into a cutout model of an M1 Abrams tank on the set, he knew what it felt like to fire high explosive rounds in a real one.

The fact is, great actors, I mean, the really great ones, don't need much help when it comes to preparation. That doesn't mean you shouldn't take the journey with them. You can be the navigator. The tour director. A great traveling companion riding shotgun. Just remember to bring good snacks.

Direction can happen anytime, anywhere. Over dinner, at craft services, or waiting for a setup. When Neil Simon observed Mike Nichols directing theater actors he marveled how "they gossiped, joked, compared restaurants, everything but the work at hand. And the play got better!"

I could never tell how much Denzel was internalizing when we'd visit an army base or go drinking with soldiers after hours. He was taciturn when he met the real version of the character he was to play. He asked respectful questions, joked with him and the other soldiers to put them at ease, but usually just listened. Most of the field officers we met were still in their late twenties, yet they would address the enlisted men, some only a few years younger, as "son." On his first day of shooting, I almost did a double take when I heard Denzel address Sean Astin this way. The next night when I looked at dailies, everything about Denzel had changed. His eyes were troubled, his posture bore an unseen burden. But he would rather die than let anyone see even a hint of the guilt or dishonor that tormented him. Instead, he would play against it. Ferociously.

"What's my character whining and moaning about? I'm fine!" he'd say to me as we worked on the script. "I'm fucking squared away!"

He was right. The audience knew exactly what had happened to him. They'd watched it on-screen. He'd commanded Sean Astin, playing the gunner, to pull the trigger on a lethal round of friendly fire. To see him deny that mistake's dominion over him was heartbreaking and ennobling. I arranged for him to talk to a local psychologist, many of whose clients were broken young men just back from the Gulf. When Denzel returned to the production office after his meeting, I asked how it had gone. He nodded solemnly. "I get it," he said.

"You going to talk to him again?"

"Nah. He wanted to get all up in my shit. Fuck that."

Meanwhile, with our budget hemorrhaging, the studio decided the solution was to fire our competent line producer and bring in a "heavy." If anything, Joe Caracciolo, a grizzled veteran who appeared in the production office in El Paso smoking a cigar as big as a howitzer, was even more sympathetic to our situation than the man they made walk the plank. For the next three months, he and David Friendly, one of the three producers along with John Davis and Joe Singer, played gin rummy, drank single malt, and conspired to keep the studio off my back. I'd come to understand this was standard procedure.

Rather than accept responsibility for their inability to read a script and deal with the implications of filming it, a studio usually prefers to think of directors as spoiled, irresponsible children with no sense of what things cost. I tried to tell them I had produced hours of television with my own money on the line for overages, but they kept talking about my "appetite," as if I was planning to eat the movie. I pointed out the pages of the script they had approved that described a massive tank battle (this is before the days of cheap CG) and suggested they didn't come for free.

In one of the more egregious idiocies of studio logic, a young VP arrived to tell me he had been tasked to cut yet another $150,000 from the budget, and that the only way he could do it was to cut scenes from the script. When I asked him what he thought we should cut, he singled out the scene where Denzel's character visits the parents of the man he has accidentally killed and asks their forgiveness. It is, as those who have seen the film know, Denzel's catharsis, the film's emotional climax. Rather than scream or throw a tantrum or hit him over the head with my director's chair, I nicely told him I was going to pretend he'd never said it, and that he should go back to L.A. and let me know once he'd seen the film if he still thought it was a good idea. Then I walked away. To his credit, after the first screening, he met my eye and nodded. That same junior executive is now a very important senior executive. In all the years since he's acquired power, he's never offered me a movie.

At last the problems seemed sorted, until I received a call from Meg's agent, who informed us that she was too terrified to go up in a helicopter. At first I thought he was kidding. She was playing a helicopter pilot. How could anyone think they were going to make a movie about flying without flying? But apparently that's exactly what some business affairs lawyer at the studio had assured the agent when he first raised this concern when negotiating her deal. It was even in Meg's contract, though no one had bothered to tell us.

Our special effects coordinator Paul Lombardi (who had cut his teeth working for his father, Joe, on *Apocalypse Now*) came to the rescue. He hollowed out the innards of a Huey helicopter until it wasn't much more than a metal shell, welded it to an enormous gimbal (a pneumatic device ordinarily used to radically rock a set in all directions), then welded the whole contraption on top of a seventeen-foot-long flatbed truck. He then had bulldozers cut and pave a three-thousand-foot road parallel to high sand cliffs. With the vehicle driving at speed, the cliffs would strobe past, giving the illusion of being in flight. Intercut with second-unit shots of a real helicopter in flight, it was impossible for the audience to know the actors were only fifteen feet off the ground. Filmmaking magic.

That didn't mean everyone else didn't have to get airborne. The rest of the actors were eager to spend as much time in the air as possible. So was our DP Roger Deakins. This was my first movie working with Roger, who began his career as a documentary cameraman shooting in war zones like Eritrea. He spent more time than I would have liked strapped into a harness, leaning his entire body out into space to capture the best angles of the men while flying. I'd never met anyone as well prepared as Roger, but also willing to throw it all away in the interest of telling a better story. He brought an extraordinary commitment to realism, a legacy of dodging bullets in the Horn of Africa. It rubbed off on the actors. He also gave great latitude to their movements, which lent spontaneity to their performances.

The moment when Matt Damon's young medic character almost falls out of the helicopter could only be accomplished by the actor doing it for real. Its power in the film is, at least in some measure, because the terror on Matt's face is genuine. But Matt never hesitated. He was twenty-two when we met, and at that time, I had no idea how far he would go in search of authenticity. A mutual friend had sent me an early draft of *Good Will Hunting* and asked if I would meet with him and discuss it. The script, although still unformed at that point, was lovely, and I was happy to make a few suggestions. (Years later I was delighted when Matt and Ben thanked me in the credits for my help.)

While casting *Courage*, Matt came to mind as I began to meet actors for the drug-addicted member of Meg Ryan's crew, Specialist Ilario. By that point, Matt was twenty-four and had done *School Ties* and a few smaller roles. He came in and read for me, and I cast him on the spot. An actor's first big role is a thing apart. A lifetime of childhood dreams, years of study, constant rejection, and the humiliation of demeaning early work can create an aura of heightened stakes that is petrifying and paralyzing.

As fate would have it, his first day of shooting was scheduled opposite Denzel. And his close-up was up first. You can tell something special is happening on set by watching the crew. Even the dolly grip, who had made hundreds of movies, was paying attention. As those two actors began to work, it was as if a spell had been cast over the set. As we finished Matt's coverage, Denzel caught my eye and nodded approvingly. Later, he took me aside. "Who is that kid?" he asked. I told him it was Matt's first big role. "Damn," he said. "Better get my game on. He almost blew me off the screen."

Matt wanted to physicalize the ravages of his character's addiction in the final scenes and went back to L.A. to lose weight. He returned, having lost so much so quickly—unsupervised—that I was worried he might not make it through filming. I knew it was a big moment in Matt's career, but was it worth him jeopardizing his health? Watching him was terrifying, but also inspiring. His performance was wonderful, and his career took off. A great actor is an athlete of the heart.

The life in some actors' eyes never seems to dim and the camera wants to know why. We call this Being Kissed by the Angel. They radiate heat the way an engine in a sports car makes the air shimmer around it; we mortals are drawn to them in the hope of being touched by their magic. Liberty contends that certain faces let in the light and glow from within while others remain opaque and reflective. He calls it movie skin.

Trying to overdetermine a star's performance can only end in tears. You don't drive a high-performance Lamborghini as if it's a truck without power steering. Its sensitivity is such that the slightest touch to the wheel can send the car skidding around a corner on two wheels. One thing is certain, you never get back anything more interesting than you give, and usually much less. If you insist on giving a line reading, it'll inevitably be worse in an actor's mouth. And if an actor is thinking about a result, it blocks the internal process that allows him to reach the emotion in an authentic way.

This was especially true of Denzel. Since *Glory*, we had both acquired a certain amount of mastery. More than that, we had come to know and trust each other. By the end of shooting *Courage*, we hardly needed to talk. Sometimes at the end of a take I might step out from behind the camera, and before I could speak, he would say, "I know, I know . . ."

And he usually did. The best example of this nonverbal collaboration took place on the final day of shooting. We were filming his character's return home. Lieutenant Colonel Nat Serling has dealt with his guilt and self-loathing and accomplished his mission of corroborating the Medal of Honor for the female pilot. His wife and children are waiting inside the house. He needs to put his life back together.

The shot Roger and I had planned was a simple one. The camera was to begin in the sky, and it was storyboarded to be a cross-dissolve from the final image of Meg in her chopper as she ascends into the heavens. (Incidentally, the only time in the movie she was *actually* flying.)

Denzel was to enter from below camera as it tilts down. I called "Action." He walked up the stone pathway carrying his briefcase, then up the steps and into the house. I called "Cut." We could easily have moved on. But in one of the rare moments of the shoot we found ourselves ahead of schedule. I knew that Roger would rather have had more clouds to match the dissolve. I caught him squinting up at the sky.

"What do you think, Rog?"

"Five more minutes, mate?"

I nodded yes. Meanwhile Denzel had walked off by himself. I think he was talking on his phone. The O.J. verdict had just come in and the Million Man March was being organized. I knew he was being pulled in several directions at once. There was no reason for him to concentrate on his performance; it was the exact kind of shot Anthony Hopkins had referred to as "N.A.R." Meanwhile, I fidgeted. Waiting for setups isn't easy for me. There's no time to read, nobody especially wants to talk to the director for fear of interrupting his concentration, and there's a limit to how many times a day I can check my watch. I sat in my chair staring at the little house. Something was off. I called out to the prop man and asked if he had any kid stuff on the truck. At my house there was always a soccer ball or a stuffed animal on the lawn.

"I've got a bike," he said.

"Perfect."

I took the bike and wheeled it into shot, then laid it across the walkway. Now it looked like a real house. I didn't tell Denzel. Five minutes later Roger gave me the high sign and I told Denzel we were ready.

Most actors tense up when you say "Action!" But if you were to attach sensors to register Denzel's heart, perspiration, and respiratory rate, my guess is you would find him in a kind of monk-like trance. His relaxation is so profound it's possible his vitals go down rather than up. His unique gift is simply being present. Each moment, each take, is happening for the first time. If this sounds obvious, I recommend trying it with a camera in your face, fifty people watching and millions on the line. I called "Action" again. Denzel walked in from below the camera again, carrying his briefcase. Midway up the walk there was now a bicycle. I can imagine another actor gracefully sidestepping it and walking past it into the house. I can even think of an actor or two who might turn back to camera and ask, "Is this supposed to be here?" But not Denzel. He looked down at the bike, stopped, put his briefcase on the ground, then reached for the handlebars and set it upright on the lawn before continuing into the house. He was a man putting his life back in order.

It's the moment in the movie where I begin to cry.

Did it occur to me that something like this might happen? Absolutely not. Do I give myself some small measure of credit for what happened? I do. Even with an actor as creative and self-contained as Denzel Washington, there are ways a director can help, whether he's aware of them or not. In most cases, it's about creating a simulacrum of reality in front of the camera where truth is the default setting. What I've come to believe is that acting isn't about being dramatic or internal, it's about not acting at all. If the costumes are right, if the set and the makeup and the lighting are right—more important, if the dialogue and the staging don't strain credibility, it should feel suspiciously simple.

Lest my portrait of Denzel risk becoming hagiography, I'll offer one slightly less admirable anecdote. Denzel had been involved with the Boys & Girls Clubs of America since we'd met. He would do everything he could to fly back to L.A. on his own dime to coach his kids' teams, and as one who coached my own son's teams, I admired his dedication. It was a Friday and I'd gone out of my way to get his work finished so he could catch an early flight. I waved goodbye and wished him good luck with the game. Later that night I turned on the TV in my hotel room to watch the Knicks in a playoff game in New York. There was Denzel, sitting courtside with Spike Lee.

On Monday morning when he walked on set and saw the look on my face, he knew he'd been busted. All he said was, "I know, I know."

TEN THINGS EVERY DIRECTOR NEEDS TO KNOW

I still tape them to the monitor.

1. This shot is in the movie.

2. There is no such thing as one more take. An actor muffs a line. The AC blows the focus. You go again. That means sacrificing something at the end of the day.

3. Everyone knows more than you, but only you know what you want.

4. Compose in depth. It's not a frame, it's a window inviting the camera into the middle of the scene.

5. Commit to your frame, crowd it with life or fill it with negative space. Do nothing halfway.

6. Coverage is God's way of giving you the chance to rewrite in the cutting room.

7. Try not to feel defeated by your day. Just do better tomorrow.

8. This is the only time you'll make this movie. (Same as #1 but bears repeating.)

9. Directing is no fun. The fun is in having directed.

10. You don't need a reason. You're the director.

CHAPTER TEN

Politics, Pop Culture, and a Pyrrhic Victory

The Siege, 1998

Coming of age as an aspiring filmmaker in the 1970s, to be politically engaged and passionate about movies were synonymous. Art and activism were mother's milk to those of us who believed it to be the artist's responsibility to militate for social justice and political change. We thrilled to Costa-Gavras's *Z* and *State of Siege*. Bertolucci's *The Conformist* and Schlöndorff's *Lost Honour of Katharina Blum* were also favorites of mine. In 1983, the TV movie I made whose unexpected success enabled me to make the transition to directing features, *Special Bulletin*, was inspired by one of the most influential political films of all time, *The Battle of Algiers*. There's a quote from Émile Zola I copied into one of my notebooks at the time. "If you ask me what I came into this world to do, I will tell you," he wrote, "I came to live out loud." That's a pretty good description of who I'd hoped to become as a director. Imagine my disappointment to discover most studio heads adhered to a very different maxim: the old Hollywood saying, "If you want to send a message, try Western Union."

I had to ask myself whether I had any responsibility other than entertaining the audience. It sounds like *Sullivan's Travels*. Do I hold up a stark mirror to ugly truths or hang a pretty curtain to hide a world in pain? Is it enough to give a couple of hours of relief from the exquisite sadness of being alive? Can a movie do both? As my films continued to do well enough financially, I began to seek out opportunities to stray from the pleasant confines of pure entertainment into what, for lack of a less pretentious phrase, I'll call "the theater of ideas."

In 1997, Lynda Obst, a producer with a deal at 20th Century Fox, sent me an original screenplay called *Blowback*. Written by Larry Wright, one of America's finest journalists, it was about a group of terrorists who bring a nuclear device into New York Harbor. Having already made a movie about a group of ecoterrorists who bring a nuclear device into Charleston Harbor (op cit., *Special Bulletin*) and seen several inauthentic movies since then about nuclear devices brought to various locales (e.g., *The Peacemaker*), I demurred.

But the spread of Islamist terrorism that was bedeviling most of Europe was something I had read a lot about. That America would eventually have to deal with the threat seemed obvious to me; in fact, we already had. On February 26, 1993, a truck bomb had exploded in a basement-level parking garage under the World Trade Center complex, killing six people and injuring more than one thousand in what was at that point the deadliest terrorism act perpetrated on U.S. soil. Had the terrorists been more capable, or just luckier, the result would have been substantially worse. Even given the little I knew about federal law enforcement, I was convinced we must already be up to our elbows in preparing for the worst. I met with Tom Rothman, president of Fox, and told him there was a movie to be made from Larry's script—not a race-against-time action movie, but an in-depth, conjectural look at how our law enforcement might deal with terrorism when it arrived on our shores. I assured Tom that it would also have some kick-ass action.

After getting the studio's blessing to rewrite the script (I honestly don't remember why we had to change the title, only that I wasn't happy about it), I asked Menno Meyjes to join me. We had never worked together but I had long been an admirer of his writing on *The Color Purple* and *Empire of the Sun*. As a

European, he knew a great deal on the subject, and as I would discover to my delight, there were few subjects Menno didn't know a great deal about. To begin our research, I called Merrick Garland, then serving as deputy attorney general to Janet Reno. Merrick and I had first met at a tea for Chicago high school students entering Harvard College in the fall of 1970. Although we were barely friends during school, he ended up dating my college girlfriend after graduation, and in yet another coincidence, while in law school he shared a house with my oldest friend from childhood, Bradley Graham, who was at Harvard Business School at the time. Years later, Brad would become a reporter and editor on the Defense Department beat at the *Washington Post*. Both men were enormous help while making *Courage Under Fire*, vouching for me to law enforcement and connecting me to experts in the field.

In the aftermath of the Oklahoma City bombing in 1995, Merrick was first on the scene and took over the federal prosecution of Timothy McVeigh. There were few people who knew more about the state of American law enforcement than he did. He became our Virgil, guiding us through the rivalries and turf wars that currently beleaguered the various agencies and animated the movie's plot. With his help, we met with current and former agents of the CIA and NSA, but it was his introduction to the FBI-NYPD Joint Terrorist Task Force that became the lodestone of our script.

At our first meeting, the Feds were friendly but tight-lipped. They considered their mission to be the crucial, final line of defense "against all enemies" of the United States—a high-stakes job performed mostly under the radar. They were rightly suspicious of liberal Hollywood filmmakers with our idealistic concerns for First Amendment guarantees. An initial tour of their Manhattan headquarters was only marginally helpful; it gave us a feel for the ambiance and rhythms of their workplace but was conspicuously absent of any information about methods and sources we couldn't have found elsewhere. The briefing we received at the end of the tour was equally short on detail, barely alluding to their techniques and sources. But as we were being escorted out of the building, a veteran field agent who happened to be a movie afficionado mentioned having liked a couple of my films and wanted to know who might be playing the lead FBI agent. When I mentioned Denzel Washington, his eyes lit up.

"Love to meet him when he's in New York," he said, offering me his card and scribbling his cell number on the back.

I asked Denzel to come to New York and invited the agent to join us for dinner. After a few glasses of wine, a couple of Hollywood anecdotes, and an autograph, he reciprocated by proudly revealing just how massive the NYPD's and FBI's counterterrorism efforts had become: profiling, surveillance, wiretapping, undercover informants, infiltration of mosques. Everything we knew to be happening abroad was happening here with little attention paid to the niceties of civil rights. He detailed how terrorist cell members had gained entry into the country by means of student visas, and how their operations were financed from abroad. He also spoke of "enhanced interrogation" techniques used by the CIA on prisoners held at black sites around the world.

Walking back to our hotel that night through the quiet streets of downtown Manhattan, we couldn't help but see the world a little differently. After Annette Bening agreed to play Denzel's CIA nemesis, she had similarly eye-opening conversations with a female agent who had operated abroad under deep cover. It was a little unsettling to see how forthcoming some in law enforcement were willing to be when they found themselves under the spell of a movie star.

I loved working with Annette. In addition to being brilliant, gracious, hardworking, and fun, she wasn't intimidated by Denzel's strength and was willing to go toe-to-toe with him. At the same time, she could always be counted on to find unexpected humor even in the most serious scenes. One night after she'd finished giving her four-month-old her 2 a.m. feeding and put her to sleep in her trailer, Annette and I were sitting in our chairs waiting for Roger Deakins to finish a huge lighting setup.

"You know, Ed," she said, with a mischievous look, "we met ten years ago."

It took me a moment, hoping I hadn't done anything untoward, but then it all came back to me. I had been in New York casting *thirtysomething* and seen Annette in a lovely play called *Coastal Disturbances*.

"I do remember," I said. "You came in to read for Ellyn and for Melissa. You were wonderful."

"Except you didn't cast me."

Knowing how well things had turned out for her since then I had the presence of mind to say, "I know. And you've never thanked me."

Denzel played the fed with studied calm, but as the story progressed, you could feel the rage rising inside him—until it exploded in a beautifully played aria when he found a naked prisoner being tortured.

The big surprise was Tony Shalhoub. I'd enjoyed his work onstage, as well as in several wildly diverse character turns. When I cast him, he had a few days left to shoot on another movie but neither its production manager nor ours anticipated a scheduling problem. That was before disaster struck his other movie and it went three weeks over schedule. I was crushed. But there was an alternative to recasting the part. Tony just had to finish work on his other movie by 4 p.m., get to LAX by five, take the red-eye to NYC, arriving on set with us at 3 a.m., never having met me, tried on a costume, or rehearsed the scene, then in subzero weather shoot a scene that had to be completed before dawn, which also happened to be his character's most dramatic moment in the movie.

In the scene, he looks desperately for his son among those Arab Americans who have been rounded up and imprisoned in a stadium, finds Denzel, and tears into him. Tony nailed it on the first take. A heartbreaking performance, it's one of the best scenes in the film. The crew, knowing what he had pulled off, burst into applause. Tony Shalhoub is the epitome of a money player.

It still being pre-9/11, the world of moviemaking in Manhattan was vastly different from what it is today. With the city's cooperation, we were able to pull off scenes of remarkable scale and authenticity. We blew up a bus in front of Peter Luger's in Brooklyn, shut down Times Square from Fortieth to Forty-Seventh Streets, and even closed the Brooklyn Bridge for a few hours to send armored vehicles and hundreds of soldiers marching across.

However, when we were in preproduction, planning all these outrageously costly sequences, and it was clear the budget was going to rise precipitously, Tom

Rothman decided we needed more star power. He convinced me to cast Bruce Willis as the general who imposes martial law on the city. Come to think of it, I'm not sure he gave me any choice if I wanted him to green-light the movie. Then again, it was risky subject matter, and without Tom having put himself on the line, it wouldn't have gotten made at all. Anyway, I had known Bruce since his days as a bartender at Cafe Central and I had worked with Demi on *About Last Night*. They were married the year after that film came out, and Liberty and I had them to dinner at our house. I figured I could make it work.

For *The Siege* (as it had come to be called), Bruce flew into New York only hours before shooting. Unlike Tony, he wasn't prepared and his performance was wooden and uncomfortable, as if he'd stepped off another set and onto ours. Paul Attanasio had come on to write some brilliant but difficult dialogue for Bruce's character, and despite my best efforts—and perhaps even attributable to the aphasia I and the rest of the world would learn of much later—Bruce barely managed to stumble his way through and the authenticity of the third act was irreparably hurt by his toothless performance.

The movie played well in previews despite some audience resistance to Bruce—so often cast as the out-of-control action hero, now playing a buttoned-down senior military officer. Denzel and Annette were considered fabulous adversaries, Tony's performance was regarded by all to be heart-wrenching, and the depiction of our country's reaction to the arrival of terrorism on our shores was strong and unsettling. But after a couple of early press interviews, I began to feel some foreboding about the story's reception by the chattering classes. I sensed resistance from both left and right: one side feared the stereotyping of Arab Americans, the other objected to the heavy-handed portrayal of law enforcement. One thing everyone seemed to agree on was that a major terrorist attack on Manhattan was implausible.

I had been contacted by a representative of the American-Arab Anti-Discrimination Committee (ADC) before shooting began; they had asked for a meeting to express their concern that our representation of the terrorists could inflame prejudice against the Muslim community. I took the meeting, though I felt mealymouthed pointing out the many positive portrayals of Arab characters in the film, and how their victimization by our government was the centerpiece of the third act. They had a legitimate grievance, but it didn't begin to outweigh my determination to tell a cautionary tale of what might be coming our way and how we might overreact should such a situation occur. I told them there was too much evidence of violent attacks by Islamic radicals all over the world not to believe it was credible that something like this could happen in America.

On the movie's opening day in November 1998, the ADC arranged protests at theaters in several cities. The demonstrations were small, but on a slow news day the message resonated with the first stirrings of journalistic wokeness; here was yet another Hollywood exploitation film turning an oppressed minority into villains. The film critics liked Denzel and Annette, hated Bruce, and were mixed about the movie. The box office was okay. The studio received several bomb threats and posted armed guards at the gates. Bedford Falls received word through a contact in the CIA that our office was being targeted. It wasn't really, we eventually learned, but only after we had security for a couple of weeks.

As the narrative of the protests was picked up by the national media, I felt obliged to respond. I wrote an op-ed in the *New York Times*.

"Insidious, incendiary and dangerous."

That is how the American-Arab Anti-Discrimination Committee has chosen to characterize my film *The Siege* in a letter sent to every major media outlet in the country. The group's objections are based on the film's depiction of radical Islamic terrorists who have chosen to attack the United States.

What the critics are saying, as best as I can understand it, is that any portrayal of the life of Muslims that includes representations of violence — no matter how well documented — is not only offensive but also inflammatory. Forget the World Trade Center and the embassy bombings in Kenya

and Tanzania; their position, simply put, is that all one billion Islamic people in the world can be portrayed only in their most positive aspect.

Even though members of this group who saw *The Siege* have pri-
vately told me they were moved by the film, the organization's official
position has been to attack it as promoting stereotypes, a stand also taken
by other Arab-American groups. But what, exactly, are these stereotypes?
The Arab-American community is as diverse and divided against itself—
politically, religiously, socially—as any vibrant community in the United
States. And this film portrays Arab-Americans as cops, landlords, people
with families, community leaders—and, yes, terrorists. In fact, the film (in
which growing fear leads to the wholesale internment of Arab-Americans)
is about stereotypes, about what happens when stereotypes are played out
to disastrous effect.

Beneath the objections of groups like the American-Arab Anti-
Discrimination Committee, I sense a fear that the image of Arabs and Muslims in America is so poor that any negative depiction, even if part of a
balanced whole, is inherently perilous. This argument has been promul-
gated before: by Jewish-Americans, Italian-Americans, and many others.
It is a time-honored expression of the insecurity of any immigrant group,
so worried about the pains of acculturation. But the logic, so emotionally
persuasive and understandable, is, I'm afraid, finally as reductionist and
disrespectful as the imputed offenses that it protests.

The single and simple conclusion *The Siege* draws is that it is impossible to generalize about Arab-Americans, that the distinction between
them and terrorists must be understood before we, as a nation, can grapple
with our fear of the "other." Only then, if push ever comes to shove in the
new war against terrorism, will we be able to respond prudently, and with
conscience. The film makes clear that even in the fight against vicious and
committed enemies, the ends, if they include the deprivation of civil liber-
ties to any group, can never justify the means.

If *The Siege* engenders a dialogue on ethnic stereotyping, on terrorism, on the increasingly cloudy legal landscape between personal rights and the public interest, then it will have accomplished far more than I might ever have imagined for a Hollywood thriller. Movies about aliens and asteroids can't offend anybody, but neither do they try to hold up a mirror to unattractive aspects of our country. And the truth sometimes hurts. In what a friend of mine calls the new American hurt game, if you're not offended by somebody, you're nobody.

These days, it seems, people wake up in the morning not only waiting to be offended, but also hoping to be offended. Central to any multicultural orthodoxy is the notion that, unless you are offended, you have no ontology.

I imagine the Army also might be offended by its portrayal in the film. Maybe the C.I.A., and Congress, and Bill Clinton, too. But I don't expect they will protest. They're used to it by now. The beauty of a pluralistic society, I've always been taught, is that it can contain the giving and taking of offenses.

This overheated chorus of lamentations began, tellingly, before the film was ever seen. But it is the job of an anti-discrimination organization to complain. Mine is to make films. I am not accustomed to defending them. What I'm trying to do as a filmmaker is to look at the world. And write about what I see. To shrink from any subject because it is hurtful or politically sensitive or politically incorrect, or Islamically incorrect, is to deny one of the most important functions of art, which is to be provocative. So, I'm sorry I offended anyone. But I'm really not.

Three years later, on September 11, 2001, at 6 a.m. Pacific, my phone rang. It was Marshall.

"Turn on the TV," he said.

The footage of the carnage was all too familiar. So were the talking heads bloviating on-air. Many of the same commentators who had pilloried me when the movie was released now called to ask if I would come on their shows and talk about how I had seen it coming. There was no pleasure in having been paying attention. In a single morning I went from pariah to pundit, trying to explain that I was much less prescient than I was given credit for. Over the next month, Marshall and I worked with many of the best writers in town on a network special memorializing the individual stories of 9/11. *America: A Tribute to Heroes* won an Emmy. Two years later, when the United States invaded Iraq for what our government believed was retaliation for an act of terrorism, Menno called from England to say, "We were right. Just not right enough."

Movies change as the cultural landscape changes around them. As the years pass, terrorism (domestic now as well as international) has become commonplace, and the movie seems to have found a curious resting place, praised for its prescience rather than its portrayal.

It puts me in mind of an epigram to one of Saki's black-hearted tales.

"Never be a pioneer," he writes. "It's the early Christian that gets the hungriest lion."

NINE THOUGHTS ON ASSISTANT DIRECTORS

An ode to the unsung heroes, from an AD fanboy

1. THE SECRET SOCIETY

Nobody outside the biz knows what an AD does, yet they and their director are symbiotic. A director becomes a director without having directed, while the AD has spent years on other directors' sets taking the best and rejecting the worst of each. A good AD essentially teaches the new director without ever letting the director know.

2. THOSE WHO SERVE

On *Glory*, Skip Cosper tolerated my Kurosawa references with bemused restraint, all the while gently saving my ass. How many times was I about to make a grand pronouncement—"Position the crane *here!*"—only to glance over my shoulder and see him quietly standing in a much better spot. Not so much showing me up as showing me the way.

3. GUARDIAN ANGEL

The AD is also responsible for safety. In four feet of mud during a night attack, I watched Skip pull a clueless extra off a mortar about to explode. Next day, he saved a camera car about to be swamped by an unexpected tide, wading into the rising surf with a rope and a hook, then swimming back with the rope in his teeth and attaching it to the generator truck's winch.

4. VOLUNTEER

When something odious needs to be done it's invariably the AD who steps forward. I've seen them bitten by spiders, peed on by infants, and abused by movie stars. They regularly suffer drunks, fans, fools, and producers—not necessarily in that order.

5. KNOW-IT-ALLS

I've known ADs who are bullfighters, weight lifters, poets, and potheads. Classical guitarists and classical scholars, former child actors and children of famous fathers. Women who grew up in the business and men who grew up on the street. Self-proclaimed experts on weather, firearms, livestock, footwear, vitamins, dental hygiene, ADs are masters of all things terrestrial. They are also armchair philosophers. Nilo Otero, my AD on *Legends of the Fall*, *Last Samurai*, and *Blood Diamond*, has an endless supply of aphorisms. My personal favorite: "Where there's no solution, there's no problem."

6. FAMILIARITY AND CONTEMPT

Not all ADs are perfect. I've also known, and fired, ADs who are screamers, bullies, or gutless company men whose only allegiance is to their next job. Even those I love can drive me nuts. Their cute little expressions and idiosyncrasies, so charming in the first week of shooting, can make me want to murder them by Day Thirty-Three (with forty still to shoot).

7. LONELY ARE THE BRAVE

By and large, I've found ADs to be solitary people. Lonely in a crowd. A disproportionate number seem to have battled drugs and alcohol. Several have ulcers. Blown-out knees. Bad feet. Often out of town, their marriages—if they last—are unconventional at best. The best ADs work a couple hundred days a year, from dawn to dusk or dusk to dawn.

8. THE PRICE

Darin Rivetti has done three movies with me. He averages four to five hours of sleep a night, never cuts in front of the chow line, and is always the first one back to work after lunch. After a six-day workweek, his off day is inevitably spent prepping the week ahead. I shudder to think of the actuarial table of an AD's life expectancy.

9. POETIC INJUSTICE

When the movie succeeds it's the director who gets all the credit. When it goes over budget, it's the AD who gets fired.

CHAPTER ELEVEN

A War Won and Lost

Traffic, 2000

One day in June 1998, I was reading an article in a magazine called the *Utne Reader*. (Remember magazines?) It described a massive drug bust gone awry in South Florida in which the DEA, the ATF, and the Miami PD were involved in a gun battle while each was running their own sting operation, all believing the other's narco-traffickers were real. This was only the latest absurdity I had read about in the preposterously named clown show that was the War on Drugs. I had read one of Steve Gaghan's first scripts and was astonished by his ability to portray different voices, as well as his political sophistication. I sent him the article and we met to discuss using it as the basis for a movie.

Our first notion was to tell it as satire, but the more we learned, the more tragic we realized the story was. At its center, in addition to the law enforcement angle, we imagined a lead character, a "friend of Bill Clinton" who had been invited into the president's cabinet as the drug czar—imagine a composite of Robert Reich and Barry McCaffrey—who not only realizes the futility of his job but that his own daughter is an addict.

As so often happens, it's impossible to keep personal experience from bleeding into the creative process. After Steve went off to do research, first to D.C. and then to the border, there followed an unusually long period of radio silence. I assumed he was having trouble writing the script. Nothing new in that. In fact, life was imitating art, and Steve was battling a drug problem of his own. It took me longer than I would have hoped to understand the severity of his problem, though I'd like to think I was compassionate and supportive once I did. There's nothing I can add to Steve's own moving account in the *New York Times* (February 2001) of his crack addiction and successful recovery, except that, despite it all, he managed to write a wonderful script. That alone is a testament not just to his genius but also to his extraordinary will.

Steve was more than a year late delivering the script when he called, panicked because Steven Soderbergh had reached him, asking about his availability to write an adaptation of the British miniseries *Traffik*.

"He's making our movie," Steve said. "What do we do?"

I sat down and watched the miniseries and realized Steve was right. It would be hard enough to get one movie made about the drug wars; the notion of competing projects was unthinkable. I recalled something Sydney once said that has always stayed with me. "It's hard enough to get any movie made, let alone a good one. No one should ever stand in its way." In that spirit I twice saw him step aside from scripts he had developed and produce them for other talented directors.

I didn't know Soderbergh, but I'd admired his work ever since *Sex, Lies, and Videotape*. I had also really enjoyed the recently released *Out of Sight*. I picked up the phone and called him. Gaghan had clearly already told him about our conflicting projects.

"There's only one thing to do," I said. "Let's combine our projects." He immediately agreed.

My deal with Steve was being financed by Fox, but when we presented them with our combined projects and Soderbergh to direct—as well as Harrison Ford playing the lead—they passed.

With Harrison committed, we felt our chances of getting it made somewhere else were good. But a few weeks later his management called to say, "Harrison doesn't think this is the kind of movie his fans want to see him in." Soderbergh was undaunted. I learned something from him then: "Act as if . . . (you're making it)," he said. And so we gamely pressed on with prep until Michael Douglas stepped in to star and Barry Diller's USA Films agreed to finance it.

Soderbergh's work on the film speaks for itself and his Oscar was well-deserved. My only contribution going forward was to try to be the best possible producer, which is to say get him all the money he needed, suggest an idea or two, and then shut up and let him do what he thought best. Only two years before, I had been sitting at the Oscars for *Shakespeare in Love*, believing we had no chance of winning, and ambivalent about it when we did. Now I was there again, this time believing we had a real chance of winning best picture. And so I perched on the edge of my seat, ready to storm the stage when my name was called. After our editor Steve Mirrione, Benicio del Toro, Steve Gaghan, and Soderbergh all won in their categories, I was sure we'd won best picture.

We didn't.

But I had a lot more fun at the after-parties than the time we'd won. And we made a great movie.

TEN TALL TALES FROM THE MAKEUP TRAILER

Directors, unchained

1. **A PRODUCTION ODYSSEY, Part I**

   The actor-director hated being in the van. He preferred to drive his Porsche. One day while on a scout in the New Mexico desert he misread a map, sped on ahead of the crew, took a wrong turn, got lost, and never made it back in time to tell the designer what colors to paint the set.

2. **A PRODUCTION ODYSSEY, Part II**

   The designer caught up with the director at a private airfield. "Get on," he said. "We'll talk on my plane." The designer climbed aboard but the director had scheduled an interview during the flight. Once they landed, he jumped into a waiting limo and vanished.

3. **A PRODUCTION ODYSSEY, Part III**

   Lacking even a toothbrush, the designer found a motel, eventually made his way back to the production office the next morning, and made the color choices himself. On the day of shooting the director arrived, took one look at the set, declared it wrong, and drove away. In his Porsche.

4. **VANITY**

   In the finale of John Milius's original script for *Jeremiah Johnson*, Redford— then thirty-five—was intended to die at the hands of a young brave who turns out to be his son. Seeing himself old and grizzled in age makeup, Redford refused to shoot it. The director (Sydney Pollack) had no choice but to fade out on the stupid theme song as the movie just sort of . . . ends.

5. **COJONES**

   By lunch on Orson Welles's first day shooting *Touch of Evil*, the studio was furious he hadn't gotten a shot. By 4 p.m. they were apoplectic. Minutes before wrap they were about to fire him when he called "Action." The three-and-a-half-minute opening shot is a classic. "Cut!" he yelled. "We're three days ahead!"

6. DOING NOTHING

The director was afraid to tell the headstrong young actor his reaction shots sucked. The editor said "Fuck it" and invited him into the cutting room. "You look like a zombie," he said. "I don't care if you're thinking about nothing, at least move your eyes." That actor is now a big star. The editor got nominated.

7. MAZURSKY REX

For *Enemies, A Love Story*, the studio wanted Paul Mazursky to cast a difficult star. When they met, the actor said, "I have only two questions. Must I screw three women? And does it have to be about the Holocaust?" "I have only one question," said Mazursky. "Why the fuck would I cast you?"

8. DIFFERENT STROKES

The legendary actor insisted on having holes cut in his pants pockets so he could hold his genitals while acting. One day the wardrobe mistress innocently sewed his pockets closed. In the middle of a take, he discovered the lack of entrée, began cursing, and stomped off the set. The wardrobe mistress was fired the next day.

9. DIRECTOR PALS

When Miloš Forman first came to America he had terrible nightmares but no time to go to therapy. Instead, he told his bad dreams to his best friend, Ivan Passer, and sent him to a therapist for interpretation. Forman became a star. Passer stayed in therapy for twenty years.

10. NINA, ON DIRECTORS

There are only two kinds of directors: those who pretend they know what they're doing and those who don't need to pretend. Consider the hack's adage: to be sure of hitting the target, shoot first, and call whatever you hit the target. Only the mediocre are always at their best.

CHAPTER TWELVE

If at First

Once and Again, 2000

From the pilot to the last episode of its third and final season, working on *Once and Again* was an unalloyed joy. Someone once said that happiness is essentially boring, especially to a director. But after the Sturm und Drang of the past few movies I'd done, I knew I could use a little boring in my life. My kids were both at pivotal moments (then again, when are they not?) and I didn't want to go on location. I stepped away from directing, focusing instead on growing Bedford Falls. With Rick Solomon and Robin Budd's help we produced several films, including Jessie Nelson's lovely *I Am Sam.* For three blissful years, I coached soccer, went to the studio at nine, and was home in time for a dinner with my family.

As for the show, the cast was exceptional; the stories were authentic, bittersweet, and genuinely emotional. The writing, by most of the same group that had done *thirtysomething,* was funny and sad, often at the same time. There was only one problem: the audience never found the show. It didn't help that the network constantly moved us from one night and time slot to another, but there was something about it that didn't sync up with the zeitgeist. Maybe the honest treatment of divorce and single parenting wasn't what the audience wanted to watch while at least half of them were living it.

Sela Ward, playing the suburban mom Lily Manning, did the best work of her career. From the very first shot of the pilot, there was something so touching and vulnerable about her. Same with Billy Campbell, as her boyfriend. Julia Whelan, in the role of Lily's eldest child, was preternaturally talented and exceptionally wise for a fifteen-year-old; Marin Hinkle was so talented in the role of Lily's sister it's little wonder her career has flourished. Jeff Nordling as Lily's ex and Susanna Thompson as Rick's could have starred in their own show. I'm not sure any of us could have predicted the emergence of Todd Field, who directed an episode in season one, as an Oscar-nominated director. And hovering above us all, floating effortlessly from one genius performance to the next was Evan Rachel Wood.

At twelve, she was that gifted child actor you come across once in a lifetime (or in my case, twice, counting Claire Danes). She had been onstage since age four and unfazed by the most demanding storylines. In such cases it can be oddly easier for a child to be relaxed in the limelight than an adult. Dakota Fanning was like that on *I Am Sam*, which Marshall and I produced in 2001. Not only did she arrive on set to star opposite Sean Penn knowing the name of everyone on the crew, but she'd also memorized the entire script. "I'm a big fan of *thirtysomething*," she told me and Marshall.

With Evan, Marshall and I would write for her whenever we could without making it too obvious that we were playing favorites. When we wrote a storyline for her about anorexia, she played it with a maturity and understanding that blew our minds. It seemed there was no challenge too difficult for her. That is, until I let my ego get in the way. We were prepping an episode where Evan's character was to begin seeing a therapist. While sitting in a casting session, it occurred to me to cast myself in the role. I often read opposite actors in auditions and enjoyed it more than I cared to admit. I'd last tried acting, with a notable lack of distinction, in high school. But I had spent twenty years since then working with the best actors in the world, observing their methods, editing their performances. And Sydney Pollack had done it, hadn't he? Also, this was surely the only way it would ever happen since no one in their right mind would cast me. How hard could it be to play a therapist? No blocking, no props, no problem. I'd just sit in a chair and listen. To Evan! No one would be watching, anyway. And why not direct it too! Quentin Tarantino puts himself in a scene or two of his movies, doesn't he?

Here is how my day as an actor proceeded.

It's nice having somebody wash my hair and lie to me about how great I looked at 5 a.m., I decide, although when I glance in the mirror I see someone resembling my father minus the hangover.

As the set call approaches, I realized hamsters have taken up residence in my stomach. The AD knocks on the door of my trailer. I spill coffee on my costume. The soundstage, on which I have spent days on end, suddenly feels unfamiliar. I trip over a C-stand. The lights, so dim behind the camera, appear much brighter as I step onto the set.

Things begin to happen very fast: a deafening bell—"Quiet for rehearsal!" On the blocking rehearsal, I forget my first line. *Suck it up, dude*, I tell myself. *You fucking wrote it.*

Another bell. Why does that man keep yelling "Quiet!" Then nothing happens. Then more nothing. "I can do this," I assure myself as I wait for someone to say "Action" and realize I'm that someone. The crew sniggers. The volume on the voice in my head is so high I'm afraid I'm talking to myself out loud.

Okay, Ed, now go open the door. Go on . . . That's right, now reach for the handle with your right hand and turn it . . . a little more . . . Good! Now hit the mark without looking down. NO! DON'T LOOK DOWN! That's right. Now, smile. SMILE! You're a therapist! You're supposed to make them feel welcome. NOW . . . say the line . . . You remember the line, don't you? DON'T YOU?? The one you've repeated in your head six hundred times. And pay no attention to the camera's cyclops eye four feet away. STOP LOOKING AT IT AND SAY THE DAMN LINE!

It takes five tries before I get it right. More or less. I say, "Cut and print," if only to stop the pain. The crew applauds. Derisively or relieved? My shirt is soaked with flop sweat. It's beginning to dawn on me there might be more to this acting thing than I thought.

Next setup should be even easier. I sit beside Evan and assume my "therapist" expression for some deep listening. I've only got a few lines, nothing more than a sentence or two each time, but just in case, I've asked Marshall to stop by and observe. After my close-up there's a long pause and I realize I've forgotten to say, "Cut." Marshall walks onto the set, leans down, and whispers in my ear. What I hear is: *"Syrchumph ikdnssst mweiss grmpchkk. Achhhh nrrrfff stchh . . ."*

Why is he talking gibberish? My heart is trip-hammering. My ears are ringing. My mouth is so dry by the time we're ready for take two, I can barely say, "Action!?"

After we cut, Marshall comes back onto the set and whispers, "Better . . ."

Better? Why? How? What did I do different? My mind is racing. He touches my shoulder and I want to cry. Sitting beside me, Evan smiles sympathetically. She knows.

ABC/Carin Baer

At last, on take seven, Marshall races onto the set, beaming.

"You did it!" he says.

I have no idea what I did. I try to regain my equilibrium off camera while waiting for the next shot. Evan jokes with the camera operator as he lines up her close-up. How can she be so relaxed? Oh, right. Drama school. Meisner. Years of experience. It's a profession, idiot.

I had done none of the preparation I ask of an actor. No backstory. No internal emotional work. My concentration was that of a meth head with ADD. Evan should have been pissed. Instead, she told me I was fun to work with. If I was her, what else could she say?

I tried watching myself in dailies and felt like throwing up. No wonder actors are so volatile. I'd often joked that the best time to work with a movie star is immediately after he's directed. I can now officially declare the same can be said of a director after he's acted. Will I be more compassionate now?

Yes? Maybe?

Will anybody see it and want to cast me?

No.

But what if I'm really right for the part?

Once I recovered from my ordeal, I had to admit I'd been too anxious and self-absorbed to gain any useful insights about acting from putting myself in front of the camera. The only possible conclusion, I decided, is that acting is essentially mysterious. Those who do it well usually can't or won't talk about it. The same can be said about directing. No matter how much Stanislavski, Adler, or Meisner you've studied, it's an instinctual, idiosyncratic calling. A director's goal isn't to understand actors, but rather to find the compassion to accept them as they are—what an acting teacher I once heard describe as "brave, beautiful, magical, terrified creatures," desperate to please, even as they resent us for our authority and influence over them.

For some actors, their insecurity is so monumental it enjoins them from unleashing their innate ability. In such cases, it takes more than a compassionate director to help them navigate their struggle. Recently I ran into an old friend, a talented actress crippled by years of self-doubt. It wasn't until she took time off to have a baby that her work began to soar. Her performance in the first movie she made upon going back to work was a revelation and won an Oscar. When I asked her what had changed, she said simply, "I realized I was enough."

Some actors, though, seem to go out of their way to defy empathy. They are fundamentally unhappy and not satisfied until everyone else around them is unhappy too. There's a nasty adage a director once told me: "How do you make an actor miserable? Cast him." One actor I endured who fits the description was a classic malcontent—hated his dialogue, his costars, and his own performance. Even worse, he persisted in calling "Cut" in the middle of a take when he didn't like how it was going. I fumed quietly until, during a complicated shot, he did it again. Finally, I exploded.

"YOU HAVE LOTS OF LINES IN THIS MOVIE!" I yelled. "I have only two. 'Action' and 'Cut.' Let me fucking say them!"

One thing for certain: Even when actors are maddening, entitled, or reactive, you have no choice but to love them. They're ripping their hearts out and showing them to the world while you sit behind the camera sipping a Starbucks. Even if you hate them, you can't kill them. Because then you'd have to recast.

The best actors are a director's dream. They shower love upon cast and crew alike and make your most ordinary writing look spontaneous and original, often investing a scene with a depth of subtext you hadn't imagined. With a single look or gesture they can tell an entire story. I've already name-checked many I've been lucky to work with, but there have been many more—Jeff Perry, Peter Sarsgaard, Michael Stuhlbarg, Tim Guinee, Lance Reddick, Regina Taylor, to name but a few—all hugely talented and paragons of professionalism. But even those I love occasionally drive me to distraction.

"WHERE THE HELL IS DENZEL??? We're losing the light! What do you mean he's having his hair cut? He has a military buzz! And what could Meg's hairdresser possibly be doing in there with her? She's wearing a helmet in the scene!"

A movie crew believes in summary judgment. To them it's binary: when actors treat them like human beings, they will throw themselves in front of a speeding bus for them, but when an actor commits the unpardonable sin of treating them like the hired help, they're dead meat. When I made my student film, I was thrilled a talented professional actor had agreed to act in it. I was less thrilled when he made my life a living hell. He had trained at the Actors Studio in the fifties and while all his former classmates had become stars, he had languished in bad episodic television. He took his revenge on the world by upbraiding me for everything I didn't know, which was everything. Years later he finally got his big break on a hit show that happened to shoot on an adjacent soundstage to *thirtysomething*. I wasn't surprised to hear from its producers that for all his success he had never rid himself of his towering rage. He was brutal to the writers, dismissive of the directors, and abusive to the crew. They hated him. In the third season, he developed lung cancer and the crew felt terrible. They knew that after treatment he would come back to work a changed man. But when he returned the following season, he was even nastier. They created a pool and took over/under bets on when he'd die. A horrible story. But true.

Some actors just can't help themselves. When I heard Shia LaBeouf wanted to play the lead in my 2018 film *Trial by Fire*, I was wary. I'd heard all the stories and watched clips of his antics on YouTube. Yet, when we met I found him to be thoughtful, self-abnegating, and the soul of sobriety. There was no question about his ability as an actor and he was dead right for the part. So, I closed my eyes, crossed my fingers, spun around three times, spit in my palms for luck, and cast him. Weeks after we made his deal and began preproduction, he sent me an over-ripe letter in the form of a free-verse poem, a small portion of which I excerpt here:

> ed, i swear on my mothers eyes
> i can get there
> don't think I don't dream of this at night
> i'm a different breed
> know this
> the closest to the T
> Truth
> it's in me
> i promise

Two weeks later I got a call from his agent. Shia was out of the movie. I asked why. The agent wasn't at all embarrassed. Just Shia being Shia, who, incidentally, hasn't spoken to me to this day, let alone written me another poem.

"I'm sorry," said the scorpion. "It's my nature."

My relationship with actors is a long-running joke in my marriage. I try to tell Liberty it has nothing to with my father and she just pats me on the head and reminds me to take out the garbage. So what if I am forever seeking the love of an elusive, narcissistic parent? My job is to transfer my fascination with these seductive shiny objects to the screen. How else can I be expected to transcend the cognitive dissonance between what I know and what I imagine? My job is to ignore their foibles and eccentricities and give over to those singular gifts for which we've come to love them.

Which brings me to the force of nature that is Tom Cruise.

CHAPTER THIRTEEN

Gaijin

The Last Samurai, 2003

I was ten years old when I first saw *Lawrence of Arabia*. Like so many filmmakers of my generation, it remains one of the films most responsible for my love of movies. Despite having since read academic studies of T. E. Lawrence and the Arab Revolt of 1916–18 that contradict some of the episodes in the movie, there remains its bold narrative, and a desire to speculate on a man's place in history that elevates it over so many would-be epics. This isn't to downplay David Lean's direction or the performances without which it surely would have remained earth-bound, but its telling offers something more than staging and scale; in addition to thousands of extras, gigantic set pieces, and huge battle scenes, it understands what makes a story epic is an appreciation of *time*, an unflinching portrayal of its central characters, and a willingness to explore a theme that distinguishes an epic from a pageant. Consider the difference between Stanley Kubrick's *Spartacus* and Mervyn LeRoy's *Quo Vadis*, and you'll get the idea.

Several of my movies had been of significant scale in a historical context, and many had war at their center. Of course, this had been the stock and trade of every dramatist from Homer to Tolstoy to Shakespeare—not to put myself in their company. Still, it's no surprise that while trolling my shelves for movie ideas, and coming upon a wonderful book about the Satsuma Rebellion in late nineteenth-century Japan—*The Nobility of Failure* by Ivan Morris—I thought there might be a film about a Westerner's entrée into what had essentially been a society all but closed to the rest of the world. When further research unearthed several Western military and trade missions to Japan at the time, and especially after learning about Saigō Takamori—known as "the Last Samurai"—and his principled resistance to the coming of Western ways, I believed I'd hit upon my next movie.

For several years John Logan and I had been wanting to work together. Well-known in years to come as the writer of so many movies, TV shows, and plays (*Gladiator*, *Skyfall*, *Penny Dreadful*, *Moulin Rouge*, among others), John was at that time still relatively new to the business. I had admired one of his first scripts, an HBO movie about the creation of *Citizen Kane* called *RKO 281*, and written him a mash note. Thus began a few years of correspondence in which we searched for something to do together. John sent me a book about Upton Sinclair's ill-fated race for governor of California, and I sent him one about William "Big Bill" Haywood and the Montana mining wars that had been the background to Dashiell Hammett's *Red Harvest*. When I sent him my research about the Tokugawa shogunate, the end of the samurai era, and the modernization of Japan, he let me know we'd hit pay dirt. When John and I met with Lorenzo di Bonaventura, then president of production at Warner Bros., it took only a half-hour pitch before he agreed to hire John to write a draft.

The work with John was as entertaining as it was productive. Our only problem was a tendency to digress into all sorts of unrelated topics. Suddenly we'd realize an hour had gone by and we'd accomplished nothing. Like me, John identified with his early years in Chicago. His first play had been about Leopold and Loeb, an infamous local murder case that had fascinated me growing up (and had inspired Hitchcock's *Rope*). We also shared a love of 1950s modern art; he would later win a Tony for his play, *Red*, about Mark Rothko. John was a bit of a changeling. Knowing at a young age that he was gay, it was initially hard for him to reconcile that with his passion for such unexpected interests as the NFL and monster movies. When I asked him why monster movies, I was moved when he explained feeling kinship with the monsters. He described being in NYC, walking around Christopher Street, which at the time was a forbidden, scary place, and realizing he belonged there, that accepting something that made him feel alien and monstrous to some people ultimately made him unique and empowered him as a writer.

After many long afternoons and voluminous faxes—John was a late adopter of computers and email, preferring to work on a battered Remington—he sent me his first draft. It was full of gorgeous work but still felt uncooked. John didn't disagree, but he had taken time off from another project to squeeze it in and the writing had taken him much longer than he had planned. Now he was committed to return to work on the other movie. Rather than wait I decided to send it to Tom Cruise, hoping he'd recognize its quality and join me in developing it further. He passed. I realized too late I had been rash to send what I knew wasn't yet the best version of the film I had in mind, but I had been too excited for its prospects to do what was necessary. I did receive a call from Russell Crowe saying he was interested in the role of Katsumoto—the film's Japanese lead. The mind reels.

It was Christmas, and there was no chance to begin the arduous process of looking for another writer, let alone persuade the studio to pay for one. I was vacationing with my family in our little cabin in Crested Butte. I have a writing room above the garage stuffed with old western artifacts I've accumulated: branding irons, rusted tools, rusted-out rifles, antique snowshoes with leather bindings. The walls are covered with faded postcards of miners, saloons, whores, and coffins of dead outlaws, their open caskets standing upright in front of the town hall with a misspelled handwritten sign hung around their necks reading, "MURDRERS." Every afternoon, thawing out after a day trying to keep up skiing with my kids, I'd huddle in front of a potbelly stove, trying to diagnose what the script was lacking. I had no plan. But there was something about the crackling fire, the dust motes in the late-day sun, the smell of pine sap, gun oil, and cracked leather that lulled me into a kind of reverie.

I found myself staring at a framed daguerreotype of a trooper of the 7th Cavalry—Custer's old regiment—and for the first time I could see our protagonist,

Nathan Algren, clearly. In earlier drafts he'd been somewhat opaque. Yet by imagining the words of his journal, written in the clipped, unemotional, observational tone he'd learned at West Point, it was as if he came alive, became knowable. Here was a way of seeing an enormous canvas of political chaos and cultural upheaval through the subjective lens of a soul-sick hero. Algren would narrate the story objectively, without prejudice, as he had been trained. Even as he grows emotionally attached to the samurai he has been told are his enemy, the detachment of his voice would never falter—until, at last, he is forced to acknowledge how he has changed and come to prize their culture and philosophy. I wrote every afternoon and often late into the night. Two weeks later, upon returning to L.A., I called Lorenzo di Bonaventura and told him I was delivering a new draft. I had done it on spec. If he didn't respond to it, he didn't have to pay me. But if he responded, I wanted him to join me in sending it to Tom Cruise again—along with a note I had written to accompany it. Tom read it a week later and said he wanted to meet.

It's hard to exaggerate the rarity of a movie star reading a submission more than once. It's rare enough for one to read a script all the way through. I met with Tom in a house he was renting in Beverly Hills. To this day, he claims I was so excited about the movie I was jumping around the living room as I demonstrated the few sword kata I had learned in my reading. I know I brought along all sorts of research: nineteenth-century tinted photographs of samurai in full armor, enchanting Japanese prints of village life, snippets of cavalry officers' diaries. It's possible I even brought him a replica of a katana (a samurai sword), shameless as it sounds.

We plunged into a conversation about the script; he was full of ideas, challenging parts of the story, embellishing others. He wanted to discuss what he would need to learn: Zen and the way of the warrior, Japanese customs, the tea ceremony, ephemera, and the notion of a good death. It was my first glimpse into why Tom's career has not just had commercial success but also such remarkable longevity. As an ardent student of movies, he would watch at least one a night. This has given him a kind of second sight, the ability to see a movie from the audience's point of view, know what they're thinking and feeling, whether they're ahead of the plot, how to understand and toy with their expectations. It's the opposite of the pseudo-intellectual approach that has sometimes gotten in my way. Tom has what I've often seen in other stars: a "stomach brain." Something either tastes right to him or it doesn't, and he trusts those instincts utterly.

What most struck me after I got to know him was his insatiable appetite to keep improving. After his breakout performance in *Risky Business*, rather than place himself alone above the title, he turned his movies into opportunities for a kind of paid apprenticeship, playing opposite Paul Newman, Dustin Hoffman, and Robert Duvall, and being directed by such masters as Ridley Scott, Oliver Stone, Martin Scorsese, and Barry Levinson. (In later years that list would grow to include Steven Spielberg, Paul Thomas Anderson, Cameron Crowe, and Stanley Kubrick.) Our conversation lasted for hours. Eventually I realized it was getting dark and I worried I had overstayed my welcome, but Tom seemed game to keep going. I told him I had to get home and stood to leave. With the force of the wrestler he had been in high school, he grabbed me by the shoulders and with inimitable intensity said, "We're going to make a movie!"

Until this moment in my career, getting a movie made had been a war of attrition. The subjects that interested me never seemed to fall neatly into a category that was easy for executives to understand, by which I mean, to sell. I'd come to expect a kind of siege mentality—haranguing, shaming, whining, bullying, and generally making myself so annoying that I occasionally managed to wear them down until they gave me a start date. Such difficult births are quite common in the business. Every year during the orgy of self-congratulations we immodestly call "awards season," you can count on someone in a tuxedo giving a tearful acceptance speech citing the decades of rejection that preceded such a halcyon moment.

So much of Hollywood studio culture is fear-based: executives afraid that the wrong decision could cost them their jobs. I was accustomed to a gradual and sometimes grudging process of acceptance, often taking several weeks of dailies, or a first cut, sometimes even a successful preview for them to get excited about what they had on their hands. The reasons a studio decides to make a film are often quite obscure unless we're talking about a superhero movie or big IP (intellectual property). On such corporate crusades, long before a single frame is filmed, a legion of marketers, accountants, and distributors have already run the numbers on its profit and loss profile, a release date has been set, and an advertising campaign is underway. But the path of a "one-off" (that's what they now call regular movies) as it struggles to swim against the mainstream is littered with revised drafts and broken hearts. Deliberately or not, a studio will do anything it can to make a script more "accessible." One thing you learn, when they call it a "passion project," you know you're in trouble.

The Last Samurai was an entirely different experience: the only time it felt like a studio was genuinely enthusiastic about what I had in mind. The movie had a green light from the moment Tom said yes. It was like the no-bid, cost-plus contracts I'd heard about between military contractors and the Defense Department. A million dollars of R&D to scout locations, hire department heads and figure out logistics? No problem. A trip to Japan to do research and meet actors? Let us make the reservations for you! You want to shoot on three continents? Great idea! Within weeks we were in headlong prep. My first trip to Japan was overwhelming; I visited museums, met historians, and traveled all over the country. There was so much I didn't know, and even more that we'd gotten wrong in the script. Since at least a third of the movie would be in Japanese, I needed help with the dialogue. The great screenwriter Yô Takeyama agreed to join me.

Vickie Thomas (the casting director whose impeccable taste I've come to rely on for twenty years) had arranged for me to meet Yôko Narahashi in Tokyo. Yôko's ostensible role would be to help cast the movie, but it was soon clear she would be much more to me than a casting director. Bicultural and brilliant—her father had been the Japanese ambassador to Sweden—she was also a theater director and a teacher with her own acting school. In addition to serving as my translator and interlocutor, her insights into the nuances of culture and behavior, on set and off, saved me from innumerable gaffs, while her intimate knowledge of her country's unusual casting traditions was a godsend. Like many institutions in Japan, casting was often hierarchical. To play a part like Katsumoto, starring opposite Tom Cruise, it was assumed that Hiroyuki Sanada—often referred to as the "Tom Cruise of Japan"—would be cast in the role. But upon meeting Ken Watanabe, I was so taken with his unusual blend of strength, humor, and emotional availability that I decided to cast him.

Upon hearing of my choice of Ken, the Japanese representatives from Warner Bros. made no secret of their displeasure. They informed the executives back in Burbank that this was a terrible faux pas. It was Hiroyuki Sanada himself who came to the rescue. By agreeing to play Ujio, Katsumoto's majordomo, he was making a strong statement in support of Ken and the movie. I couldn't have known that after surviving a battle with leukemia years before, Ken had found himself in debt to shady managers; at that time, the Yakuza was heavily involved in the business. To pay them off, for several years he had been obliged to play whatever roles on Japanese TV came his way, no matter how uninspiring, and it had hurt his career. In our early rehearsals, Ken seemed somewhat tentative, but Sanada's deference never failed to endow his presence with the necessary aplomb. Day by day as his self-confidence grew, so did Ken's performance. By the time we were ready to shoot, he had grown into the role, owning not just his size as the character, but as a leading man going mano a mano with the biggest movie star in the world.

While reading a book about the Meiji dynasty I had seen a picture of an ancient monastery and asked if we could visit it. It turned out that the seven-hundred-year-old Buddhist compound was located atop a mountain outside Himeji, a midsized city. To reach it required taking a rickety funicular. But once there, walking the hand-hewn floors through temples shrouded in clouds was like being cast back in time. When I told the Warner physical production people I wanted to use it as Katsumoto's home, I expected to be laughed out of their office. But I had forgotten this was a Tom Cruise movie. They figured out a way to make it work. There were just as many things I would have liked to shoot in Japan that proved too costly; there simply wasn't the kind of open space and vistas we needed to stand in for the pastoral splendor of nineteenth-century Japan. I had been to New Zealand once before with my wife and kids for a backpacking trip on the Routeburn Track, a three-day trek through alpine meadows, emerald-green tarns, prehistoric ferns, and spectacular vistas. It was a north-south mountain range, as was Japan's. Lily Kilvert, John Toll, and I spent weeks flying up and down the North and South Islands in a helicopter ordinarily reserved for the prime minister (a Tom Cruise movie, remember?) until we found a pristine valley in which to build Katsumoto's village. There, Lily would bring Japanese carpenters to build the houses in the traditional *sashimono* style of wood joinery without nails. She also began planting rice paddies that wouldn't be shot until the following spring.

Back in L.A., it was a cold, rainy winter. One wet evening, Marshall and I were scheduled to meet with Tom about the script. In addition to helping me produce the movie, Marshall had joined me in the rewrite—not only because the burdens of preproduction were beginning to overwhelm me, but because, much as I hated to admit it, I knew his unique gift would bring the script to the next level. Also, because he insisted. He has a great love of the epic form, and his ideas and criticisms, however painful to hear, were brilliant. Tom quickly recognized Marshall's ear for dialogue as well as his gift for sly humor and began to rely on him. This became something I depended on more and more as the demands of shooting drew closer.

After Marshall and I finished another draft, I got a call from Robert Towne's assistant asking if I was available to meet. I knew that Towne—one of the few living writers in my personal pantheon—had an informal arrangement with Tom whereby he sometimes quietly rewrote his movies. I drove over to his house in the Pacific Palisades, harboring more than a little dread. Had Tom asked him to rewrite us? It turned out Towne didn't want to talk about the script, except to point out several things he'd enjoyed. Apparently, he just wanted to take my measure. Still, as we spent a pleasant couple of hours talking about John Fante novels, it did feel like he was giving me his blessing.

That night, Marshall and I arrived at Tom's house for a meeting and were told he was down at the tennis court. We followed a winding path through the fog toward the sound of strange percussive whacks, each accompanied by loud, guttural cries. Below us, we could barely make out five spectral figures hacking at each other with wooden swords. Though principal photography was still six months away, Tom was already working out every day, determined to do the scene where Algren takes on four assailants in a single take without a cut, *chanbara* style, as in the old samurai movies. No stuntman was going to play his part.

There was one stunt we knew would be too dangerous. The moment the samurai are first revealed, emerging on horseback out of the misty forest, needed to be violent and terrifying. As we had written it, Algren, a former cavalry officer, draws his saber and fights while on horseback. As the conclusion of the sequence, Marshall and I had imagined him getting T-boned—his horse deliberately struck by another horseman, with Algren knocked to the ground and his horse falling on top of him. There was no way to do the stunt with Tom on a real horse, where the slightest wrong movement could put his head in the path of a swinging metal sword, nor could we really have one horse hit another, let alone have Tom's horse fall on top of him. So how to do it?

These days it would all be done with CG, but that was still years away. To shoot it in cuts using a stuntman would inevitably look staged and give the gag away. It was Paul Lombardi, our special effects guru, who suggested building an animatronic horse. It took months of experimentation, repeated failure, and re-imagination, but six months and a million dollars later, Tom Cruise is fighting on horseback in the middle of a melee, or so it appears, and the real Tom Cruise has a live horse falling on him. I've never counted how many seconds of the fake horse—Wilbur, as he affectionately came to be known—are in the final cut, and I defy anyone to identify him without going frame by frame. All I know is they're the most expensive frames of any film I've ever shot.

Our first day of shooting was in the Buddhist monastery. Riding up the funicular at dawn, we were enveloped by clouds. Moments later we broke through to be confronted with what looked for all the world like a cliché—the perfectly round, bright-red sun of the Nippon flag rising over distant mountains and setting the ancient temples aglow. Soon after, the entire crew gathered under the gaze of a fourteen-foot-high Buddha. Surrounded by hundreds of lit candles and dizzying incense, we accepted the monks' blessings of good luck for the film. At lunch they even made us seasonal bento boxes of sashimi adorned with colorful fall leaves. It was as magical a time as I've ever had on set.

After lunch we were to shoot the first scenes to be performed entirely in Japanese. I'll admit to being a bit nervous, yet as soon as the actors began to speak, I realized that although I couldn't understand the words, their intentions were perfectly clear. At first, I'd confer with Yôko after every take. Did their performances seem natural? Were their line readings correct? If I had an adjustment, she would communicate it to the actors. But after a while, I began to allow my instincts to guide me. These were scenes we'd written ourselves, after all, so it made sense I might be able to follow along with its beats and rhythms. It was, I suppose, what directing silent films must have been like. Most surprising was how many times I'd see Yôko nod her head after I said I preferred a particular take. Remarkably, it was often her favorite as well. I was especially pleased as Ken's sense of humor began to inform his performance. Over the course of a taxing shoot, that quality would prove to be a saving grace. He is one of the most delightful, soulful men I've ever met.

We shot in Japan for two weeks, mostly in Kyoto. After we wrapped on the last night, Sanada took Ken, Marshall, Yôko, and me to his favorite karaoke bar. I walked in expecting something glitzy and high end. It was just the opposite. No bigger than a ship's stateroom, there were only five seats at the bar, and Sanada had reserved the place just for us. It's possible he knew just how boisterous we would get. When Sanada entered, I thought the bartender was going to faint. It turned out, in addition to Yôko's many talents, she was also a songwriter whose tunes were there on the jukebox. Ken turned out to have a spectacular voice and loved to sing American pop standards. (He would go on to be nominated for a Tony for his performance in *The King and I*.) One of my favorite memories of all time is seeing Marshall, a nondrinker, shit-faced for the first time in our long friendship, clutching the mic and crooning "Danny Boy" at the top of his voice in a rich basso profundo.

We flew back to L.A. for the second leg of our worldwide production. It's hard to describe my wonder and delight as I walked onto the Burbank lot and found the famous New York Street completely transformed into Tokyo, 1876.

1975. Winnetka, Illinois. Home from Paris to visit my mom. Funny how much you can tell about a relationship from a single picture.

Courtesy of the author

Early days at AFI with Marshall Herskovitz. "I couldn't risk becoming your enemy, so I became your friend."

American Film Institute © 1976. Courtesy of American Film Institute

Melanie Griffith was nineteen when she acted in my AFI student film. I was twenty-two. She had already worked with Arthur Penn. I was still trying to figure out where to put the camera.

Courtesy of the author

Special Bulletin was an improbable notion that changed our careers and our lives. It was political, experimental, and provocative. We never thought it could get made. Its success encouraged us to keep reaching.

"You know the problem with you, Danny? Your *face!*" By demonstrating his talents as a comic straight man to Jim Belushi in *About Last Night*, Rob Lowe saved himself from a lifetime of playing pretty boys.

Rob and Demi seemed unusually comfortable and unabashed in their bedroom scenes. Only later did I learn they'd hooked up years before. The director is always the last to know.

When *thirtysomething* won the Emmy for Outstanding Drama Series over *LA Law* in our first season, it so enraged Steven Bochco that he never spoke to me again.

*Javier Mendoza, Herald Examiner Collection/
Los Angeles Public Library*

In the *thirtysomething* offices with Liberty Godshall, my wife and a prized member of the writing staff. Here, she's suggesting I know nothing about women and need to rewrite the whole episode. I am pretending to laugh.

Courtesy of the author

Our first, last, and only cast and writers' party, May 1991. Lots of tears and fears. We were ready for it to end but couldn't have known how lucky we had been.

Courtesy of the author

Had I not done *About Last Night* and *thirtysomething*, I never could have made *Glory*. It wasn't just gaining experience as a director, it was watching everybody else's extraordinary work and stealing from it shamelessly.

Denzel, Morgan, Andre, and Jihmi were in a state of rapture. They were hearing music I couldn't imagine. The best I could do was humble myself and serve the story as best I could.

Some actors have an innate moral authority. They are incapable of doing anything inauthentic. To have two such actors in a scene was spellbinding. I was often so mesmerized I forgot to say "cut."

When *Glory* began prep, the studio was led to believe we were making a little movie. Each week they watched in horror as it grew in scale. Yet they never said, no. Then again, they never quite said yes, either.

In the movie, after Col. Shaw dies, Trip picks up the flag before he too is killed. In truth, it was Sgt. William Carney, seriously wounded, who carried it back to the Union lines, and was the first Black man awarded the Medal of Honor.

Ed Solomon and I working on a scene from *Leaving Normal*. We had a great time. The cast was stellar. Alaska was amazing. Everyone got along. If only anyone had gone to see the movie.

Directing the ensemble in *Legends of the Fall* brought its unique challenges. The four leads came from such diverse backgrounds and training, at times I felt like an interpreter at the UN, except I was translating English to English.

It's not enough that a movie star be handsome, and it's not just the way light and shadow plays on their bone structure. It's something ineffable in their inner life. We don't know what's going on behind their eyes, but we desperately want to.

The saga of the Ludlows is told by the character of One Stab; his dark and bloody tale hurtles forward through the years, choosing behavior over psychological explanation.

My friend, editor, and scourge, Steve Rosenblum, paying a rare visit to the set of *Legends of the Fall*. He prefers the sanctity of his tiny, dark cutting room where he plays rock 'n' roll at earsplitting decibels.

I always found a small role for Liberty's father, Ray. This wasn't to butter up my wife. It's hard to find an older man with the innate dignity to feel comfortable doing a bit part. Plus, he was my lucky charm.

Meg did all the combat training on *Courage Under Fire* alongside Matt, Lou, Tim, and Seth. She bossed them around just as a Huey helicopter crew chief would. She was, however, terrified of flying.

After making several movies together, we hardly had to talk. At the end of a take, I'd step out from behind the camera. Before I could speak, he'd say, "I know, I know . . ."

Roger Deakins' challenge as director of photography? Create the shock and awe of a tank battle in the Iraq desert lit by burning oil wells, rockets, and explosions—in El Paso.

After finishing his first scene with Matt, Denzel took me aside and said, "I gotta get my game on. That kid almost blew me off the screen."

It takes confidence to go toe-to-toe with Denzel, but Annette made a great sparring partner in *The Siege*. Tony Shaloub, an actor's actor, gave a heartbreaking performance as an Arab-American FBI agent.

We shut down the Brooklyn Bridge as hundreds of troops and armored vehicles crossed the river. Productions of this physical scale are increasingly rare. Soon, it will all be CGI and something ineffable will be lost.

Shooting *The Last Samurai* on the steps of a two-thousand-year-old monastery in Himeji. Predictably, Marshall is telling me what's wrong with the script.

Tom sees his movies from the audience's point of view. It's the opposite of the pseudo-intellectual approach that has sometimes gotten in my way. He has a "stomach brain." Something either tastes right or it doesn't, and he trusts those instincts utterly.

Ken had done mostly TV, but I was taken with his strength, humor, and emotional availability. Casting is often hierarchical in Japan, and the local reps were at first unhappy. Once they saw him go mano a mano with the biggest movie star in the world (and later, get nominated for an Oscar), they changed their tune.

I grew up watching *Lawrence of Arabia*. No matter how much I tried, David Lean's direction has never been rivaled in its staging and scale. We did our best to imitate its appreciation of time, its unflinching portrayal of its characters, and its willingness to explore themes that distinguish it from a costume pageant.

Samurai was my second film with John Toll. After winning the Oscar for *Legends of the Fall*, he won another for *Braveheart*. Not one to rest on his laurels, John was even harder on himself than I remembered.

Our first family trip to Africa, January 2000. Liberty and the kids would return often. It was here that the seeds of *Blood Diamond* were sown.

Critics like to talk about chemistry. But what is it really? Good writing, talented actors, and a director serving as host, matchmaker, camp counselor, and group therapist.

Trying to film horrors that happened in real life is wrenching. You want to be truthful but not exploitative, accurate but also captivating. All you have to rely on is the moral clarity of your intentions.

There's a unique feeling of dread on the set when you're about to shoot a dangerous action sequence. No matter how much preparation, no matter how many safety meetings, no one is able to breathe until the shot is in the can.

By the end of shooting, Djimon and Leo were bruised, battered, and worn out. Like two great athletes, they left it all on the field and raised the level of each other's game.

Daniel read the script for *Defiance* overnight and wrote back the next morning to say yes. I later learned his father was among the first British soldiers to enter the concentration camp of Bergen-Belsen.

A prudish attitude in *Love and Other Drugs*, an adult comedy about Viagra, would have been ridiculous. Jake and Annie understood this. Their affection for each other was matched by their good humor.

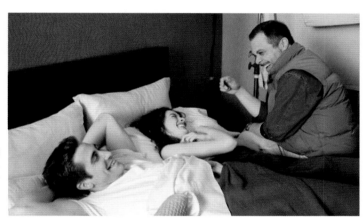

Annie is emotionally available and open. She had done brave, heartbreaking work on more challenging scenes in the film. Yet as the finale approached, I could tell she was anxious.

How to make a thriller about chess? In the case of *Pawn Sacrifice*: Cast Liev Schreiber and Tobey Maguire to star, and get Brad Young to shoot, Steve Rosenblum to cut, James Howard to score. Then add water and stir gently.

I thought I knew all there was to know about directing actors before working with Laura Dern. But her mentoring of Jack O'Connell was revelatory. She deserves to share my director's credit on *Trial by Fire*.

Lily's production design was a marvel: every detail from the live eels to the wood joinery. Same with costume designer Ngila Dickson's hand-painted kimonos and gleaming armor.

On our first day of shooting in Burbank, I happened to glance behind me and see Steven Spielberg. Moments later, David Fincher appeared, and then Cameron Crowe. How coincidental that they'd all "just happened" to be on the lot that day. I would later discover each was courting Tom to be in their movies and this was a chance to get a bit of face time. I will confess to being the tiniest bit self-conscious giving direction with that intimidating trio on my six (as they say in *Top Gun*). But their visit prompted an oddly charming and very revealing reaction from Tom. While Fincher, Crowe, Marshall, and I were chatting behind my chair, the still photographer asked if he could take a picture. Tom must have been with Spielberg at the time, but when he heard about it, he asked for a copy and had himself photoshopped into the shot. Apparently, even movie stars have FOMO.

Courtesy of the author

Shooting went well the first week, and then we hit our first speed bump. It seems the neighboring houses had grown tired of the noise caused by productions shooting deep into the night and had gotten wind that we were planning more late nights by the little pond at the border of the studio known as "Gilligan's Lagoon." That's where we had built a set for Katsumoto's Tokyo home. As a compromise we agreed to shoot split days—from noon until midnight—rather than work all night long.

We had already agreed not to use black powder in the antique rifles—again, because of the noise. The solution by the armorer was to turn the weapons into what essentially were battery-operated toys. When the trigger was pulled, a flash would appear, followed by a puff of smoke. The sound would then be added in post. It sounded swell in theory, but from the outset of shooting Katsumoto's escape we discovered the gag rarely worked, and even when it did, it took far too long to reload for the next take. After only an hour of shooting we were several hours behind.

Going into the second night of filming the sequence, we had lost at least half a day and I was getting worried. How would the studio respond to us falling behind so soon? To executives always ready to panic about the budget, it would augur worse to come. At lunch—in this case, that meant 6 p.m.—I was scheduled to have a meeting with the marketing department. Sweaty and stinking from the pond, I walked into a huge conference room and found it brimming with no less than forty smiling faces. For an hour they regaled me with their plans for the movie's release: billboards, talk shows, magazine covers, trailers, international premieres. I did my best to pay attention while unable to banish the single thought hammering my brain—*We're behind. We're behind. How bad will it be tonight?*

It got worse. A couple of hours later, while still moving at a crawl, I was waiting for a lighting setup that was taking much too long (night lighting setups *always* take too long) and anxiety-mainlining peanut M&M's at the craft services table when Tom ambled up. He greeted me with his usual, peppy "How's it going?!" I wasn't in the mood to respond in kind.

"I don't know," I moaned, "the sequence isn't really working. Those stupid guns are killing us. We're already behind and I'm worried we're going to have to come back and reshoot at least half of it." He listened as I went on. Then he looked off into the night.

"Hmmm . . ."

That was all he said before touching my shoulder and walking away. I stood there, confused. Couldn't he tell I was upset? Had he been in this situation so many times that he just took it in stride? It was then that I began to realize the gulf between my experience and Tom's. No matter how many movies I'd made until then, no matter how many battles I'd had with studios, or times I'd gone over schedule, there was still some part of me that needed to be a good boy.

When I ran into Marshall, I recounted my non-conversation with Tom. Marshall smiled and said, "He knows there's not going to be a card in the credits that says, 'This movie was made on schedule.'" Then he touched my shoulder exactly the way Tom had done and headed back to the set. Later that night, as I was setting up a shot, Cruise was passing by and stopped. "How ya doing, boss?"

"Better," I said.

"Good, GOOD! You know what we get to do tonight?"

"What?"

"MAKE A MOVIE!"

As he walked away, I realized I'd missed the subtext of our earlier interaction. It had been Tom's nonconfrontational way of reminding me I was the director, and that directing was a samurai job. He didn't want to see me shaken. We were going to be shooting for another hundred days. If I was willing to compromise now, I might compromise tomorrow, and that's not the way he rolled.

I called the studio in the morning and told them we needed to reshoot.

They didn't say a word in protest.

A fter New Year's, our huge traveling circus moved to its third continent. New Zealand was a dream. My family and I stole a delirious week in a house by the Tasman Sea before production started up again. The bracing weather changed hourly as storms moved in and out while we explored snowcapped mountains, shadowed glens of dense ferns, and fog-shrouded fjords. My daughter learned to surf, and my son went backpacking. I even had time to remember I was married. Sooner than I would have liked, Kevin de la Noy called to say I needed to come into the production office. Kevin had taken over as line producer once the scope of our ambitions revealed the need for someone of his unique genius. I had first met Kevin fifteen years before when he was the location scout on the first incarnation of *Shakespeare in Love*. In the years since, this English logistics genius had risen to rockstar status: planning the logistics for the climactic battle in *Braveheart*, organizing the beach assault in *Saving Private Ryan*. I could hear in his usually jolly voice that he was beginning to suspect his greatest challenge loomed in the weeks ahead.

There are few Japanese in New Zealand. How then to populate the cities, seaports, and villages we had built? The answer was obvious: bring them over. This would prove harder than it seemed. In addition to auditioning thousands of "fighting extras" so as to find seven hundred with the ability to learn nineteenth-century fighting tactics, rounding up another couple hundred women and children, getting them all the necessary visas, and then leasing the 747s to fly them in, Kevin had to create an entire colony of translators, doctors, and chefs to accommodate them all.

Our base of operations was New Plymouth, a small oil-and-gas town on the North Island. Within a week it looked like an occupying army had taken over. Every laborer with a pickup truck was put to work, every piece of heavy machinery was commandeered. The restaurants and hotels were booming. As the extras came to recognize me as their *meishu* (a classier honorific than "director"), I couldn't walk down the street to buy toothpaste without accepting and returning any number of gracious bows. Not that I minded.

In addition to the Japanese cast I had hired Tony Goldwyn as Colonel Bagley, Algren's former superior officer in the 7th Cavalry, and Billy Connolly as Sergeant Zebulon Gant, in what I liked to think of as the Victor McLaglen role—the gruff, stalwart noncom straight out of a John Ford movie. Tony, a talented director himself, was a joy to be with, on set and off, while Billy was irrepressibly funny in the way I imagined working with Robin Williams must have been. At times I literally had to beg him to stop making us laugh so we could get back to work. Ken Watanabe's commanding performance continued to thrill me while I came to count on Sanada's vast experience in martial arts (known as *Seiten wo Tsuke*, literally "reach beyond the blue sky") to help me stage the many fighting scenes. Koyuki, the actress playing the role of Taka, Algren's reluctant host, was the greatest revelation. Her understanding of period behavior was expressed with exquisite simplicity and elevated every scene.

Working with Tom was joyous, challenging, and exhausting. His energy was intimidating. It may sound surprising, but the one formative experience we had in common was that we both wrestled in high school. Like all wrestlers, we shared a tolerance for hard work and punishment. Tom was in every scene for 120 shooting days, yet he never showed the slightest sign of fatigue, not even after getting the shit kicked out of him by Sanada take after take in the mud and pouring rain. Tom likes to think of himself as being chased by a shark, which he means metaphorically. I hope. His mantra when giving notes is, "How can we ratchet up the pressure on my character?" By which he means, he wants a bigger shark.

He is also legendarily, at times *maddeningly*, self-confident, no matter if it's about doing a dangerous stunt or a six-page dialogue in a single take. But there were times that very self-assurance could look opaque on film. And it was the opposite of what I wanted to see in him when, on the eve of the final battle, he has to say goodbye to Higen, the son of the man he killed. We were to shoot the scene at magic hour, an ineffably beautiful time in the village we'd constructed in New Zealand. Given that Algren knows he probably won't ever see it again, I thought the fading light was appropriate. But it also meant Tom would have time for no more than a single take. This, I thought, gave it a degree of difficulty much higher than the most difficult stunt. If I hoped to get him to the right emotional place, I felt I needed to touch some vulnerable part in him that I'd yet to see him reveal in the movie.

I don't mean to suggest he wasn't completely open to my direction. If I had asked him to do a scene while standing on his head, I'm convinced he would have been willing to try. If I had said, "Listen, Tom, could you be just a tad more emotionally revealing in this scene?" he would have given his all. But the result would have invariably ended up feeling forced—precisely because he was trying to give me what I wanted.

I didn't want him to *try* to make something happen. I wanted it to happen.

While filming their earlier scenes together I had noticed how sweet and attentive Tom had been with the young actor playing Higen. Over the months of getting to know Tom, I'd also observed how close he was to his eight-year-old son, Connor. As the crew scurried to make ready, we were already losing the light. I took Tom aside.

"Tell me about your son," I said.

He looked at me, surprised. I knew Connor had just returned to L.A. and Tom wouldn't be seeing him for a while. For a moment Tom was quiet. And then he began to talk. It doesn't matter what he said in those few short moments in the fading light. I watched as he looked inward, and a window seemed to open and his eyes softened.

"Go," I said, gently nudging him into position on the porch. He nailed the scene with the depth of feeling I had loved in his best performances. I should also mention his Japanese pronunciation was spot-on.

The light was gone. The AD called, "Wrap." As Tom walked past me on his way down the mountain, he caught my eye and mouthed, "Thank you."

Preparing for the final battle scene was the largest challenge most of us had ever faced. Since the film business had long ago rightly outlawed trip wires to make horses fall, and knowing that the ASPCA kept a close watch on film sets to guarantee the proper treatment of animals, one of Kevin's ideas that at first seemed extravagant but later proved ingenious was to hire Alejandro Cobo and his team of Spanish gypsy riders to come to New Zealand six months before shooting, round up a herd of young horses, and teach them how to fall—in fact, to enjoy falling. What these horsemen understood was that young animals were like children at play. Nothing was more fun than to hurl themselves into space toward a soft landing in pits full of mulch and sawdust.

By far the best demonstration of Kevin's logistical brilliance was to figure out how to get the seven hundred dress extras to the set before dawn, through hair and makeup, into armor, onto buses, then to the battlefield, lined up in formation in time for shooting, back to the mess tent for lunch, then out again to work the afternoon, then back again at wrap and into what came to be called "the sausage factory," where it would all happen again in reverse. Kevin's cost-benefit analysis had determined it would be more efficient to hire several additional buses and remove every other row of seats, thus allowing the soldiers, now clad in full armor and carrying weapons, an easier time getting on and off. His time-motion study had concluded this would cut a day's shooting—a savings of $300,000 compared to a few thousand hiring the extra buses.

Kevin once explained to me his "coast of Norway" theory of budgeting. On a typical map, Norway's coastline is approximately 100,000 kilometers long, but on a more detailed map, you can make out twists and turns in the coastline that you couldn't have seen before. Now the coast of Norway is 100,300 kilometers. Once you get a topographical map you see that you must include elevations. It gets worse when you actually try to *walk* the coast and discover the need to build a bridge across a stream or hire a boat to cross a fjord and so on, until the coast of Norway is now thousands of kilometers longer than you first thought. "It's 100,915, second longest in the world!" Kevin would exclaim triumphantly. "Like our budget, it grows every day and I'm the one measuring it!" Until getting to know Kevin, I had never quite understood how the tiny island of England had once ruled the world. After watching him work, I wondered how they'd ever lost the Raj.

The final battle would also prove to be the longest and most complex sequence I had yet faced as a director—especially when you realize it didn't benefit from CG. This meant endless sessions with a storyboard artist, countless meetings with department heads, hours spent planning the fights with our stunt coordinator. But the biggest obstacle was totally unexpected. Midway through production, my back had begun to ache at the end of the day. By the time we reached New Zealand I was having deep sciatic pain from my buttocks all the way down into the toes on my left foot. I had never contemplated the meaning of "a pain in the ass," but once experienced, its miseries were never far from my . . . mind. The production found a physical therapist to work with me, at first at home, and then all through the shooting day. His ministrations would ease the severity for an hour or so, but then the pain would come roaring back. Eventually I couldn't stand upright for more than fifteen minutes at a time. Squatting would alleviate the agony long enough for me to give direction and watch the monitor, but by the last month of shooting I was counting the hours until we wrapped.

But before we could shoot the final battle, we had to fight the battle of the budget. Despite the studio's enthusiasm and largesse, it was never their intention to give us carte blanche, even on a Tom Cruise movie. Kevin was sending thousands of detailed memos back to his bosses at Warner Bros., overwhelming them with their sheer volume, confounding and paralyzing them as costs continued to climb. The danger in making a movie the studio is excited about is that every department can't help but seek a level of execution they've never had the chance to reach before. So, with the best of intentions, it becomes a movie about stunts, or sets, or hair and makeup. Too soon, the perfect becomes the enemy of the good. Marshall called the production people at the studio and said simply, "Let's cut to the chase, the final battle is going to take two weeks more than scheduled and cost several million dollars more than budgeted."

They went nuts, later claiming no one had ever been so arrogant and high-handed. Apparently, they weren't accustomed to people telling them the truth. I was on set while Marshall took the next call, this one from a studio executive who launched into a diatribe filled with accusations of bad faith and betrayal. Rather than acknowledge the difficulty in accomplishing the demands of the script, he attributed the problem to my "appetite," and worse, to Marshall's inability to control me as the producer. It was a mistake few people ever make twice with Marshall. In the quiet, resolute voice I have come to love and fear, he simply said, "Then maybe you'd better find a new director and producer."

We never received another call, and when the same executive visited the set to observe the battle, he showered us with compliments, sucked up to Tom, and was back on a plane for L.A. within thirty-six hours. He then went out of his way to trash Marshall's reputation all over town and try to sabotage our relationship with the president of the studio.

At the moment, however, none of that was our concern. Men, horses, and cannon stood ready. Special effects technicians' fingers hovered over buttons that would set off explosions throughout the battlefield. Eight cameras were rolling. There was nothing left for me to do but say "Action" and watch. Still, I paused for just a second, trying to remember to breathe, to take in the beauty and madness of what we were doing. Two years before, John Logan and I had sat in my office imagining just such a moment.

Tom had insisted on being in the center of the crashing lines. It was a huge risk. Should an overzealous stuntman or a clueless extra make a horrible misstep, he could be seriously injured. That morning at dawn I had stopped by Tom's "pain cave," the trailer where he and Ken worked out in preparation for the action sequences. Tom had worked hard to build a rapport with Ken, knowing the stronger his costar's performance, the better his would be, too. I wanted to make sure Tom knew what he was getting himself into being in the center of the charge. Before I could finish my words of caution, Tom grabbed Ken's shoulder in one hand and mine in the other, and practically shouted in our faces:

"DO YOU KNOW WHAT WE GET TO DO TODAY?!!! Ken yelled back without hesitation: WE GET TO MAKE . . . A . . . MOVIE!"

I couldn't help but grin. Their childlike joy was unalloyed and infectious.

Tom Cruise is a movie star. Also, a complete enigma. This unknowability could also describe many other such celestial creatures I have known. Even as they portray the most extreme emotions on-screen, they tend to be utterly guarded in their personal lives. Is it compensation for an innate fear of revealing their inner lives and thus diminishing the public myth, or are those secret parts just so much less interesting?

The answer didn't much matter. This movie was happening because Tom had given himself to it unconditionally and with abandon. He had helped me realize a dream and I was grateful for it.

I looked down at the verdant field with soldiers, horses, and flags spread out like in the museum dioramas I had studied as a kid, or better still, the toy soldiers I had played with for hours on the floor of my bedroom. At last, I called "Action!"

We shot the battle for two weeks. Every night I would lie in bed, sleepless, trying to devise original ways to stage men killing each other. It was downright ghoulish. Each day in the lunch tent I would cross out another of the hundreds of storyboards displayed for all to study. Tom and Ken had trained for weeks to be able to ride in the final charge. And then it was on! Fifty horses pounding forward! Suddenly Ken's horse stumbled and he was catapulted in the air. Everyone said a silent prayer as he lay there on the ground. You could almost hear the collective sigh of relief when he stood up and began to clown around, laughing and doing a silly happy dance to the delight of the extras. When he was nominated for an Oscar—the first Japanese actor to be so honored—I couldn't help but smile and hope he was doing another happy dance.

At wrap on the last day, I noticed the seven hundred extras marching single file toward the waiting buses. Suddenly overcome with gratitude for all they had done—standing for hours, waiting, in wool uniforms, often without food or water under a hot sun—I impulsively hurried over and reached out to shake hands with the first man in line. Not to be outdone, the person behind him wanted to shake hands too. It took over an hour, all of it in overtime on Warner Bros.' tab, but I shook every hand.

Two days after returning home, I had surgery for foraminal stenosis (in lay terms, an impinged S-4/S-5 nerve). I was up and walking the next day and it's never bothered me again. But as I walked through downtown Santa Monica in the days to come, something felt amiss.

No one was bowing to me.

The Last Samurai was nominated for four Oscars, including Lily Kilvert for art direction, Ngila Dickson for costumes, and Ken Watanabe for best supporting actor. It was my greatest commercial success worldwide. Most gratifying was its embrace in Japan, where it broke all box office records for an American film.

It wasn't *Lawrence of Arabia*, but we tried.

TEN TIPS, TRICKS, AND TIRADES

A writer-director's omnibus

1. **PRIMING THE PUMP**

   Always leave something undone at the end of your writing day. You'll have a running start in the morning. Think about your script in the moments between waking and rising. There's an image in your head, you don't know why. The elves came while you were sleeping.

2. **HOMEWORK**

   Study great scripts not to imitate, but to learn the architecture. Internalize the beats and tropes of genre to understand the audience's expectations and then subvert them. Picasso could paint beautiful portraits before he rearranged the faces.

3. **MAKE IT EASY, Part I**

   Do the actors' work for them. When you play a scene in your head, put yourself inside each character and ask if they're true to themselves or merely serving the plot. Subtext gives them something to play.

4. **MAKE IT EASY, Part II**

   Try recording a conversation when people are unaware, then transcribe it. Real speech is fragmented and redundant. Sentences without subjects, paragraphs full of ellipses. If your dialogue sounds like writing, cut it. Your most clever, articulate lines should be the first to go.

5. **THE STUDIO READ**

   Don't do the art director's job. Long descriptions are for novelists. If the mise-en-scène isn't clear from the dialogue, there's something wrong with the scene. Read an Alvin Sargent script. It's like watching a movie rather than reading one.

6. **YOUR OUTLINE, Part I**

   It's the first thing you create and the first thing you abandon. No matter how much thought you've given to the armature of a story, it's impossible to anticipate how much or how little a scene can accomplish. Your left brain is off the clock, let your right brain be your guide.

7. YOUR OUTLINE, Part II

If you're at a loss for what should happen next, ask yourself, "What would *really* happen?" Certain obligatory beats can enliven your script with a dramatic obstacle. Others are so obvious: try leaving them out and let the ellipses tell the story.

8. FLASHBACKS

Sometimes they're essential, often redundant. If you count on them to understand a character's motivation, there's something wrong with your "present" story. Is the counternarrative intrinsically interesting or a crutch? Can your script work without it?

9. REWRITES #5–10

Ask yourself, "Have I served all the supporting characters equally? Do I love them all?" Write a draft paying special attention to each part in turn. Are their voices unique? Do they have arcs of their own? A script is no better than its weakest character.

10. EXPOSITION

Nothing is more grating than expository dialogue. In life, no one says something to somebody who already knows what they'd say. Jim Brooks is the master. From *Broadcast News*: "I'll meet you at the place near the thing where we went that time." Genius.

CHAPTER FOURTEEN

The Child Is the Jewel

Blood Diamond, 2006

After the success of *The Last Samurai*, Warner Bros. was eager to find another film for me to direct. A script entitled *Okavango* had been in development at the studio for several years when they sent it to me. It was the story of an American mercenary who hears of an extraordinary diamond from an African farmer who has escaped from forced labor in the mines. After a compelling opening, the story devolved into a series of rather ordinary adventure-movie tropes in which the two men overcame all sorts of *Indiana Jones*–like obstacles to steal the diamond and return safely to civilization.

I happened to know a little bit—the operative word being *little*—about the eleven-year-long civil war in Sierra Leone that had finally ended in 2002 and realized there might be an opportunity to rewrite the script to portray an authentic version of its causes and its tragedy. In the guise of an action movie, while exploring an unexpected relationship between the two men from different worlds, I could also shine a light on the depredations of the diamond industry and its role in the exploitation of the third world. I told Alan Horn, then president of the studio, that I'd like to reimagine the project. He gave his blessing, and I rolled up my sleeves.

Having worked as a journalist before becoming a filmmaker, my approach to telling stories based in history or nonfiction has always been to begin doing my own research. To that end, I began to read everything I could about the subject; there was an abundance of brilliant reporting. This led me to several people whose lives had been directly influenced by the conflict.

Meredith Ogilvie-Thompson had worked for many years as an investigative journalist in South Africa. She had also, ironically enough, been married for several years to a member of the De Beers family. There was little about the diamond industry she didn't know (and despise). She walked me, step-by-step, through the circumstances by which De Beers' stranglehold on the market in rough diamonds was complicit in financing the bloody Sierra Leone conflict. With her guidance and by virtue of her connections, I visited mines, read spreadsheets and secret memos, peered at rough stones through microscopes, traveled through four continents to talk to jewelers, dealers, smugglers, politicians, captains of industry, mercenaries, NGO do-gooders, and corporate spin doctors. What I learned was as complex and rife with contradiction as Africa itself: as faceted and mysterious, one might even say, as a diamond—a thing both rare and yet abundant, a beautiful object born of ugliness, something indestructible that has also caused so much destruction.

Throughout my travels I kept hearing about a group called Global Witness. I soon learned it was a campaigning organization based in London that, in its work on the issue of conflict stones, had coined the phrase "blood diamond." Just as important, their tireless efforts to bring together all the stakeholders in the industry had led to the establishment of the Kimberly Process, an international initiative to increase transparency and oversight in the diamond industry, and to eliminate trade in rough diamonds sold by rebel groups to fund conflict against legitimate governments. Charmian Gooch, Patrick Alley, and Simon Taylor—the founders of Global Witness—became invaluable sources of contacts, information, and emotional support.

One day as I journeyed down the rabbit hole of Google, I came upon a link to a documentary called *Cry Freetown*, claiming to include footage of a rebel attack on the capital of Sierra Leone, where some of the worst horrors of the war took place. I entered my credit card information, skeptical about its veracity but eager to find images of things I had heretofore only read about, no matter how ugly and painful. When the VHS tape arrived, I was surprised to find a handwritten note attached. "If this is the same Edward Zwick who made some of my favorite films, please feel free to contact me. I would be happy to help you in any way possible." It was signed, "Sorious Samura."

There are moments in the making of a film when you realize you'd rather be lucky than good. *Blood Diamond* would not have been the same movie had I not encountered Sorious. His help was incalculable, and his personal story was as heroic as any fiction I could write. As a young journalist in Freetown, trapped in the middle of a brutal urban assault in which hundreds died, he had chosen to remain in harm's way. Believing the world needed to know what was happening in his country, he risked death time and again using a cheap video camera to record the horrors that surrounded him. After shooting several hours of material, he stowed away on a cargo ship and illegally entered England only to find the TV networks unwilling to put his material on air because its resolution wasn't up to broadcast standards.

Rather than accept defeat, and lacking a work permit, he took a job as a short-order cook and was paid under the table to earn enough money to buy proper video equipment. He then returned to the war-torn city, again placing himself amid the violence, and filming it even more graphically. He somehow made it back to London and eventually managed to have it broadcast on CNN. For his efforts he was awarded a BAFTA, an Emmy, and a Peabody. Sorious's official title on *Blood Diamond* was as a consultant, but to me he was a moral compass and an inspiration.

In Sierra Leone, after eleven years of civil war over control of the diamond fields, in which tens of thousands died or were mutilated and ninety percent of the country's population was made homeless, there was almost no infrastructure left of what was once a lovely, prosperous, and gentle nation. No sewers, few schools, little health care, and only occasional electricity. It had been such fertile ground for the expression of evil, where the human capacity for cruelty was starkly revealed. I heard about a local trying to explain the depredations that had befallen his country. "We tink da devil got loose," he said.

Freetown was a shattered city. Its streets were riddled with craters, walls pockmarked with bullet holes. A campaign worker from Global Witness taught me a lesson he believed to be the one unifying truth about Africa: that throughout the history of the continent, whenever anything of value is found, the locals die in misery, their sons become child soldiers, and their daughters are made into sex slaves. The story had been the same for ivory, rubber, oil, gold, and diamonds. After hundreds of years of slavery and colonization, the global exploitation of its precious resources is the final humiliation. It was obvious there wasn't the infrastructure to support production of a large-scale movie in Sierra Leone, so from there I flew to Maputo, Mozambique.

Leaving the airport, I passed a mural dedicated to the martyrs of the struggle against the colonialist oppressor: Portugal. It featured a raised fist clenching an AK-47, the same weapon found on the Mozambican flag. On the Avenida Karl Marx, car horns seemed to be another way of talking; on the Avenida Mao Tse Tung, people were yelling, their pointing fingers and raised voices punctuated by pats on the back and sudden explosions of laughter. Eventually, things began to blur and strobe as we sped past. Soon my capacity to assimilate it all began to shut down. But the street scene went on and on, block after block. There was simply too much to see.

The crowds pressed too close, the hustlers and hookers and harassing peddlers called incessantly from the sidewalk, and the cripples, beggars, and amputees who lay in wait at every stoplight did not look away no matter how benignly I ignored them or how summarily I refused their entreaties. Even to roll down the window was to admit the smoke of burning garbage mixed with a diesel exhaust so dense it momentarily took my breath away. And so, from the stillness of the car, I observed a little girl digging a hole by the side of the road in which to bury her dead dog. Framed by the tinted windshield, two boys hunted frogs in a storm drain. A teenage boy draped himself over a girl in the pleated skirt and long socks of a high school uniform.

Over the following days, I saw children playing everywhere in what seemed to me to be miserable circumstances. It confounded my preconception of poverty, deprivation, and suffering—until I recalled that the happiness of children is concerned with the miracle of the moment. Life lived in the street—especially when home was a corrugated shack, baked and blistering in the heat—seemed to carry on at all hours. Construction workers took advantage of the early morning hours before the oppressive sun sapped the energy of even the most determined crew. Wherever one man was working, three others stood around and watched. Newsboys hawked the morning papers as traffic crawled to a stop to allow a flock of laughing schoolchildren to cross the street. Street vendors flogged the hand-me-down cultural detritus of forgotten Western fads: faded T-shirts with corporate logos, blue jeans cut unfashionably high at the waist, sports jerseys of long-retired superstars.

At noon, families picnicked in the meager shade of denuded trees on the median strips of broad boulevards cratered by fifteen years of civil war or civic neglect. Five-year-olds took care of infants; ten-year-olds roamed in packs or stood idly by the roadside waiting for something, anything, to happen; teenagers hawked pens, fake gold chains, mass-produced "hand" carvings, and bootleg DVDs. The sidewalk cafés, some no more than huts with hand-painted signs, others with crumbling colonial facades, were boisterous by early afternoon.

The city grew even more alive at night. Boys in secondhand Gap T-shirts chatted up girls in tight halter tops and short skirts. Freed from the swelter of the day, people were more animated, swaying to the Kwaito music that spilled out into the street from the clubs, many of them open and packed, at least on weekends, until dawn. Death and disease hovered over it all. Were it not for the HIV/AIDS awareness ribbons painted on walls and billboards, there would be no evidence of the plague that was said to infect one-in-four. Rather, what I sensed was the opposite: a kind of overt, even ebullient sexuality. Women who learned to walk with forty-pound bags balanced on their heads develop a statuesque carriage. They met your eye directly, their gaze frank and unashamed. Meanwhile, the men on the street lounged in dark doorways, their bodies lean and sinewy, their shirts pasted to their skin, sweat shining on their faces as they called to every woman who passed. How to think of abstinence, as the U.S.-financed AIDS education policy preached, when sex was the only pleasure many could afford?

We left the capital and began scouting locations for where to build the diamond mine. One satanically hot afternoon in a barren, ruined village, as I sought refuge in the shade of a mud-thatched hut, a cluster of children were crowding around calling out, "Sweet . . . ? . . . Sweet?" Then I heard what sounded like singing nearby. Following the voices, I came upon a corrugated lean-to and peered inside. There in the dark, cool shade, a hundred people, white-robed, crowded shoulder to shoulder, were clapping and swaying to a rapturous hymn, literally shouting out the glory of God. It would have seemed absurd had it not been so inspiring. I couldn't decide whether to weep for love or for pity. Everything I saw bespoke of the immanence of life and at the same time its exquisite sadness. It was daunting to take in so much new information, to see so many inexplicable things—I felt overwhelmed by the privilege and overcome by the opportunity. I could only hope that making this movie would have some resonance—if not import, at least a cry in the darkness.

After a scouting day tromping through head-high grassland, we returned to the hotel for dinner. The night was steamy and sweltering yet I had chills. Sweat beaded on my scalp, my throat began to ache. If I was at home, it might have signaled the onset of a cold, or even the flu, but fever has a different significance in Africa. My first thought was malaria. I did the math. The incubatory period for the virus is between ten and fourteen days. We'd only been scouting for a week. Food poisoning, maybe? A common enough occurrence in even the most sanitary Mozambican kitchen.

I called Marshall, forgetting about the time difference, and woke him. A hypochondriac-adjacent, he was always ready for a conversation about illness, his or anyone else's, for that matter. I'm not convinced Marshall has ever read a novel but based on the number of medical journals he reads regularly he could be counted on for the latest remedies as well as the direst in possible outcomes.

Marshall happily ran down the catalogue of diseases I might have caught, warned me to expect imminent, explosive diarrhea, and reassured me that Cipro should take care of it within hours. Months later he came to Africa with an entire suitcase serving as a traveling pharmacy. He stayed for exactly one week, claimed to have acquired an intestinal parasite, and was back in L.A. in time to visit the travel doctor the following afternoon. For what it's worth, he was fine.

That night in my hotel room, there was no gastrointestinal event. Instead at midnight I awakened with night sweats. The sheets were soaked. I took two Advil and fell back into a semi-delirious sleep. At dawn the fever broke again, and I dragged my ass to breakfast feeling as though I'd run a marathon in my dreams. I shrugged off the notion of a brain tumor and concentrated instead on the list of possible maladies: hepatitis A or B, tetanus, typhus, dengue fever—yet I'd had inoculations for all these and more. I remembered an old routine by the Firesign Theatre called "Beat the Reaper," in which a contestant is deliberately infected by an unknown agent and must diagnose his symptoms as they take hold before dying onstage. Somehow it seems less funny now.

We climbed into a van at seven the next morning. Scouting days are brutally long, but I needed to take advantage of every hour of daylight during my time in Mozambique. Hour after hour was spent traveling bumpy roads staring out the window at empty landscapes, and then coming upon a place, unremarkable in every aspect except for the vague memory of having seen a photo of it, taken in different light from a more flattering angle that in no way resembled the spot where I now stood squinting and scratching my head trying to visualize an imagined reality of actors, extras, sets, and costumes. It cast a dark, brooding atmosphere over a day already made tense by an endless litany of calls from the studio, inevitably with bad cell reception, demanding that I focus on cast deals, script issues, and budget crises—when all I wanted was to crawl back into the hotel bed and try to recuperate from the incessant fever and a headache that felt as if I'd been hit by one of those armor-piercing, depleted uranium rounds used in the Iraq War to penetrate a tank's outer shell.

At last, after a couple days of this I was back in the van on the way to the airport for the return flight. The air-conditioning was freezing yet I'd sweated through my shirt again as I cycled between nausea and panic. En route to London, the flight attendant eyed me warily and brought me another blanket. When my teeth began to chatter, the pilot came on the intercom to ask if there was a doctor on the plane. There wasn't. Passengers changed seats to move as far away from me as possible. When we arrived at Heathrow, I was greeted by three men in hazmat suits and taken to a sterile room. There, a jovial tropical diseases doctor lifted my pants leg to examine an angry, swollen lesion, and called out to his nurse, "Darling, come take a look at this . . . *Rickettsia africae*. Isn't it a lovely one?! Haven't seen one this gorgeous in years!"

In other words, African tick-bite fever.

He shot me full of meds and I slept the entire twelve-hour flight to L.A., hallucinating the whole way.

After a couple weeks spent in L.A. struggling with Warner Bros. over the budget, I returned to Africa. Accompanying me was Kevin de la Noy, the line producer whose genius was in no small part responsible for *The Last Samurai*, and Vickie Thomas, the casting director I counted on not just for her taste but also her refusal to settle for anything less than the perfect actor for a role. In addition to finding extraordinary African talent for the supporting parts, her coup was discovering the kids to play the child soldiers. Somewhere in the vast townships of Johannesburg, she located a program in which at-risk adolescents were given the chance to join improvisational acting workshops, not in hope of becoming professional actors, but rather to gain such life skills as communication, anger management, and collaboration. Without those kids' fearlessness in doing some of the things I asked of them, a crucial element of the story would have been lost.

When it came to casting the role of the diamond smuggler Danny Archer, Leonardo DiCaprio was always foremost in my mind, and remained there even as I met with other actors about playing the part. I had never worked with him and was told he would be difficult to pin down, and that his process of deciding what movies to do was arcane and shrouded in mystery. Nothing could have been further from the truth. To my astonishment, one of the most sought-after movie stars in the world also turned out to be the most unpretentious. Once he read the script, we arranged to meet. After he gave me a quick tour of his jaw-dropping collection of movie posters—considered by many to be the finest in the world—we sat in his garden and talked about Danny Archer. Leo's questions were probing and insightful. He didn't commit right away, nor did I expect he would. But at the end of our meeting, he asked if we could meet again. In the interim I gave serious thought to his notes about the character and returned with ideas. He seemed to like what I had come up with and soon said yes; it was as straightforward a process as any I had experienced and working with him was like that from that moment on.

His most defining quality was a dogged determination to have his ideas given real consideration—not necessarily that they be accepted carte blanche, but always discussed at length, sometimes at great length, and sometimes, I'll admit, with a redundancy that made me want to tear my hair out. In the realpolitik of Hollywood, he knew the movie might never have been made without him, and certainly not at the scale or with the means I was being given, yet he never expressed his ideas as anything more than suggestions. It was an intense and intensely gratifying collaboration between actor and director. Invariably, once I understood what he was getting at, and figured out how to express it in the script, his contributions never failed to make the movie better.

Departing from the first-writer's intentions, Marshall and I had reimagined Leo's character from that of a gung-ho American mercenary to an embittered "Rhodesian" (Zimbabwean) ex-soldier. That he believes himself to be as African as the Mende fisherman he treats so badly was central to Leo's interpretation of the part. Crucially, he was unconcerned about making his character unsympathetic to the audience. In fact, he went out of his way to reveal aspects of Archer's vestigial apartheid sensibility: the subtle disparaging phrases and slurs, and the superior tone that evoked a society that had rid itself of a racist policy but not yet eliminated its entrenched culture of racism.

Watching dailies after our first week of shooting, the DP—Eduardo Serra, a lifelong idol of mine—said something about our lead actor that I've never forgotten: "No matter how many bad things he says, or even the cruel things he does, the audience somehow knows there is good inside of Leo," he said. "He is a fallen angel, but he still reaches for the stars."

Is it possible this is the essence of his stardom?

Long before arriving on set, Leo worked for weeks with Tim Monich on perfecting his accent. In addition to breaking down a dialect to its vowels, consonants, and emphases, Tim's technique was to locate several native speakers of the same age and background as the character and put them on tape. Together, he and Leo would discuss which specific person among them best embodied the subtleties of sound and attitude that would define him. Upon arriving in South Africa, where we would shoot the early scenes, Leo took it to the next level—hanging out with real-life versions of his character, drinking Jägermeister with them in seedy bars, soaking up the ambiance, emulating their tics and jargon, even passing as one of them as he assimilated their affect as if he'd served with them in the bush.

Leo was a rock during a grueling shoot. (Years later his work in *The Revenant* would be testament to that same resilience.) Midway through production, just as we were to begin shooting the toughest action sequences, he aggravated a torn hamstring. After each shot, he stepped behind a makeshift curtain, dropped his pants, and a physical therapist did his best to stretch him out and alleviate the pain. He never complained, and we never lost a minute of production time. Each day he just gutted it out.

Like Denzel's, Leo's work was never less than revelatory, and it was a rare moment that I felt the need to impose myself on his process. After working with so many gifted artists, I'd come to be wary of too much direction, especially with genius actors. A menu of ideas can often be confusing and weaken your ability to offer important notes when you have them. Better to say nothing and appear thoughtful than say something inconsequential and reveal you don't know what the hell you're talking about.

With Leo, I soon realized the best gift I could give him was being straight-forward with my thoughts while giving him the illusion of having all the time he needed. Leo's senses were so acute he'd always know if I was worried about the schedule. He'd see me looking at my watch and *tsk*. Even given the late-night calls I was getting from the studio executives worried about budget overages, if I appeared to be more concerned with "making our day" than with doing good work, I risked hampering the spontaneity and ease of his performance. The best thing I ever did while shooting *Blood Diamond* was throw away my watch.

One day as were leaving a tiny village, I saw earth-moving equipment waiting to move in. I asked the location manager what was happening, and he told me someone had arranged for a new well to be dug. When I investigated, I discovered this wasn't the first time Leo had quietly donated the funds to leave a place in better shape than we had found it. Eventually, this was adopted as the studio's policy. In this, and in some many other areas of his life, Leo walks it like he talks it.

When I was first thinking about the part of Solomon Vandy, a poor fisherman caught up in a world beyond his control, I received a call out of the blue from Russell Crowe. "You must cast Djimon Hounsou," he said. "He's majestic!" As generous a gesture as that was, Russell needn't have bothered. I can't recall ever considering anyone else for the role. I'd first admired Djimon's work in *Amistad* and *Gladiator*, and more recently in a lovely, less-known film by Jim Sheridan, called *In America*.

What I couldn't have known is that Djimon lived between two worlds. Born the fifth child to a poor family in Benin that he still supports, as a teenager he'd found his way to Paris where he was discovered by the famous fashion designer Thierry Mugler, and quickly became a top model. Not long after, he began doing music videos, eventually rising to starring roles. His portrayal of Solomon brought to the movie the kind of authenticity and confusion that only someone who had experienced such things could understand. At the same time, his ferocity as a father willing to go to any lengths for the sake of his family was as labile a performance as I had ever seen.

It's not easy stepping into a role opposite one of the biggest stars in the world.

I'd watched Ken Watanabe struggle briefly before rising magnificently to the challenge. But Djimon's unique admixture of innate sweetness leavened by volcanic anger was a formidable match for Leo. They quickly formed a deep bond. Anything less couldn't have created the necessary trust that allowed them to explore the emotional places their scenes required them to go.

To play Maddy Bowen, an investigative journalist, I needed someone who could translate the complicated workings of the diamond industry and have the words sound like second nature. I'd been a fan of Jennifer Connelly's since her work on *Requiem for a Dream* and *House of Sand and Fog*. In addition to her obvious beauty, I'd always sensed a keen intelligence in her performances, and it was clear from the moment we first talked about the role that she could hold her own opposite Leo and Djimon.

Her preparation was intense. Jenny (as she likes to be called) spent time with other journalists who had worked in Africa, even going so far as to begin carrying and shooting on the streets of Manhattan with the same Leica SLR she would later use in the movie. I remember her recounting an eccentric detail that a woman reporter had told her about how she helped keep her sanity while in the bush. "One thing I always carry in my pack," the journalist told her, "is a pair of heels. It reminds me not to forget I'm also a woman."

She is also quite a badass. During a rough stunt in which her car plunges through dense jungle while under fire from rebels' AK-47s, she got so knocked around that she suffered two herniated discs and a concussion—yet insisted on finishing the day's shooting before seeking treatment. But the key to making her character work was the personal passion she invested in scenes that might otherwise have come off as expository. The intensity of her character's desire to get the story had to rival Danny's quest for the diamond and Solomon's desperate search for his lost child.

The scene where Jenny coaxes Leo to tell her the story of his traumatic and violent childhood is a master class in active listening; such a level of concentration is much harder than it appears. Without her avidity, her keen interest in his every word, the moment could easily have become clichéd, or worse, bathetic. Audiences tend not to recognize that listening is a skill, but other actors recognize its irreplaceable value.

Playing opposite an active listener makes both actors better. If you look closely, you can always tell who is really listening and who is just getting ready to say their line.

There's only one instance of even the mildest misbehavior that I can think of when it comes to these three terrific actors, and it's more a testament to their camaraderie than anything else. It seems Leo was currently between gorgeous girlfriends. One morning I walked into the makeup trailer as I often did to discuss the day's work with him. I found him in the chair waiting for his turn and noticed he was paging through a Victoria's Secret catalogue.

"What are you doing?" I asked.

Jenny was in the chair beside him. Without even looking over, she said, "Shopping."

And that's all the dish I've got about the three of them. The boring truth is that it was a joy working with such generous, talented people. Leo and Djimon were both nominated for Oscars. Jenny deserved one too.

B*lood Diamond* was the first film I was to make with composer James Newton Howard, after James Horner's tragic death. The process was so gratifying that we have since gone on to do several more. James is the most unexpected blend of film sense, pop sensibility, and classical instinct. Having begun his professional career as the keyboardist in Elton John's band, he is first and foremost a wonderful musician. (Interestingly, not every composer is, nor needs to be.) James's process is improvisational at first; I treasure the hours I have spent in his studio, sitting quietly, marveling at his capacity to tease out themes. I've also come to expect those moments that he feels stymied and wrung dry. At times I'm the one responsible for his pain. I am at best a half-assed musician. I play guitar badly and piano worse. Having taken a musical theory class or two, I am a composer's staunchest ally and worst nightmare. I have just enough vocabulary to articulate the nature of my problem with a cue, but no ability at all to suggest how to fix it. Fortunately, James has deep reservoirs of patience and after a glass or two of wine and a night's sleep we've never failed to find a solution we both endorse.

At the heart of every story is a sound—something so deep it resonates like a pressure in your chest. It is this feeling that the composer seeks to make heard: to give voice to a movie's inner life, its soul, if such a thing can be said of film. I adore the score to *Blood Diamond*. Somehow James managed to find an idiom that combined the wildness of the journey of the three leads with their deepest inner longings. In the weeks that followed James's initial composing, on a dark dubbing stage, the raw music was married to the film—tweaked and enhanced in the secret depths of the mixing board, until in the end it was as if the score disappeared entirely—so much that the moviegoer in the darkened theater forgets there is any music at all other than in his imagination, and that the only percussion he hears is the beating of his own heart. That's the idea, anyway.

Sydney Pollack came to an early preview and really liked the movie. He had had his own profound experience of Africa and was eager to hear about mine. At lunch a week later, he seemed uncharacteristically subdued. After one of the most enviable careers in town—a streak of award-winning hits that included *The Way We Were, Tootsie,* and *Out of Africa*—he'd made a few in a row that hadn't done well, the latest after a six-year hiatus.

When I first met Sydney, it's possible I saw in him a surrogate father, an older man I admired who honored me in turn for my talent and ambition. He and my father were of the same generation, with more than a passing physical resemblance, and even some similar mannerisms. But as we sat at lunch that day, I realized something had changed in our relationship. We were peers now, both battered, bloodied but unbowed. We talked openly about our lives, our kids, our marriages. We stayed at lunch a long time. By the time we were ready to leave, his spirits had risen considerably. He said he was halfway to persuading Redford to do a great script he was developing. It pleased me that he let me pick up the check.

In the weeks before the movie's release, De Beers spent millions on a PR campaign denouncing the film while heralding the good works they had done in Botswana. Predictably enough, their disinformation neglected to mention the company's appalling role in Sierra Leone's civil war. When De Beer's surrogate, the World Diamond Council, called upon Warner Bros. to add a disclaimer to the film pointing out the many toothless reforms the diamond industry had undertaken, Alan Horn refused to dignify their request and stood by the film. A straightforward good guy, Alan is also quite politically conscious—he has been board chair of the Natural Resources Defense Council for many years.

During the press junket, I was often asked about my political intentions in making the film. Did I believe a Hollywood movie could change things? This is a question I had often asked myself. The answer isn't simple. Films are necessarily reductionist. They take complex subjects and distill them, which often requires oversimplifying them. If you've done your job, the audience takes away a few potent images, in the case of *Blood Diamond*, say, child soldiers holding AK-47s.

The word *infantry* is an ancient word, having evolved from the Latin *infans*, meaning child. The term suggests that children have been forced to do unspeakable things for hundreds of years, yet no one had ever shown it on-screen. I felt there was a way, even in a Hollywood film with flirty dialogue and movie stars, that I could disseminate those images into popular culture. The same was true of characterizing the role of diamonds in a civil war. By describing a situation that was little understood and had never been dramatized, I felt it might engender a dialogue about the exploitation of resources in the third world.

My hope as a Hollywood filmmaker who at times has chosen to dramatize provocative subjects is to reach beyond the natural constituency for such subjects. I'm betting some eighteen-year-old will walk into a multiplex in pursuit of a good movie with great actors, maybe even some action, and be surprised to find himself thinking deeper about something he might never have encountered otherwise. Maybe he'll someday watch a documentary about it, or God help me, read a book.

The old Hollywood adage about calling Western Union if you want to send a message has stuck for a reason. Audiences don't go to the movies to be lectured; if it feels like medicine, or too worthy, they'll turn off. But I believe if a film is genuinely entertaining, if the politics are an organic part of a great story rather than being grafted on with an obvious agenda, you've got a chance to draw them in and give them something extra in the bargain. I can't help but recall what my college English professor called the Spencerian Edict—to teach and delight. Every director knows there's meaning created every time you juxtapose one piece of film with another. It's just a question of how engaging and how subversive it is.

I've made several so-called political films, yet I think some of the television Marshall and I have been involved in is just as radical. In *My So-Called Life* we were honoring what it meant to be a fifteen-year-old girl at a time in the culture when no one was acknowledging their voices. Likewise, *thirtysomething*, which to some seemed to be a show about privileged, whining yuppies, addressed such difficult subjects as ambivalence in marriage, competition in friendships, and the consequences of one's choices. For better and worse, though my films haven't always been entirely successful in addressing what I saw as urgent social and political issues, I suppose you could say what I've wanted is a place at the table.

So, in answer to the question at the press junket, about whether a film can effect change, I say no. But we do what we can with what we have. Change comes slowly; the exact moment of a paradigm shift is often hard to identify. One hundred and fifty-nine years ago in this country a man could own another man. Less than sixty years ago there were still Jim Crow laws. Thirty-five years ago, we thought little of drinking and driving, and it was fine to smoke in restaurants or on airplanes. Consider how much network television brought same-sex couples into people's living rooms, hastening the course of marriage equality. One voice is added to another until it becomes a rising chorus. Sooner or later, it reaches a tipping point and change happens. Václav Havel, a constant inspiration to me, says it better than I ever could.

"Either we have hope with us, or we don't. It is an orientation of the spirit, an orientation of the heart. Hope is definitely not the same thing as optimism. It is not the conviction that something will turn out well, but the certainty that something makes sense, regardless of how it turns out. It is hope, above all, which gives us the strength to live and continually try new things."

———————

Blood Diamond did well at the box office, but it didn't set the world on fire. Soon after its release I had lunch with Alan Horn. "I love this movie," he said. "I'm proud of it and I'm going to hang the poster in my office. But it's the last one of its kind we'll ever make."

"But why?" I asked.

"Because it cost one hundred million dollars to make and the studio only made a forty-million-dollar profit," he said, shrugging. "Our corporate bosses expect us to meet a P and L projection every quarter. It's more profitable for us to lose seventy-five million on one release and then make three hundred fifty million on the next. Those are the multiples we're working in these days. A big movie just for adults can't do that anymore. And forty million doesn't move the needle on our stock price."

What he was trying to tell me, I now realize, was that the business I had longed to be part of since I was a kid, and a career that had surpassed my wildest dreams and expectations, was changing irrevocably. But even then, I couldn't have known just how different it would become, and how quickly it would happen.

I had come to Hollywood to reinvent myself in the image of the great writers and directors I had always admired—of the 1930s and 1940s as much as the 1970s. More than anything, I had wanted to make a certain *kind* of movie, the kind that lit up my boyhood imagination—but until that moment in Alan's office I hadn't realized the time for such a dream was already beginning to fade away.

Given the shrinking studio appetite for grown-up movies, there are never more than a few ambitious projects getting made at any one time. That was true when I made *Blood Diamond*, but has become especially more so in a landscape now dominated by superheroes and the Marvel Universe. The comic book super-hero has taken the place of the complex antihero. In the meantime, new, talented directors are minted every day—at Sundance, Comedy Central, AFI, and on their iPhones. It's like being a gunfighter in the classic westerns I still love. There's always someone younger and faster coming to town.

On television, what I once thought of as a story is now called a "streamer." I don't depreciate serialized storytelling as a form. It worked for Charles Dickens's *Pickwick Papers* in 1836, it worked for William Randolph Hearst with *The Perils of Pauline* in 1914, and God knows, I have had more than my share of success in the various TV series Marshall and I created. But with its insistence on obligatory cliffhangers at the conclusion of each episode, the storytelling in the new age of streaming platforms seems deliberately crafted to create a kind of anxiety artfully designed to induce gorging rather than fulfillment, conversation rather than catharsis, consumption instead of closure. The thoughtful has given way to the marketable, and the complex idea replaced by the fifteen-second TikTok.

When I left Alan's office, I had to assess how important it was to me that the offers kept coming. I wanted to leave a scar on the world even as I needed to pay for my kids' college tuition. It's true that I'd chosen to work with movie stars, but only when I admired their talent and believed them to be right for the part. And the subjects I chose to make movies about had never really been affected by commercial considerations. But the pressure to hold on to one's commercial viability is enormous. To what lengths would I go to keep it? Choose the upbeat ending rather than the downer because it will score better at the preview? Sign on to direct a movie because the idea is based on pre-sold IP and can be marketed in a single sentence to compete with aliens and vampires and impossible missions? I'd long ago become reconciled that I would never reach the heights of those careers I admired. But the alternative would be to aim low and hit the target.

Making a movie carves out a little piece of your soul. You give up home and hearth in exchange for an anonymous hotel room, fourteen-hour days, constant stress, and the unimaginable frustration of trying to be an artist in a process dictated by time and money. It's always been an article of faith with me that it must be worth it, even given the real possibility of colossal failure. Only if my belief in what I'm trying to accomplish is so ridiculously outsized that it can sustain me for two years do I have a chance of holding an audience's interest for two hours. Despite all that, I wasn't ready to give up the good fight.

So, instead of a lucrative offer for a movie about an alien serial killer, I chose to make a personal movie about tough Jews.

TWELVE RUMINATIONS OF A WRITER-DIRECTOR

Practices, precepts, and prescriptions

1. SENDING YOUR SCRIPT

Is it ready? Who should you let read it before you hit Send? Do you want criticism or are you looking for praise? A reader should be able to turn to any page at random and be able to tell whether it's worth his time. Too harsh? Not when your career depends on it.

2. TAKING THEIR NOTES

The great Japanese screenwriter Yô Takeyama has the best advice: "Never say 'no'," he says. Instead say "Interesting note!" Say "Oh! I'll try that!" And most important, always say *"Yes!"* (Then the lower you bow, the less you mean it.)

3. MOVIES VS. TV

The conventional wisdom used to be that movies were told in sequences while television relied on scenes. This was simple economics: a sequence took a long time to shoot and television had shorter schedules. As streaming budgets grow, this is changing. Hallelujah!

4. AN UNSEEN HAND

There's a time in every first draft when you despair. This is a hormonal condition common to all writers. The only remedy is to put it away and take a walk. By morning, you might find it better than you feared. Perhaps the elves came overnight and worked on it. Still, you'll rewrite it.

5. LARCENY

It's axiomatic that good artists borrow and great artists steal. In fact, every artist is a thief; some are just sneakier than others. Just as painters have always learned by imitation, you take what's been tried and put it in your own voice until one day you find you actually have a voice. And then someone steals from you.

6. **IF AT FIRST**

Reshooting doesn't necessarily make a movie better. But it rarely makes it worse. Rewriting, on the other hand, isn't elective surgery. You open up the patient to remove his appendix but before sewing him up discover he needs a heart transplant. It's like pulling a thread on your favorite sweater and the whole sleeve falls off.

7. **STRANGER THAN FICTION**

What does it mean that a film is "based on" true events? Such movies are often judged on how closely they adhere to "the permanent record." But is Oliver Stone a historian? Is Quentin Tarantino? Nope. We are filmmakers who make up stories "about" history.

8. **FACTS ARE THE ENEMIES OF TRUTH**

What happens when historical facts don't conform to the unities of structure? Is it possible to convey the essence without ticking every factual box, or worse, bowdlerizing the truth? All you can do is keep faith with your intents and purposes. *Se non è vero, è ben trovato.*

9. **SENTIMENT VS. SENTIMENTALITY**

Emotion for its own sake is bathos. The actress who talks to her dead husband at his graveside makes our skin crawl, yet the grieving widow who refuses to cry while removing his clothes from their closet makes our eyes well up. Chekhov instructs us that "to move the heart, write more coldly."

10. **EXPOSITION**

The audience is as smart as we are. They're hip to the same tropes we writers depend on and are often way ahead of us. Yet they delight when we foil their expectations. The worst part of a bad movie is when, rather than hearing the characters, we realize we are listening to the studio notes meeting.

11. TRAGEDY

Tragedy is restful. We know life only goes in one direction. When Lear gives away his kingdom, when Macbeth has Banquo killed, when Blanche DuBois loses Belle Reve, the conclusion is foretold. As characters move ineluctably toward an inevitable end, we can't help but identify. We are all tragic heroes.

12. COMEDY

Comedy is anxiety. Fall into a manhole and we end up in the hospital, yet Chaplin avoids them in a whimsical ballet. If a house falls on us, we get crushed, yet Keaton is unaware. We howl as Bowfinger dodges traffic or Ken Pile drops a safe on a dog in *A Fish Called Wanda*. Comedy is tragedy without consequences. Plus laughs.

CHAPTER FIFTEEN

Shadows of Valiant Ancestors

Defiance, 2008

My paternal grandfather Itchky was a tough Jew. I'm named after him; my Hebrew name is Yitzhak. In 1920s Chicago his five brothers ("the Uncles," as they were known in my family), Dovie, Fat, Zus, Zell, and Jules, were "betting commissioners" (read, bookies) for the Capone mob. As a boy I secretly relished my family's unsavory past.

Of course, I had more conventional heroes too. Like my non-Jewish schoolmates I thrilled to World War II accounts like *PT 109*, or those of the leatherneck marines of Guadalcanal. Hidden inside my Hebrew-school texts were typical war comics of the time; Sergeant Rock and Nick Fury were particular favorites. But other tales distinguished my adolescence from that of my gentile friends, stories whispered only when the grown-ups believed me to be out of earshot, accounts of lost relatives and places with unpronounceable names, accompanied often by tears and sighs.

Eventually I came to know the grainy out-of-focus images of hollow-eyed survivors in striped pajamas or corpses piled high in freshly dug pits or saw the documentaries with panning shots of living skeletons clinging to barbed wire. Such grisly iconography of passivity and victimization became, to an adolescent boy, not only a morbid obsession but also a source of shame.

And so, in 1996, before heading off to El Paso to shoot *Courage Under Fire*, I was sitting in Dodger Stadium with my childhood friend Clay Frohman. A veteran screenwriter, he told me about an obituary he'd read in the *New York Times* about a man named Tuvia Bielski, who'd survived the Holocaust by living in the forests of Belarus. He had tracked down a book about him by Nechama Tec called *Defiance* and suggested there was a movie in his story. I groaned, "Not another movie about victims."

"No," he said. "This is a story about Jewish heroes. Like the Maccabees, only better."

He was right. The triumph of the four Bielski brothers, Tuvia, Zus, Asael, and Aron, who fought the Nazis in the deep forests of Belarus and saved twelve hundred lives, was unlike anything I had ever read about that dark time. Rather than passive scapegoats wearing yellow stars, here were fighters in fur *chapkas* (hats) brandishing submachine guns. Instead of helplessness and submission, here were rage and resistance. The uprising in the Warsaw ghetto seemed to stand alone in the popular imagination as the only moment in which organized opposition took root. Yet while pursuing his story, I would learn that the impulse to fight back was in fact everywhere: from the streets of Vilnius to the forests of Bialystok to the concrete slabs of the Sobibor and Treblinka camps, thousands of Jews did whatever they could to resist genocide against overwhelming odds.

More often than not, the heroes of Hollywood cinema are imaginary. Luke Skywalker battles the Galactic Empire, Frodo Baggins duels with the Dark Lord. We have Spider-Man, Batman, and Iron Man, but few ordinary men. Because the closer one looks at real-life heroes, the less they conform to the simple verities Hollywood finds easiest to peddle.

But the Bielski brothers were men of flesh and blood. It was said "they were like blocks of wood," raised wild in the forest. Uneducated, unsophisticated, volatile, sexually predacious, fiercely loyal, at times murderous, at times merciful, they were the least likely of leaders. Yet these flawed men confronted daunting moral decisions: whether to seek vengeance or rescue others, how to re-create a sense of community among those who had lost everything, how to keep faith alive when all evidence was that God had turned away, and gradually, reluctantly even, they rose to the task, discovering in themselves something extraordinary.

Learning of their defiant acts awakened in me something utterly primitive and deeply personal, a wave of awe, humility, and admiration. There was outrage too. Why, I wondered, had I not known these stories when growing up? Could it be that the necessary commemoration of six million dead had eclipsed the stories of those who struggled and survived?

Defiance was a story that needed to be told.

Clay began his research at the Holocaust Memorial Museum in Washington, D.C. Entering the impressive rotunda, he encountered a huge photo of the first American G.I.s to walk through the gates of the Ohrdruf concentration camp. As Clay looked up at the sea of young American faces, he found himself peering at one oddly familiar young soldier wearing little round glasses. He looked closer. It was his father.

Fox 2000 developed our first draft and then summarily passed when we turned it in. Every other studio that read it did the same. Yet Clay and I continued to work on our own, writing draft after draft—ten years in all. They say when the student is ready the teacher will appear; the same can be said of a film, and a movie star.

In 2005, while prepping *Blood Diamond* I was en route to Mozambique on the endless L.A.-to-London flight when chance and circumstance finally favored us. Sitting across from me was Daniel Craig. He was heading home to begin production on his first Bond movie, *Casino Royale*. It's hard to say which of us was more anxious. Dan was being trolled by the London tabloids, enduring taunts as the "Blonde Bond." His work to that point had been as a gifted character actor. He knew other actors' careers had been dwarfed by the role of Bond and wasn't at all sure he had made the right choice. Meanwhile, I was intimidated by the prospect of shooting a big movie in Africa. Also, by being away from home for so long. We shared what we both knew to be our first-world problems, traded email addresses, toasted each other with Ambien, and went to sleep.

Dan and I didn't speak for two years. During that span, Warner Bros. released *Blood Diamond* while Clay and I finished yet another draft of *Defiance*. Reading the new version, it struck me that Daniel would be perfect for the part of Tuvia, the eldest Bielski brother. I took a flyer and sent him the script. He read it in bed the night it arrived and, to my astonishment and delight, wrote back the next day to say yes.

He was moved by the script. I was floored. It was only the first of many times he would astonish me. I later learned that his father, Tim, was among the first British soldiers to enter the concentration camp of Bergen-Belsen. Fittingly, I found this out from Dan's girlfriend, as it was unlike him to talk about himself.

Rather than go the studio route, I decided to look for independent financing. Based on Daniel's apotheosis as the new James Bond, we were able to secure funding from Don Starr and his company, Grosvenor Park.

Once the production was a reality, I began thinking about who could play Zus, the second eldest Bielski brother. I'd loved everything Liev Schreiber had done on Broadway and off, from *Glengarry Glen Ross* to *Macbeth*. His unique blend of skill, size, and raw power seemed perfect. We met for dinner in spring 2007, after one of his performances in Eric Bogosian's *Talk Radio*. An actor's actor whose work in the classical repertory is often considered the finest of his generation, Liev was such an engaging conversationalist that it wasn't until I noticed the waiters putting chairs on the tops of tables that I realized the restaurant was closing. His thoughts on his character were direct, provocative, and funny. That would describe Liev as well. That someone with such facility for language could so convincingly portray Zus, a loutish, casually violent miller's son, is only the surface evidence of his genius.

When, a few years later, I cast him as chess grandmaster Boris Spassky in *Pawn Sacrifice*, a role that demanded he perform scenes entirely in Russian, the Russian actors playing opposite him swore he was a native speaker. He was the perfect implosive foil to Tobey Maguire's opaque, emotionally volatile Bobby Fischer, and his stillness and subtlety of reaction in the close-ups during the matches rivaled the finest silent movie acting since John Barrymore.

To play young Asael Bielski I chose Jamie Bell, who had been marvelous at fourteen in Stephen Daldry's film adaptation of *Billy Elliott*. At twenty-two, like Asael, he was no longer a boy but not yet a grown man. This moment of suspension was precisely the story I wanted to tell about a young man who comes into his own in the harshest of conditions. Daniel, in particular, forged a strong bond with Jamie, taking on the kind of fraternal, protective role an elder brother would have in such circumstances.

George MacKay was only fifteen when I cast him as Aron Bielski, the youngest brother. To my horror, he arrived on set for his first day of shooting with his face swollen by a black eye—having run into a lamppost, or so I was told. Though barely able to see, he insisted he was able to work. I scrambled and wrote in a difficult stunt to justify his condition, which George performed with aplomb. He immediately became a favorite of the actors playing his older brothers, who treated him with exactly the kind of rough good humor you might expect. Whatever we put George through was nothing compared to the beating he was to take eleven years later as the lead in Sam Mendes's extraordinary WWI saga of the lost soldier in *1917*.

We began filming in August 2007 in Lithuania, just across the border from Belarus, where the Bielski brothers had built their hidden camp. Dwarfed by pines so immense and thick the sunlight rarely penetrated, we worked from dawn until dark in the damp, mossy hollows, never growing accustomed to a perpetual half-light so dim that even at midday we needed super-fast lenses to gain enough exposure to shoot. Most mornings a low-hanging fog would rise from nearby bogs, enveloping and chilling us to the bone.

Arriving on the set before first light, hundreds of spectral figures, dress extras clothed in tatters, with blankets wrapped around their heads, would huddle together for warmth. These hollow-eyed men, women, and children were haunting replicas of those who had lived and died on this very ground. They seemed to suggest we were not only presuming to honor the dead but conjuring forth their spirits as well.

Toward the end of the first Friday of shooting, Liev, Clay, and I were standing together in the partisans' camp when one of the extras approached us and asked if they could have a Sabbath kiddush at wrap. He explained they were part of the tiny group of Jews still living in what was once the largest and most vibrant Jewish community in Eastern Europe. It would mean a lot to them, he said, as well as be a blessing for the film.

As it grew dark, craft services provided bread and wine while the special effects team lit oil lanterns. An aged rabbi stepped forward and as he intoned the prayer, I looked over and saw Liev's face, full of feeling in the flickering light. He had told me his research for the movie had allowed him to dig deeper into his Jewish roots and I assumed he was thinking of his own ancestors. I knew Liev's maternal grandfather had emigrated from Ukraine to the U.S.—so it came as no surprise when I heard after Russia invaded that country in 2022 that he was among the first celebrities to work with the World Central Kitchen, cooking 1,984 pounds of brisket to provide a traditional Passover meal for refugees of the war.

To work at northern latitudes is to be acutely aware of winter's approach. By September there was frost on the ground. By mid-October we were knee-deep in snow. By November dawn wasn't until 8 a.m., and the pale sun began to fade by three. Despite our sophisticated outerwear, we were always cold. Yet for three long winters, with subzero temperatures and a mind-numbing wind off the Baltic that brought Hitler's assault on Russia to a frostbitten halt, the Bielski partisans wrapped themselves in skins and rags, braved starvation, and dug burrows into the hillsides, living like moles.

If it can be said a director's job is to create an aura of verisimilitude, then it was as if my work were being helped by an unseen hand. There was no need to instruct the actors to shiver; they were shivering for real. When I once dared compliment Dan—who I don't think ever once took refuge from the cold in his trailer—at the end of a scene, he looked perplexed. "Not hard to act cold when you're freezing your nuts off," he said. In other words, no conversation about Stanislavski was required to communicate a motivation as simple as survival. Whether an actor was digging a trench, peeling a potato, or loading a weapon with frozen fingers, the story was telling itself.

One moment in the film epitomizes Dan the actor and the man. The refugee camp is overrun; the end is near. His character was to give a ringing speech exhorting the Jews not to give up. But what if he is terrified and unable to speak? What if someone else steps up? Movie stars can be . . . uh . . . selfish when someone takes away their words. *It's my fucking scene!* When I suggested to Dan that Jamie might give the speech instead, Dan was quiet for a moment, then simply said, "Right." Later, as he watched Jamie nail it, there were smiling tears in his eyes. Relationships with actors while you're working together can seem as intimate as love affairs. Until they fall in love with their next director, that is. I can't say I got to know Dan well. I only know we spent a Lithuanian winter freezing our nuts off and I love him still.

While looking through the camera on the wintry set, it occurred to me that directing isn't about directing actors at all, it's about directing *myself.* Sometimes, while standing alone in the dark forest, I would drift off, projecting myself into the scene I was filming. Inevitably, as I imagined myself rooting in the frozen ground with a sharpened spoon, or standing sentry in the icy twilight on the lookout for German patrols, I couldn't help but ask myself a single humbling question: How would I have fared in the forest? Would I have dared go into the forest at all?

Directing a film inevitably becomes personal for me. This one, though, felt as if some private boundaries had been breached. The faces of the local extras looked like mine; their bodies were shaped like my body. Even their Eastern European inflections sounded familiar. And when the grown sons of the Bielskis visited the set and sat laughing and crying while telling stories about their parents,

I couldn't help but stare. Because these loud, funny, warm, rough men were utterly recognizable. They reminded me of the Uncles.

During their visit, I suddenly remembered when, for a high school assignment, I had recorded a series of conversations with my other grandfather—my mother's father, an upstanding dress manufacturer—only a year before his death. His narrative of his traumatic flight at age fourteen from Poland included descriptions of the several brothers and sisters who had stayed behind. "All of them lost," he whispered. "All sent to the camps. Except for one, that is. A tough character, that brother, a *vilde chaya*, a brawler. He wanted to fight. He went to the forest. And we never heard from him again."

As I compared a faded photo of my grandfather to those I had collected while researching the film—drawn faces clutching captured weapons in the Belarusian snowscape, staring bravely into the lens—I was struck by the resemblances. It occurred to me that here was yet another uncle in the family mythology. Was the one who had stayed behind the real hero of the bunch?

Defiance was personal to Liev of course, too. Weeks after the Bielskis visited the set, while shooting a scene in which the brothers discover a mass grave, I found Liev standing not far from our re-creation—a ghoulish pit filled with pale, naked bodies. In the cruelest of ironies, Liev had stumbled upon a small concrete plinth, mostly overgrown with weeds, commemorating the slaughter of three thousand Jews in these same woods. As I walked over to stand beside him, I saw his face was wet with tears.

"These were my people," he said.

In November my friend Leon Wieseltier, at that time the literary editor of *The New Republic*, came to visit the set. One night as we stood in ankle-deep snow, I talked about how much these months in the forest had affected me. After a reflective silence he said, "The forest has always been a place of transformation. Think of the lost children in Grimms' fairy tales, or the characters in *Twelfth Night*. And now it has changed you too. Is this perhaps why you made this movie?"

I've had time to consider that question for a while now, asking myself if I knew all along how emotionally involved I would become. The truth is, a director's reasons for making a film often can't be understood until many years after the fact, if indeed they can ever be fully understood. During my time in Hollywood, I've banged heads with more than a few hard-nosed Jews. I've worked with Samuel Z. Arkoff, Ray Stark, and Harvey Weinstein, and while they liked to talk like gangsters, I can't say I ever feared for my life.

I was born far removed from the depredations of the Holocaust. And the odds of my fighting back, had I been there, are overwhelmingly six million to a few thousand against it. Yet I have come to understand that resistance has many faces and continues long after the fighting has stopped. Scholars struggle to preserve history by writing books, archivists create museums to raise consciousness, memoirists bear witness, reopening old wounds in the belief that in pain is the preservation of memory. Keeping faith, it can be said, is yet another form of resistance. Meanwhile songwriters and novelists (and filmmakers too) dramatize events of long ago, believing their art can bring the dead to life, if for only an hour or two in our imagination.

On the last day of filming, as the December forest became a fortress of snow, I stared at a photograph I had pasted onto the inside cover of my script. The fading daguerreotype was taken at Ellis Island and had accompanied my paternal grandfather's application for citizenship (abnegating "all allegiance to the Czar of Russia"). I couldn't help but feel he had been with me all along, and that I had made this film to affirm the connection between my safe, assimilated life and the lives of those hardened, proud relatives of my childhood.

As they had done for so many others, the Bielskis had led me home.

I had been on location in Lithuania when I heard Sydney Pollack was sick. By the time I got back to town and visited him, he was very weak. His illness had come on fast. Only months before he had been making plans for a comeback; he was going to direct *Recount* for HBO. I didn't stay long. He made a good effort to make it seem like a normal conversation, asking how the filming had gone, what was it like working with Daniel Craig—he always wanted to talk about the actors—and I kept the conversation light, making a few jokes about Lithuania in a bad Eastern European accent. I wanted to tell him how important he'd been to me, but when I began, he shook his head and lifted his hand—he didn't want to hear it. Sydney had always hated sentimentality. He was tired, and I didn't want to overstay my welcome. But as I stood to leave, he raised himself against the pillows, leaned forward, and touched my arm. "Enjoy it, kid," he said.

Best advice I ever got.

Four months later, James, Steve Rosenblum, and I flew to England to record the score. We were in Abbey Road Studios—yes, that Abbey Road—waiting to begin the session when James sat down at an old battered upright piano in the corner and began banging out "Martha My Dear." It was on this very piano in this very room that Paul had recorded it. Closing my eyes, it could have been 1968, and I was there with the lads. Later, when Josh Bell, one of the world's foremost violinists, arrived, I was in for yet another musical treat. As he began to play James's score, the power and virtuosity of his solos was overwhelming. It was all there: the loss, the ferocity, the despair, the nobility. Everyone in the booth was weeping. For good reason—James was later nominated for an Oscar for his work.

At an early, private screening of the film back in Los Angeles, Kirk Douglas, ninety-two at the time, put in a surprise appearance. After the credits, with the aid of a walker, he made his way to me through the crowd. His speech had been badly affected by his stroke but his strength as he grabbed me by the shoulders was still impressive. He leaned in and whispered in my ear, "Thaah . . . wahz . . . mahh . . . moovie."

He was right. Had I made it in 1962, Kirk would have been my hands-down first choice to play Tuvia. When I told the story to Daniel Craig, he smiled and nodded. The next morning, I received a hand-delivered note on Kirk's personal stationery that made me cry. In a barely legible scrawl, he had written, "You owe me a night's sleep."

From that moment on, if ever I've been in doubt about writing to someone whose work has moved me, I think about Kirk and send the note. The old pros knew what it was all about.

After a moving premiere at New York's Museum of Jewish Heritage, we took the film to Europe. After almost every screening, no matter the country, an aging Holocaust survivor would come forward and ask if they could describe their experience. Some had been in the forest with the Bielskis, others had hidden in cellars or on local farms. One evening in Israel I felt someone tugging my coat and turned around. I looked down to find a stooped, wizened woman smiling broadly. She drew herself up to her full height of five feet and, in thickly accented English, stated proudly for all to hear, "I blew up the train."

Soon after, I was back in L.A., in a doctor's office having some stitches removed—the result of an embarrassing incident with a kitchen knife. Sitting beside me in the waiting room was another withered, birdlike woman. At first I thought it might be yet another Holocaust survivor, but after a moment I realized it was Nina Foch. "I have an extremely rare blood condition," she explained, as if coolly analyzing the premise of a scene in front of her class. She told me she'd seen *Blood Diamond*, and thought it was strong. "The DiCaprio boy is quite good," she said. "He reminded me of Monty before his accident." (She meant Montgomery Clift. As Nina would have said, "Look it up.")

When the nurse announced it was time for her to see the doctor, she seized my wrist in a surprisingly powerful grip. "You must promise to come talk to the students in my class!" she said with her uniquely intimidating ferocity. "I've been working on several new techniques for young actors."

"Of course," I told her.

She patted my injured hand as she stood. Despite her diminished frame, the years of practicing the Alexander Technique were evident in her proud posture as she walked away. "I'll call you," she said over her shoulder.

The call I received was to inform me of her memorial service. In her eulogy, fighting back tears, Julie Andrews said, "Norma Desmond had nothing on Nina."

CHAPTER SIXTEEN

In Sickness and in Health

Love & Other Drugs, 2010

I was diagnosed with non-Hodgkin's lymphoma on November 12, 2008. On that same day I received a green light from 20th Century Fox to start casting *Love & Other Drugs*. That I might be directing a movie about illness while fighting an illness was an irony that didn't go unnoticed.

A very good script, *Pharma*—written by Charles Randolph—had been sent to me by Leonardo DiCaprio's manager. He told me that Leo liked the script but felt it needed a rewrite, and asked if Marshall and I would be willing to do that with him in mind. Having had such a happy experience with Leo on *Blood Diamond*, Marshall and I read the script and said yes. We liked the idea of seeing him do a behavioral comedy, and we thought the rest of the world would too. It would also be a nice change of pace for me after the epic dramas I'd been making. The TV shows were all relationship-based stories, but not since *About Last Night* had I done a comedy. While still retaining Randolph's biting satire about the pharmaceutical industry, we concentrated on the relationship between Jamie Randall, the Viagra salesman, and Maggie Murdock, the girl with whom he falls in love and discovers is suffering from early onset Parkinson's disease.

After finishing our draft, we sent it to Leo's manager only to learn that Leo had, in fact, never read the earlier script, knew nothing about the project, and no matter how much he might like this one, he was committed to make another movie. Rather than take a hit out on the manager, I sent the script to two actors who I thought would be great.

When I sat down with Jake Gyllenhaal, I saw qualities in him that surprised me: a piercing intellect, an offbeat humor, and a penchant for wild flights of fancy I'd never seen on-screen. Then, seeing him in drag on *Saturday Night Live* singing a falsetto version of "And I Am Telling You" had only confirmed that instinct. By the end of the meeting, he was in. Anne Hathaway was more cautious. She felt her character's capacity for denial and her fear of the future warranted deeper exploration in the script, and that such a depiction would dovetail nicely with the movie's themes of love and death. Marshall and I loved her notes and did a pass on the script focusing on them. Jake, who was an extraordinary ally throughout, helped woo her as well. She read the new version and said yes.

By that time, I was about to start treatment. The cocktail I was to be given was called R-CHOP: an acronym for rituximab, cyclophosphamide, doxorubicin, vincristine, and prednisone. I was to receive an infusion lasting five hours, once every three weeks, for eighteen weeks, at which point I would be scanned to see if the cancer had progressed. The doctors would then give me a prognosis. If all went well, I would be out of treatment in enough time to make a start date on the movie in the spring. If not, well . . . I tried not to think about that.

I took Jake to lunch and let him know what was going on. He didn't hesitate. He said he would do whatever I needed, and that he was committed to me and the movie. Anne's eyes filled with tears when I told her, and she responded in the same way Jake had. It was my turn to cry. I couldn't help glancing around, wondering what the other diners thought was happening at our table. I conspicuously didn't tell the studio. I knew they would panic that I might not be insurable to work. My oncologist, who had been through this before with patients in the movie business, suggested I wait and see if the initial scan, which I would undergo in six weeks, indicated I was responding well to the meds, in which case he could write a letter to the insurance company that might indemnify me.

I began treatment the following week. The first infusion didn't induce many side effects—except the prednisone, that is—a major dose of steroids that revved me up so high that Liberty woke to find me cleaning my closet in the middle of the night. The second treatment kicked my ass and began a catalogue of miseries that would define my life for the next three and a half months. Being sick is like learning a new language for a journey to a foreign country you've never especially wanted to visit. I considered starting a blog entitled *The Daily Indignity* to describe the odyssey. The physical symptoms, although bearable, were mostly garden variety: hair loss, nausea, meds to treat nausea that instead caused constipation, stool softeners, neuropathy, bone pain, and fatigue. At the end of the day, chemotherapy is a very medieval approach, not unlike bloodletting, in which they kill you just a little bit in order to cure you.

As my hair fell out, I decided I needed to wear a wig. It wasn't so much out of vanity as it revealed my fear of having people in the business know I was sick. I couldn't help but recall one of the African ADs on *Blood Diamond* describe what happens when an alpha lion grows weak and is expelled from the pride. As his teeth fall out, he is forced to follow at a distance, surviving on the pre-chewed scraps the younger lions have left behind. I'm a bit appalled at having thought about this rather than, say, my chances of survival. Whether irrational or not, it reveals a deep-seated response to the competition and ageism in Hollywood I had internalized over the years.

Of course, it was also no more and no less than the reckoning with mortality we all face someday, and after a couple of weeks I said fuck it and got a beret. But I was reminded of a popular Tibetan saying: "When a man confronts a leopard on a narrow ledge, there is no way to avoid the situation." My mother was an extremely loving person whose exuberant warmth was leavened by a wicked sense of humor. Whenever I'd complain about something not working out as I had planned, she would invariably respond, "Honey, one thing you can count on in life . . . You're going to get everything that's coming to you."

I'm not sure this is what she was referring to, but it's possible her wit was just mordant enough to include it as a possibility. I gutted out the next months, forcing myself to exercise, sometimes falling asleep in the middle of a meeting, tempering fatalism with aggressive denial, magical thinking with cussed determination.

I've often wondered if cancer changed me as a director. The answer is unequivocally yes, but so did marriage, family, having children, success, failure, and the death of my parents. This isn't to suggest that being sick didn't impact me, quite the contrary, but neither did it define me. And the possibility of making a movie should I manage to survive this crucible was as positive a motivation as any self-help book, therapy, or support group. Of course, I can't possibly leave out the outpouring of love and support I had from my wife and children. So, too, from Marshall and Richard Kramer. Clay Frohman came and watched baseball with me until I'd invariably pass out by the sixth inning, and Bill Broyles, writer of *Apollo 13*, collaborator, and lifelong friend, checked in daily after sending Zuni bear fetishes to watch over me during treatment. My assistant of more years than I care to count, Troy Putney, was a rock. I couldn't have attempted something as foolhardy as prepping a movie without his attentiveness and nurturing.

My first scan had shown remarkable progress with the treatment. This didn't mean I could avoid the full eighteen weeks, but it gave me the strength to endure the remainder with grim determination. By the second scan I was in full remission. Three weeks after finishing chemo I was on the set in Pittsburgh.

Now I had to make a movie.

Many times during treatment while I lay in bed, moaning, I had confronted the thought that I might never get to make another film. Now that I was back at it, each day felt like stolen time. I had never taken such pleasure in the process. Hours scouting in the van? Sure! Endless production meetings? Yes, please. Shooting in the freezing rain? Bring it on.

To be fair, I'd occasionally nod off in my chair while waiting for a lighting setup, and for the first time in countless shooting days I learned where to find my trailer so I could nap at lunch. Pieter Jan Brugge, my friend since film school, a talented director himself and a producer of *Glory, Defiance*, and now *Love & Other Drugs*, never let on just how much he covered for me during those first few weeks. Likewise, Steve Rosenblum, editing with me yet again, went out of his way to let me know when I could skip dailies and get to bed early. Jake and Annie (as she was known to cast and crew), meanwhile, were avid and prepared; rehearsing with them was the highlight of each day.

Jake and I had a very amusing and telling interaction early on. The character of Jamie he was to play was, not to put too fine a point on it . . . a dog. His job as a salesman takes second place to his vocation, which is hitting on women. That wasn't Jake's style at all. Not to say he didn't do just fine with women—at the time he was seeing Reese Witherspoon—but his "game" wasn't overt. Rather, I knew he would downplay his charm and lead with his innate authenticity. My job was to explode all that, along with any inhibitions he might have.

One night while the two of us were at dinner, an attractive girl walked past on her way to the bathroom. I noticed Jake eyeing her.

"Go for it," I said.

"What?"

"Go get her phone number."

"No."

"You want to play this guy? Let's see you do it."

At first he thought I was joking. When he realized I was serious, he tried to protest but I gave him my best O.G. director stare—the kind I've perfected over the years as if to say, *Are you an actor or aren't you?* Grumbling, shaking his head, he headed for the bathroom. Minutes later he reappeared. Initially I couldn't tell by his expression what had happened. But he couldn't hold back his grin for long and he tossed the napkin on the table. On it was scrawled a phone number.

"Now, can I eat my dinner?" he asked.

I'm not suggesting my little real-life improv had an overwhelming effect on his performance, or in real life, for that matter, but he was damn good in those scenes where he's trying to score with Maggie when he first meets her. (Later, while we were in London for the European premiere, he introduced me to his new girl-friend, Taylor Swift. I'm just sayin' . . .)

My process with Annie was quite the opposite. Her comedy chops were never in question. We did our research together, talked to doctors, visited hospitals, and met with several young women in the same situation as her character. Their stories were wonderful, and often counterintuitive. More than one of them talked about how important sex was to them. Sure, there was the endorphin rush and the feeling of how it made them feel young and desirable, but they also made a point of telling us their tremors were always less intense after they had abandoned themselves to lovemaking.

In addition to signing on Hank Azaria, Oliver Platt, and Judy Greer, three of the funniest comic actors in town, as key supporting cast members, I hired Josh Gad for his first movie role as Jamie's wealthy brother, and he crushed it; he made a delightful third wheel to Jamie and Maggie's efforts to be a couple. I went out of my way to make sure Josh and Jake spent time together before shooting; Josh's irrepressible, madcap humor could be counted on to lighten Jake up. He took special pleasure in making fun of the nudity he was about to do. On the last day of shooting, Josh gave me this picture as a wrap gift.

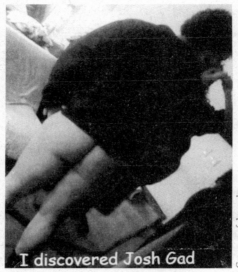

I discovered Josh Gad

Courtesy of the author

In life, sex is impulsive and improvisational. Filmed sex is anything but. The admixture of lights, lenses, modesty, politics, body image, and MPAA ratings—not to mention an audience of even a small crew—resembles a clusterfuck more than it does lovemaking. Everyone dreads a sex scene. The actors worry about being exploited. The director worries about being the exploiter. I'm sure the presence of an intimacy consultant (a new wrinkle I've yet to experience) can help. But only porn stars seem comfortable turning a private act into a public performance. The fact is many people (read, Americans) are uncomfortable watching sex, especially when it's gratuitous.

Sometimes, though, it's just as disingenuous not to include such important behavior in a relationship. Especially in a movie that aspires to being authentic about men and women. So, what to do? Not unlike the depiction of violence, if the scene served the narrative, if it advanced the story, it deserved to be in; if it existed merely to titillate, it was out. The only possible approach was to regard it as just another scene. And make damn sure everyone involved was comfortable with it.

In *thirtysomething*, Ken Olin and Patty Wettig were married in real life. They were married to others on TV and played many bedroom scenes with humor and forbearance. Was such faux Bloomsbury difficult? No. They tended not to watch when the other was shooting. In *Legends of the Fall*, Brad Pitt and Julia Ormand were great platonic friends, yet Julia was wary before they filmed their steamy moments. Once they began shooting, though, she took the lead with remarkable vigor. Brad's greatest concern was having makeup applied to his butt.

A prudish attitude in *Love & Other Drugs*, a comedy about Viagra, would have been ridiculous. Jake and Annie understood this. They were affectionate with each other, and good humored. We had two weeks of rehearsal. It was literally the three of us in a room, playing, talking about the books that moved us, and watching some pretty racy sex scenes from other movies. It was a little awkward at first, but we got over it soon enough. We were professionals looking at work we'd admired that also just happened to turn us on. We looked at *Don't Look Now*, *Sex and Lucia*, and many more. We explored the range of what we liked and what would make Jake look great and Annie look beautiful. We discussed what they were comfortable with and what would be going too far. A scene with Rock Hudson and Doris Day with the covers pulled up to their necks was at one end of the spectrum, Michael Winterbottom's *9 Songs*, where the actors were really having sex, was at the other end.

It was the same process we would have applied to any other scene. In the past, whenever I'd watch a movie about people who were sleeping together, it inevitably pulled me out of the story to see them being so modest in front of each other. She'd have her body covered up to her neck and then you'd have the shot of his bare ass in the walk-to-the-shower shot. What we were going for was an authentic cinematic representation of two people in love, the antithesis of the sex scene in the spy movie where the story pauses and the hero goes to bed with the girl as the camera travels lasciviously over her body and you know she's going to die in the next reel. Instead, I would ask them to consider their characters' experience: "How many times have you made love? What do you do afterward? What does it suggest is happening emotionally if you sit up rather than keep holding each other?" The idea was that issues like nudity and intimacy were secondary to those questions.

After doing everything properly for days on end, disrobing at the last minute, having two wardrobe supervisors standing by to put their robes back on between takes, it soon got boring and the absurdity of all the effort became clear. Every time Annie would put on her robe, it would rub off all her body makeup and it would take twenty minutes to reapply it. Eventually, modesty gave way to comedy as Annie told her wardrobe supervisor in her best cop voice, "Step. Away. From the actors!" Things got even sillier on a day the schedule called for them to be in bed from first shot to wrap while wearing nothing but a strategically placed little chamois "merkin" taped to their nether parts. "Very strong tape, please," Jake called to the wardrobe supervisor, "the same kind you used on *Pirates of the Caribbean* to keep their wigs on!"

Some moments were less silly, though, not in terms of sex but of safety. No matter how carefully choreographed and rehearsed a scene may be, things can change in the heat of the moment. In the scene when they impulsively have sex in the kitchen, banging into the stove, knocking pots and pans to the floor as they tear each other's clothes off, it was obvious neither of them could wear padding. Afterward, I remember Annie trying not to let Jake see that she was badly bruised. When he noticed, he was genuinely distraught. Throughout the movie, it was moving to see how tender and caring they were toward each other.

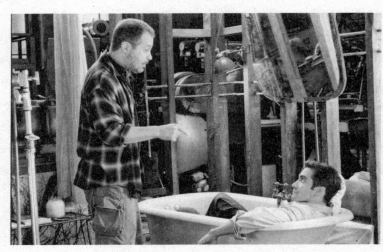

Their affection for each other was matched by their kindness toward me. On the last day of shooting, they had the prop department create an award they called "the Golden Merkin"—a genital cover-up (unspecified as to whose) sprayed with gold paint and mounted on a wooden plaque with a brass plate bearing my name and the date. They gave it to me at wrap, and I joined them in bed for a picture. It was intended to be a private shot, but the unit photographer gave it to the studio marketing department by mistake, who loved it, then created what appears to be a composite image—with me photoshopped out—which was used as the poster for the movie. There's a metaphor in that about directing, but I'm not sure I'm ready to confront it.

More often than not, films build to some kind of catharsis: a moment of personal revelation or deep emotion. For many actors, these depths are easily explored. For some, they are a dark, impenetrable forest that can only be entered at great cost.

For better or worse, tears are easy signifiers of emotion. Some actors are ugly criers, their faces contorting into monster masks. Others discharge copious amounts of snot. Many become even more beautiful, their wet faces shining with dew. Actors are alike in dreading such scenes. Even given time to prepare, say, by using sense recall, or listening to music, to authentically reach such depths of feeling as the camera turns and the crew looks on, is a kind of practical magic. There are shortcuts. A tear blower is a little tube filled with menthol crystals. Blown into an actor's eyes, the tear ducts become irritated, and waterworks often follow. Most actors think it's a cheap trick. Also, it reddens the eyes and doesn't always work.

Anne Hathaway is a gamer. Emotionally available, and always willing. She had already done brave, heartbreaking work on more challenging scenes in the film. Yet as the finale approached, I could tell she was anxious. With two great actors, it's hard to choose whose close-up to shoot first unless you're willing to compromise the lighting and shoot both at the same time, which isn't fair to the DP, not to mention to two beautiful faces in the finale of a romantic comedy. I asked Jake to go first. He was every bit as anxious but agreed without hesitation. As we rolled, though, it just wasn't happening, and he knew it. Off camera, Anne could see he was having trouble and realized he needed help. It's impossible to exaggerate how much one actor's work influences another's. But as Jake found the magic and his performance blossomed, I happened to glance off camera and saw Anne's face wet with tears. She was giving herself to him completely. A 180-degree reverse of camera direction takes time. Anne stood alone, waiting, listening to music, trying to stay inside herself. When at last we rolled, despite Jake's equally generous work off camera, she couldn't get there. Take after take she kept trying. Finally, she took me aside and whispered, "I'm dry."

She knew I wanted her to cry. And I had made it worse by acknowledging it.

"Annie," I said, putting my arm around her, "you are great in this movie. There is absolutely no need to cry in this scene."

At which point she burst into tears, and I called, "Roll . . ."

Love & Other Drugs was my second personal film in a row. Much of the film was shot in hospitals. Between setups I would wander the corridors, catching random glimpses of a patient alone in bed, a couple holding hands in a waiting area, or a family gathered around a sick loved one. I would pause to look closer than I might have in times past, identifying with each tableau. My experience of making the movie was so profound that, at times, the line would blur between what I was shooting and what I was feeling. When, in the penultimate scene, Jamie finds Maggie's message about wanting what she has, I could barely hold it together.

"This," she says. "This moment right now. It doesn't matter if I have ten thousand more moments like this, or just this one, because it's all the same. Yeah . . . just that. Right now. This moment. I have *this*."

My experience with Annie was as magical and gratifying as any I'd ever had. She understood the ordeal I'd undergone with great compassion and there are moments in her performance that are unerringly familiar. At wrap she wrote me the most beautiful note; I still have it pasted into one of my notebooks. Soon after, I showed her an original script Marshall and I had just finished and asked her to play the female lead. After reading it, she had some great suggestions that we incorporated in our rewrite, which she read and loved and immediately said yes.

Three weeks later her manager called. Annie wasn't going to do it. No explanation. Actors never want to be the ones who say no. It's their prerogative, of course. Still, I wish she had told me herself. We've run into each other several times since then over the years and are genuinely glad to see each other. Neither of us has ever mentioned it.

Hollywood.

ME AND DAMIEN CHAZELLE

A Hollywood parable

1. **INCOMING**

   It's 2021. I'm sitting at home, conspicuously not writing, waiting for the latest submission not to be read by a movie star, and a call not to be returned by an executive, when I get a text from a young agent at CAA asking me to call.

2. **INTEREST**

   After playing phone tag, he tells me there's "interest" from Damien Chazelle in me playing a role in his new movie, *Babylon*. At first, I wonder if I'm being pranked, but he insists it's on the level and would I like to take a look at the script? Well, duh . . .

3. **THE SCRIPT**

   It's 175 pages. Dense. Paragraphs of single-spaced description. Profane, dirty, entertaining, and overheated. I do what every self-respecting actor does, which is to say I check to see how big my part might be.

4. **TIME MANAGEMENT**

   My character (see how it's already *my* character?) appears in ten scenes spread over a three-month schedule. I've admired Damien's movies but have never enjoyed watching someone else direct. It makes me antsy, anxious, and envious.

5. **POSITIVES**

   It's nice to be asked. I know Damien a bit. He's a good guy. I check IMDb to see who else is in the movie: some are actors I've worked with, others I'd love to get to know. I imagine hanging out on set sipping Perrier with Ryan Gosling.

6. **NEGATIVES**

   I'm in the middle of a new script and negotiating to direct an indie. Also, there are travel plans with my wife. Would I have to shave off my beard? I grew it while making my first movie. It was in the DGA contract along with the obligatory baseball cap.

7. DOUBTS

No schedule ever holds. What happens when it goes over? My part is basically one line per scene—with a speech in the finale that will inevitably be cut. I mean, in a 175-page script, who's more expendable, me or Margot Robbie?

8. THE JURY

I poll my friends. Some say I'm an idiot to say no. Increased visibility. Hanging with the cool kids. A director friend says I'll be the O.G., feeling diminished and boring everyone with war stories while they're trying to concentrate.

9. TEMPTATION

I think about how often Spielberg invites other directors to do small parts: Truffaut in *Close Encounters*, Cameron Crowe in *Minority Report*. I'm leaning toward yes. Bu then I consider my commitment to my own projects. So . . . work or vanity?

10. THE VERDICT

Saying no to any offer makes me anxious. Nonetheless I decide to demur. I'm about to call but the agent calls first. "They've decided to go another way," he says. Do I laugh or cry? Is it possible to be flattered and rejected? Only in Hollywood.

CHAPTER SEVENTEEN

Onward

Pawn Sacrifice, Jack Reacher, Trial by Fire, 2012–2020

I've been in remission now, on and off, for sixteen years. When the power of one wonder drug has waned, there's been a new one to take its place. I am either a miracle of modern science or a canary in the coal mine. My old friend Jerry Groopman, who somehow manages to be a brilliant writer and teacher while serving as chief of experimental medicine at Beth Israel, calls it "playing whack-a-mole."

"With my life," I tell him.

Since my initial diagnosis, I've directed three movies, produced two others, made a TV series, a pilot, and two documentaries. Marshall says I work like something is chasing me. It is. Considering the alternative, it all feels like I'm playing with house money.

Lately, the stories that interest me have been smaller, intimate films, mostly because those I have made in the past—movies for grown-ups on a large scale—just aren't being made these days. Scale means more than budget. It's an essential color on a director's palette. These days, big movies with movie stars and all the bells and whistles tend to be about superheroes and comic books. This isn't grousing. It is what it is. Though I do try to imagine what effect there might be on a young filmmaker whose only experience of storytelling is sitting alone in a room, or on his computer, or on his phone. Something more than the box office will be lost not to have participated in the communal moment unique to a theater filled with warm bodies. And what happens if the theatrical experience, itself already in decline pre-Covid, continues to forfeit its place in our cultural imagination? To paraphrase the adage: "If a movie falls in the forest and only one person sees it at a time, is it still a movie?"

When I was in my thirties and first invited to join the Academy, I was assigned to a committee whose purpose was to offer (or deny) membership to other directors. Its chairman was the formidable Richard Brooks. The other members were such fierce lions as John Frankenheimer, Peter Bogdanovich, Dick Donner, and Paul Mazursky. Anything I had gone through once, they had done countless times. I had just directed *Glory*. I was the youngest of the group by a wide margin, and justifiably intimidated. Once a month I would sit, agog, as Frankenheimer talked about directing Sinatra in *The Manchurian Candidate*, or Brooks told stories about Burt Lancaster and Robert Ryan in *The Professionals*, and Bogdanovich held forth, having met and interviewed everyone who had ever called "Action."

After a while, even amid the joking and good fellowship, I began to sense a dark subtext in the room. Eventually, I realized no one ever talked about what they were working on because none of them were working. And they weren't happy about it. As I got to know them, in private moments, usually after several drinks, they would talk about what it felt like after the caravan has moved on. It wasn't the money they missed, they had plenty. Nor was it the meetings or the phone ringing, the offers, or the interviews. It was the inimitable feeling of being connected to a piece of work, utterly and passionately, switched on as only an artist can be.

I've tried to think about how much they must have longed for that fire in their belly, what Martha Graham called "a blessed unrest." To this day, when I am sleepless it's because I am writing or directing in my head. I honestly can't ever remember waking up in the morning and saying, "Shit, I have to go to work today." I know there will come a time when I must confront the same reality as those same directors I so admired. Everyone falls out of favor eventually, whether from changing tastes, ageism, or failing health, it's in the cards.

I observe the talented young directors coming up with admiration tinged with a certain wariness. Too many of their films seem not at all interested in holding up a mirror to contemporary life, its issues and contradictions. I'm not suggesting their movies need to be explicitly political, but to me, the best stories are those that try to make sense of chaos. They insist on interpretation even when information seems to refuse it, especially at a time when the very notion of "truth" is under assault. Throughout history, popular storytellers have always been the default moralists of their time. To abjure that obligation in the name of creating mindless "entertainment" is to surrender a kind of sacred duty. It's not enough to make films that drown out the growing sound of screaming in the world beyond the Hollywood bubble.

I guess what I'm saying, is that if a film isn't about something, it's about nothing. And even as they display astonishing technical virtuosity, I can't help but notice when they also choose to abandon the reality principle so crucial in having an audience relate to a story. This is understandable given all the new toys in their toolbox. But when the camera defies the laws of physics, passing through keyholes or careening around walls, or the obvious use of CG stunts or extensions makes the audience wonder "how did they do that?" it feels like they've chosen the sizzle over the steak. The minute we start *oohing* and *ahhing* because the whole scene was filmed in one uninterrupted five-minute dolly shot—which, by the way, isn't really that hard to do—it means we've been pulled out of the story emotionally. And something is irrevocably lost.

Because, to me, movies are about the story, not the director. If I have a credo, it's that everything be sacrificed at the altar of meaning and emotion, including my ego. I'd like to think one reason so many of the performances I've directed have gotten the kind of recognition they have is because I've never felt the need to compete with the actors for the audience's attention. If this sounds like a special pleading trying to explain a career that has never attained celebrity status, you haven't understood a thing I've been writing about. I've had more than my share of success. And praise makes you its prisoner. It's the spike in your arm where the first taste is free. And when it comes from the critics, it's the hangman saying you have a pretty neck. If I choose to read the good reviews, I'd better read the bad ones, too. And not pretend I don't read them. It's like porn. Nobody watches it, but somehow, it's a multibillion-dollar industry.

The reasons I've set out to make a particular movie have often been mysterious, even to me, and sometimes they've changed as a movie revealed what it wanted to be. Sometimes I've been surprised when the deeper wellsprings of my intentions aren't revealed to me until long after. Most of all, I pray there's something unshakable in a story's DNA that sustains me through the setbacks and heartbreaks I've come to expect. The hardest time for me is between projects. Like those giants of my youth I came to know as a young director, I don't do well with idleness. Whether as a writer, director, or producer, I've had to invent my own universe every day. My job is to create capital, such as it is, out of nothing. This requires a cussed determination to face the frustrations and inevitable rejections of trying to get a movie made. As much as it sometimes makes me want to scream, throw my phone, curl up in the fetal position, sob uncontrollably, get drunk, eat a pint of ice cream, or all of the above, there is really only one thing to do. *Grit* is the word my mother would have used.

So, I sit down to write. But where to begin? I can't write the same script again, make the same movie over and over. I watch favorite films, not to refer to them—meta is boring, also too easy—but rather to be inspired and goad myself to keep pushing. A long career is made or broken by material: writing it, finding it, developing it. There are always lots of good shooters and any number of one-hit wonders. Yet very few continue to generate projects that actors want to play, and studios want to make. For better and worse, I've struggled to do it for nearly five decades.

After an obligatory number of false starts and disappointing early drafts, I manage to write something I believe in, and begin pushing a new boulder up a steep hill. Movies aren't born. They fight their way to life. And the struggle can wear you down. I send the script to a movie star's manager, who says, "I love the script for him." It means her assistant read it. When the movie star's "covering agent" says, "I love the script for him," it means the actor is technically available and needs an offer to read it. When the movie star's "responsible agent" says, "My client loves the script," it means the actor has notes. When the movie star's lawyer says the same thing, it means he's going to make the negotiations as painful as possible. When the movie star himself says, "*I* love the script," it means he wants to know who's going to rewrite it.

And then comes the same process with the studio. When the creative executive says, "We're gonna make this movie," it means she'll try to get the VP to read it. When the VP says he'll make it, it means he's read positive coverage. When the EVP says it, it means she'll take credit for finding it if the president of production likes it. When the president of production says it, it means he needs to tell the CEO which actor is starring in it. And at last, when the CEO says, "We're gonna make this movie," it means it'll get made if he still has his job in six months.

One day, while Menno Meyjes and I were dealing with an especially galling set of studio notes, he said something that should be tattooed on every director's bicep: "Working in Hollywood is a series of small humiliations interrupted by bigger ones." Because there's often a secret loathing between artists and management that's toxic and ultimately destructive to the process. They tend to think of us as irresponsible children while we in turn consider them venal philistines. Yet we also love each other. Or say we do. Certainly, we are dependent on each other. They give us millions to indulge our fantasies. We make them millions to send their kids to private school. We lunch together, schmooze at parties. They visit us on the set and celebrate with us when we succeed. When we fail, not so much. And when they call something a passion project, it means they're patronizing you and never intend to make it.

After fifty years of getting their notes, the sum creative contribution from all but a few truly gifted executives might be reduced to four words: "Faster. Dumber. More likable." Every script "needs work," every first cut is "eighty percent there."

In the new millennial Hollywood, the legacy of Silicon Valley start-up culture is felt everywhere. Everything is decided by "the group." An idea needs to be "socialized." But since when is consensus the best way to judge art? Is homogeneity really the goal? Each year they introduce a crop of new phrases: "edge it up," "backload it," "unpack it," "lean into it." At such moments I remember Cameron Crowe describing an executive as someone who claims to know the way, doesn't have a map, and can't drive a car. As Steven Soderbergh once told an executive, "You confuse having an opinion with having an idea."

Before each film I've had to ask myself, "Am I a retail businessman, or do I care most about expressing my personal vision with millions of other people's money?" It's not a simple question. The answer affects every decision, from script to casting to release. My films have to enjoy at least a certain amount of commercial success if I want to keep getting them made. Then again, the best definition of *success* I ever heard was going from failure to failure without loss of enthusiasm.

No matter how much good fortune I've had, I always feel like I'm never more than a big failure away from movie jail. Happily, I'm also never more than a hit away from being paroled. Even if a movie happens to be a hit, things are never simple. Success is essentially mysterious; marvelous, unidentifiable forces in the universe have converged to make a movie exceed my imagination. Did *I* think of that camera move, or was it the dolly grip? What if it hadn't rained that day and I had shot the crucial scene in bright sunlight the way it was originally intended? Only in humiliating failure have I ever been willing to open myself to the harsh self-scrutiny that leads to growth as an artist. In success, the revisionist history claims everyone loved each other and can't wait to work together again, which wasn't necessarily the case. Sometimes I think little is learned from success except maybe a greater fear of failure.

There's a famous story about Fred Zinnemann at age seventy-five, winner of four Oscars, director of twenty-five films, who found himself in a meeting with a young development executive. To break the ice, she politely asked, "So tell me what you've been up to . . ." To which he politely responded, "You first." I will admit to getting a little tired of that same young executive (by another name)

telling me he grew up watching my movies and that I'm one of the reasons he's
in the business. Whenever that happens, I know I'm not getting hired. There's a
confusing, bittersweet quality to being complimented on old work. It suggests a
distance between how they see me and how I see myself. I've even heard myself
described as a "throwback" to an earlier era of filmmaking, which I'd like to think
is flattering, but I'm not so sure that's how it was intended. I certainly don't feel
like a rarified antique, but neither did the veterans I encountered as a young director; in fact, they were probably no older than I am now. I tend to think of myself
as a young professional who has defied the Fates for fifty years by getting up in the
morning, rolling up my sleeves, and doing a day's work for a day's pay, albeit on
a ridiculous pay scale. Professionals do some things they love because they love
them, and some they don't love, or even like. But they do them all as *if* they love
them. Only another filmmaker can truly know the struggle, the compromise, the
pain, the disappointment, and exquisite sadness of making a movie, no matter if
it turns out to be a hit or a flop. That's why when two directors meet, they share a
knowing look and are inclined to lovingly embrace. We're not competitors, we're
survivors.

How I've managed to balance the life of an artist with that of a husband and
father is impossible to envision without having lucked into the right marriage. Even as I write this, I can imagine Liberty in the background saying: "You
mean the one with Marshall?"

It's an old joke between us, but it belies a deeper, unresolvable tension. Just
how divisive is the sailor's time at sea? And is it worth the hurt it causes at home?
This has been the refrain in my head over the years as I've lain awake listening
to the rattle of the hotel ice machine in the hall, knowing I have missed my son's
soccer final, or my daughter's recital, or my father-in-law's funeral.

While working on this book, Liberty offered a sheaf of letters we exchanged
over the years while I was on location. It's more than a litany of all I have missed,
it is evidence of the dark chasms in our relationship while I was away. In one,

she recounts a hilarious episode of suspecting our fifteen-year-old son of having sex with his girlfriend in our daughter's playhouse and not wanting to find out. I respond in kind with the anecdote about an actor's insistence that he have holes cut in the pockets of his pants so he can hold his privates while performing. In an especially tone-deaf letter I offer a glowing description of Meg Ryan's commitment to her performance. Liberty counters with a vivid account of having stayed up all night with two kids, both with ear infections. And there is worse: each letter evoking a moment of public and personal history—fears about climate collapse, the invasion of Iraq, the specter of a Trump presidency—amid equally dire doubts about the state of our marriage. But there is better, too: glowing reports about our children, shining report cards, sports victories, and ardent expressions of desire that give John Donne a run for his money.

Taken together, they are moving, and often painful to read. Though our exchanges vary from the newsy to the passionate to the foreboding, and my wife is as supportive and funny and invested in my work as anyone could wish, there are times when she makes no attempt to hide a certain detachment and an earned quotient of unspoken, banked rage at my ability to compartmentalize my career from my real life. For my part, I seem to be constantly yearning for her and home, abjectly guilty about being away, but just as blithely able to forget everything but the next day's shooting schedule. It occurs to me that our marriage, perhaps every long marriage, is like the sea. One day the sea is green, the next day blue, the day after gray, and then green again. Why was I so confident it would always change back?

Today, the sea is green once again. Liberty—often my first reader—has read what I have written and approves, but not without a certain amount of irony and rue. Our children have grown sturdy and able. They are both cooked and out in the world. The home fires are still burning. And our marriage abides. None of it could have happened without her. But she knows that.

One thing I learned in the cutting room: always come into a scene at the last possible moment and get the hell out as soon as possible. But before

writing "Fade Out," I realize there are several movies and TV shows that haven't
been given their due in these pages: also, the many friends and collaborators who
I will no doubt hear from for not having singled them out. Twenty-five years after
producing Jason Katim's first TV series, *Relativity*, he and I were able to have a
great time working together on a Netflix series about space exploration called
Away. Steve Gaghan lives down the street so I don't feel the need to mention
our disastrous experience making *Abandon*. I haven't even mentioned Marshall's
gorgeous and subversive movie about the courtesans of the sixteenth century,
Dangerous Beauty, which seems to grow in reputation each year, and for which I
received a barely deserved producer credit. On *Pawn Sacrifice*, Tobey Maguire and
I banged heads at times, but his performance is very special, and we came away
good friends; I only wish more people had seen it. Liev Schreiber's performance
in it is miraculous, too, just as it was in *Defiance*. If I'm lucky, we'll get to make a
third movie together, although I suspect he might prefer that his whole part not be
in Russian. *Jack Reacher: Never Go Back*, which Tom Cruise and I made in 2016,
fizzled at the box office. I blame myself (and my willing accomplice, Don Granger)
for thinking the audience might enjoy a mash-up of *Jack Reacher* and *Paper Moon*,
when in fact they just wanted more red meat. I had a wonderful time working
with Cobie Smulders, and I certainly don't blame Tom for not being six two—as
the novelist Lee Child described his protagonist—and should Tom happen to call
about making a third movie together, I'll definitely pick up.

Two explicitly political films didn't set the world on fire yet still hold a place
in my heart: *Birth of a Nation* was a project for which we all had great hopes
but, sadly, its director-star Nate Parker's personal issues ended up overshadowing
an important story. Allyn Stewart and Alex Soros knew how much *Trial by Fire*
meant to me, and together as producers, made it happen. We were proud of adding its voice to the rising chorus of those speaking up against capital punishment.
If I'm not smart enough to work with Laura Dern again, I have only myself to
blame. Our collaboration was a love fest from day one. She is movie royalty.

Meanwhile Marshall and I are hoping to shoot a feature we've written about sixteenth-century Morocco. We're also adapting a Stephen King novel for JJ Abrams—starring Leonardo DiCaprio—all while writing another original screenplay. The odds are one will get made, the other won't, and the third will languish in purgatory until its fate is decided. There's a special place in my heart for the projects I've developed over the years that never got made. Marshall and I have several specs we still dream of making gathering dust on the shelf. Chris McQuarrie and I worked on and off for four years on a script we abandoned. I collaborated with Winnie Holzman on a sparkling romantic comedy about shrinks in love that never made it to the starting line. Tony Kushner and I had a couple of meetings about adapting *The Mayor of Castro Street*. I was thrilled by the possibility of working with him, but we couldn't agree on an approach. And Bill Broyles and I have been slogging away on a script about the Siege of Khe Sanh (a tragic, heroic chapter of the war in Vietnam) for twenty years. Last year it seemed to have some traction, then *poof*! . . . disappeared back into the ether. Same with Bob Odenkirk and an original L.A. noir. A final count would probably reveal at least as many projects that died in utero as those that thrived and made it to the theaters. The real question is, would my career have been any different if those that didn't get made were the ones that did, and vice versa? Too Zen? Ask any director which of his movies is his favorite, and the only possible answer is, "The one I haven't made yet."

I've worked with so many warm, talented people, thousands probably. We've shared the giddy hilarity of night shoots, the half-awake wanderings into the lunch tent at dawn, and the occasional miracle of dailies. We've found things funny when it's all gone wrong and watched in stunned disbelief when something actually works. Most of them I'll never see again. This, I suppose, is the promiscuity of the life we've chosen. Early in my career I was thrilled to find myself working with a renowned actress, a Tony Award–winning doyenne of the New York stage. I'd imagined us becoming good friends, sitting for hours drinking dirty martinis as I listened to her stories about life in the theater. Despite us working well together, she kept her distance. Finally, at the wrap party, I got up the nerve to ask her why. After her third vodka, she turned to me and said, "Too many fucking goodbyes."

This was clearly her adaptation to the uncertain, contingent circumstances of the life all of us in "the business" have chosen. My contingencies just happen to be more vivid than most these days. Years of waiting, dashed plans, false hopes, more medical tests, and then the phone rings: "Hi. Oh, my God, that's fantastic! Cambodia? I've always wanted to shoot there! A scout next week? No problem, I'll just tell Liberty I'll be out of town for our anniversary. Again."

Once the cast is set and we're on location, I know well enough what making the movie will be like. I have long ago come to accept that no one really wants to talk to a director while he's shooting. And the truth is, I'd rather they don't even try. Anxiety surrounds me like a toxic cloud. Marty Scorsese legendarily attaches huge rear-view mirrors to his monitor—the kind truckers use on semis—so he can be sure no one is lurking behind him as he watches the shot. I have often been told that I seem possessed and act along with the actors while watching them. My face contorts, I squirm in my chair, doing everything I can to will them to safely walk the tightrope of a difficult scene. It's a little bit like willing a pitcher not to throw a gopher ball as he tosses the final inning of a perfect game. It's exhausting.

After a few days of working with me, the crew will realize it's best not to try engaging me in anything resembling a human moment. Just pat my shoulder and move on. Though they harken to my every word and the actors listen avidly when I give direction, the truth is nobody will pay attention to how I feel. Nor should they. They shouldn't be wondering if my stomach is in knots; they need to concentrate on the scene at hand. For better or worse, the director is a sphinx, a benign monolith like the camera itself. I become accessible only in the moments I choose to emerge from behind the camera and deliberately disrupt a cast or crew member in process. Otherwise, I will accept the loneliness of being self-contained. Alienation is part of the gig.

Inevitably, there will come a moment on the shoot when I'll have absolutely no idea what to say. The actors await my verdict on a take. A hush falls over the set as all eyes focus on me. The default at that moment is to announce, "Let's go again," as if I know what I'm looking for and giving the actors a chance to find it for themselves. Sometimes the scene actually gets better.

After a few weeks of shooting, days will fall into a familiar, blurry pattern. After thirteen hours of work, I'll call wrap. I'll be jangled, frustrated, defeated by all I haven't accomplished, convinced nothing will cut together, let alone measure up to the exalted vision in my head. Curled into the back seat on the ride home in my filthy clothes I'll try to replay the day's work but won't be able to keep my eyes open as the adrenaline of the day drains from my body. By the time I've finished reviewing dailies, it'll almost be nine. I'll stumble back into my anonymous hotel room leaving a trail of dirty clothes on the floor, fall into the unmade bed, and pass out.

For about four hours.

I'll then wake with my heart racing and my fists clenched. For a moment I'll struggle to remember what city I'm in, let alone what movie I'm making. Bizarre images will linger from a turbulent half-sleep, and I'll realize I've been reshooting the day's work, only this time in an ominous Dalí dreamscape, the director's equivalent to facing an exam for a class you didn't know you were taking. I'll formulate a plan for the next day's work, vowing to hold true to my vision of the script rather than compromise for the sake of staying on schedule. I'll scribble notes on scraps of paper: bits of dialogue, ideas for shots, reminders to actors and department heads. Sometimes in the pocket of an old jacket I'll find notes from other movies, ink smeared and crumpled, their meaning long ago forgotten.

I'll try to close my eyes, praying for another hour or two of half-sleep, and finally manage to drift off for what feels like seconds before the alarm crashes in. Resentfully I'll tread the dark water just below the surface of consciousness, desperate to steal a few minutes more in oblivion, but the years of discipline and duty, fueled by the rising tide of anxiety, are too ingrained. I'll open my eyes, fight off a wave of nausea, and begin to get dressed.

At such moments I'll honestly begin to think making movies is a young man's game, that I know too much about the inevitable compromises and disappointment of falling short of one's expectations, not to mention the ineffable price paid in the abandonment of family, friends, and the comforts of home. But then that day on the set, something incandescent will happen, or that night in dailies an image will exceed what I thought I had seen while shooting it, or the editor will show me a few scenes cut together, and I will suddenly be heartened, even buoyant, having glimpsed the possibility that the discrete parts of a story—so deconstructed, prosaic, even inconsequential in the process of filming them—might eventually coalesce into something passable, possibly even good.

And so, I'll lace up my muddy boots in the darkness, clomp down the stairs, and walk out into the uncertain light, ready to face the new day with a smile.

Acknowledgments

To me, writing a screenplay with its three-act structure, abbreviated description, and abundant dialogue is a familiar exercise. Deciding to write a book with no set structure, little dialogue, and interminable prose felt like setting off on a pioneer's journey without map or compass, not unlike the studio executives I so blithely traduce. Had it not been for some firm guidance and bracing moral support I would have lost my way. The same can be said of a career. It is to those cherished few who offered their counsel these past two years, as well as the countless others who encouraged me, excoriated me, taught me, and joined me over the course of a lifetime learning a craft, that I owe thanks.

Marshall Herskovitz has had more than enough screen time in this book. I hope his desperate longing for attention is at least temporarily mollified by his many mentions.

Steve Rosenblum is probably embarrassed by my overheated encomiums, so I won't add to his suffering.

Richard Kramer has been my first reader, as well as my first phone call in the morning since the day, almost fifty years ago, we took each other's measure in the Fox commissary. Having long ago tired of hearing my reruns, he never stopped hocking me to put them on paper.

Bill Broyles's mastery of the writer's dark arts is outdone only by his genius for friendship, his remarkable children, and his commitment to convincing me to write this damn book.

Adam Gopnik was the first to read what I thought was a completed manuscript. After finishing it in one sitting, he challenged me in much the same way I
have presumed to confront actors. "I was so entertained," he said. "But where are
you in it?" His words, then and throughout the process, goaded me to go further,
dig deeper.

Kurt Andersen was an early advocate and an invaluable midwife in getting
this book published. Likewise, Roger Rosenblatt, longtime friend and teacher, by
encouraging me to read chapters out loud for his late, lamented brainchild, "Write
America." And Patrick Radden Keefe recognized a book latent in my tweets long
before I did. Alessandra Stanley and Graydon Carter were the first to believe it
worth publishing. I still owe them a fancy dinner.

Bob Bookman read an early manuscript, declared that it deserved to be a
book, and rolled up his sleeves to make it happen. John Burnham joined in and
made essential calls. In desperate need of someone to shepherd me through pub-
lication, I was lucky enough to convince Gail Ross to come aboard. Her wisdom
and tender care have been invaluable.

This being my maiden voyage as an author, I relied even more heavily on the
seasoned professionals at Simon & Schuster, who suffered my ignorance of the
process with patience and good humor. My deepest thanks to Aimee Bell, who
read the manuscript overnight and said yes. My editor Max Meltzer's firm, learned,
and sympathetic hand is felt everywhere. Now that we're done, does this mean I
have to find someone else to call to discuss all things great and inconsequential?
To Jennifer Bergstrom, who wrote the check, to Caroline Pallotta, Jonathan Evans,
Brigid Black, Kate Kenney-Peterson, and Jaime Putorti, who made it into a book,
and to Jennifer Robinson, who devoted herself to getting people to read it, bless
you all.

It took years for Nina Foch's teachings to sink in and even longer for me to
get over my fear of her disapproval. More high priestess than pedagogue, whether
explicitly quoted or filtered through my own experience, her DNA can be found
everywhere in these pages. Her influence on my movies was seminal. I also need to
evoke several earlier drama teachers, each of whom left their mark on a precocious

theater kid: John Baumhart, Red Buerger, and Mark Lamos as part of the remarkable New Trier High School Performing Arts Division; George Hamlin, Robert Chapman, Franco Colavecchia, and Doug Schwalbe for four invaluable years at Harvard's Loeb Drama Center; Jean Firstenberg, Jan Kadar, Bob Gazzale, and everyone at AFI for everything that has followed.

As tutor for my senior thesis in college and so much more, Marty Peretz introduced me to George Orwell's essays and essentially said, "Write like this." Alan Munro and I first worked together when he created the storyboards for *Glory*. A gifted director himself, over fifteen movies his genius has been essential to my process. Throughout the years, Bedford Falls has been my haven, my clubhouse, and my rock; Rick Solomon and all those who have grazed out of our refrigerator have been an extended family—most of all, Troy Putney, who has offered brilliant insight on every piece of work we have produced, all while providing companionship, dark humor, and a nurturing hand.

My children, Jesse and Frankie, are both writers. Doomed by what appears to be the literary family curse, their destiny has been evident since childhood, when their astute observations and unabashed criticisms of my work were irrefutable, if occasionally maddening. From the moment they were born, they have been my best life lessons and my unfailing inspiration.

Every writer needs a soulmate in the struggle. Despite my best efforts, I worry that I've failed to accurately depict the antic, joyous life force that is my wife, Liberty. Anyone who's ever read her stuff also knows she's the real writer in the family. Yet for fortysomething years, with more grace and less umbrage than I deserve, she has tolerated me getting all the kudos. I won't dare claim to be unable to express my gratitude, because I imagine her saying, "Try . . ."

Edward Zwick
Santa Monica, 2023

About the Author

Ed Zwick is an Academy Award– and Emmy Award–winning director, writer, and producer of film and television. A graduate of Harvard and the AFI Conservatory, he lives in Los Angeles with his wife, Liberty Godshall.